DEMOCRACY AND DEVELOPMENT IN TURKEY

C.H. DODD

DEMOCRACY AND DEVELOPMENT IN TURKEY

DEMOCRACY AND DEVELOPMENT IN TURKEY

C.H.DODD

The Eothen Press

Preface and Acknowledgements

This book is an expanded version of lectures given to first year students in the University of Hull. An introductory chapter provides basic information, after which particular aspects of Turkish politics are dealt with at greater depth. The subjects discussed cover most of the field of Turkish politics, but there are certain areas which are omitted from detailed treatment, including the role of Parliament, the Constitutional Court and the Council of State. Insufficient research has as yet been done on these and a number of lesser, but still important, topics to provide material for worth-while discussion.

The particular importance of Turkish politics for students of politics generally lies in the struggle of a state with a long and varied political tradition to combine economic and social development with a democratic political system. It is not easy to find a state in, or on the fringes of, the third world like Turkey which has tried as hard or as long as Turkey to accommodate these two powerful movements of the modern world. The problems which arise from the attempt to reconcile what are often regarded as irreconcilables underlie much of the discussion in this book.

The sources which have been employed are mainly secondary in nature; primary material has been used where particular gaps have had to be, and could be, filled, but my acknowledgement of the work of others can never be adequate. Works both in Turkish and in European languages have been used, but with English readers in mind I have given more prominence in references to work in English.

For help with information about recent research by Turkish scholars I am particularly indebted to Prof. Dr. Nermin Abadan-Unat of the Faculty of Political Science, Ankara University, and to Professors Ergun Özbudun and Rona Aybay of the same Faculty. I am also grateful for help to Dr. Kemali Sayıbaşılı of the Middle East Technical University, Ankara, and for the opportunity of conversations with former colleagues there. For enlightenment in many respects I am indebted to the work of Prof. Dr. Şerif Mardin and other members of the Boğaziçi University,

Istanbul, particularly to Prof. Dr. Suna Kili, Dr. Metin Heper and Dr. Sabri Sayarı. Prof. Dr. İlter Turan of Istanbul also kindly helped with material.

To Dr. W.M. Hale of the University of Durham I owe a particular debt of gratitude not only for his always ready help, but also for reading the whole of the manuscript and for many helpful suggestions for improvement. A similar service was also rendered by Mr. T.P. McNeill of the Department of Politics in the University of Hull, who, with other colleagues, have generously helped in the task of making Turkish politics better known by participating in the teaching of the subject.

Professor D.A. Rustow and the Princeton University Press kindly gave permission to reproduce a lengthy quotation from *Political Culture and Political Development*, ed. by L.W. Pye and S. Verba, ©1965 by Princeton University Press. To Prof. Dr. Ergun Özbudun and the Princeton University Press I gratefully acknowledge permission to reproduce the map of Turkish agricultural regions. Oceana Publications, Inc., New York, allowed the reproduction of extracts from Constitutions of the Countries of the World: Turkey, ed. by A.P. Blaustein and F. Gisbert (translated by İlhan Arsel). Two visits to Turkey to collect material and to maintain academic contacts were financed by the British Academy, whose help in this regard was of very great value.

For typing the manuscript I am grateful to Judith Murden, and for composing it for printing with great care I am indebted to Helen Parker. Mel Ward, Mrs. Doris Sharp and the staff of the University of Hull's print room contributed greatly to the smooth production of the book. Finally, I should like to acknowledge a particular debt of gratitude to Gary Sargeant who, in addition to much valuable advice, supervised all stages of production and designed the cover.

This book is dedicated to the 150 or more students in Hull who each year read Turkish politics as part of a first year course and to those who devote themselves to further study of the subject in their third year.

Hull, 1979   C.H.D.

CONTENTS

Transcription, Pronunciation of
Turkish Words and Abbreviations

Save for those with an established English form, like Pasha, Ottoman Turkish words have been transcribed into modern Turkish orthography. For those who like to know how the Turkish words in the text are pronounced the following notes on the pronunciation of certain letters should remove the principal difficulties.

ç is pronounced as j in judge

c is pronounced as ch in church

g is pronounced as g in gate

ğ is pronounced as y after e and i, but is otherwise
                                  hardly sounded except that it
                                  lengthens a preceding a or i

j is pronounced as j in French *jour*

ı is pronounced as i in fit

i is pronounced as i in first

ö is pronounced as eu in French *deux*

u is pronounced as u in bull

ü is pronounced as u in French *lune*

ş is pronounced as sh in ship

In the text the Republican People's Party (*Cumhuriyet Halk Partisi*) is usually shortened to People's Party and the Worker's Party of Turkey (*Türkiye İşçi Partisi*) to Worker's Party.

CHAPTER I

INTRODUCTION:
HISTORY SOCIETY AND GOVERNMENT

HISTORY

Some peoples of the world have achieved greatness at one time or another in their history and the Turks are one of these peoples. Their origins are obscure, and they do not appear in history until the sixth century. The Chinese knew them as nomadic inhabitants of parts of Siberia, where they left their first written traces. Then they, or other Turks, moved south and west to settle in Central Asia, where they abutted on the Muslim, and chiefly Arab, Middle East. In the later troubled years of the mediaeval Arab empire, the Turks found ready employment in the Arab Empire as mercenaries. This was the thin end of a wedge, for in the eleventh century, under leaders of a Seljuk line, the Turks set up a kingdom in Baghdad, nominally under the Arab Caliph. These Turks soon became Muslims, and orthodox Muslims at that, in the high traditions of Islam; and by this time the Turks in the recruiting ground of Central Asia had become Muslim too.

Yet not all Turks, and certainly not the nomadic Turks, the Turkomans, took kindly either to the severe orthodoxy of the classic Islamic state, or to its practice of tax-gathering. These Turkomans found religious solace in the more folksy, and often more mystic, forms of religion spread by itinerant preachers and merchants sympathetic to the unorthodox Shi'ite "heresy". The Turkomans also found scope for their military prowess not only as Seljuk soldiers, but also, and more important, as self-organized raiding warriors for the faith (*Ghazi's*) on the borders of the declining Byzantine Empire. Not only were land and booty theirs if they could take them; they could also justify their aggression by pointing to their duty as Muslims to carry war to the unbeliever. The Seljuks variously aided and abetted the Turkomans, as when they defeated the Byzantines at Manzikert in 1071; but they also restrained them from attacking the Byzantines if it suited them to do so, especially after establishing their dynasty in Konya in Central Anatolia in the twelfth century. Nevertheless, and despite set-backs due to the western Crusades, the Turkoman irregulars continued to capture, Turkify and Islamicize Anatolia. A fillip to this forward surge was provided by defeat of the restraining Seljuks by the Mongols in 1243; moreover, many of the local Byzantine populations, including their leaders, seemed to prefer the Turkish yoke to the Byzantine, adopted Islam and joined the Turkish ranks.

The Rise and Fall of the Ottoman Empire

One of the successful Turkish leaders, or emirs, under whom Turkoman irregulars gathered at the end of the thirteenth century was a certain Osman, whose emirate in North West Anatolia was strategically well placed for further attacks on the declining Byzantine power. These *Osmanli*, or Ottoman, Turks captured Bursa in 1326, established themselves on the European shore of the Dardanelles in 1364, defeated the Serbs at Kossovo in 1389, and, after raiding as far north as Hungary, destroyed the best that European knighthood could muster at Nicopolis in 1396. Masters of the Balkans, they had no great difficulty in taking Constantinople in 1453 after recovering remarkably from a catastrophic defeat at the hands of Timurlane the Mongol at Ankara in 1402.

The Ottomans now entered upon their glorious century which concluded, to hazard a date, with the death of their sun king the Sultan Süleyman, the Law Giver, in 1566. During this golden age Belgrade was captured and consolidated as an Ottoman bastion, the Hungarians were massacred at Mohacs in 1526 (when Süleyman claimed he buried 24,000 Hungarians) and the mighty Hapsburgs had to pay tribute for part of Hungary. In 1529 Vienna itself was besieged, though without success—a significant portent. Meanwhile, the Ottomans were over-running the Islamic East— Syria, Egypt, Iraq and the North African littoral, as far as the Straits of Gibraltar—though the Shi'ite Persians were never vanquished and continued to constitute an exhausting second front for the Ottomans. One particular jewel was the capture of Rhodes from the formidable Knights of St. John.

The failure before Vienna was a straw in the wind. There were many more conquests including Podolia and part of the Ukraine— and as late as 1676. Then again in 1683 the Ottomans were back once more hammering at the gates of Vienna, though again without success. The later victories were short-lived however. The outer ring of European territory was soon to be lost. Podolia, Hungary and Transylvania were signed away by the Treaty of Carlowitz in 1699. Then after a century of stalemate, which included some Ottoman successes, a Russian war was concluded with the Treaty of Küçük Kaynarca which in 1774 led to the loss of Ottoman territories on the Black Sea coast, including the Crimea. The early nineteenth century saw the rebellion of the Ottoman Governor of Egypt, Mohammed Ali. When he penetrated deep into Anatolia the Turks had to call in the Russians to help, though they never actually had to ask them to fight. This cost them a treaty of defensive alliance (*Hünkâr İskelesi*, 1833), but it also brought Britain and France to the rescue of the now woefully stricken Empire. Yet, whilst helping to hold Russia at bay, Britain and France could not prevent the further disintegration of the Empire through the corrosive forces of liberalism and nationalism working through the Ottoman non-Turkish and non-Islamic subjects. Indeed liberalism and nationalism were just as significant European exports as the economic, military and administrative efficiency which thoughtful Ottomans really wished to import from the West. By the first world war the European and African domains had dropped away; by the end of the war not even the Muslim Arab heartlands remained.

Modernization

The reasons for the rise and decline of the Ottoman Empire must be among the most complex in history, but only the bare outlines are suggested here.[1] Certainly the growth of the Empire owed much to vigorous Sultans, religious and sheer expansive zeal, and to a highly integrated and mutually supportive civilian and military organization which included the famed Janissaries, a highly trained army recruited from the sons of Christian subjects of the Empire; they were converted to Islam and trained to owe allegiance to none but the Sultan. There were other contributory factors like the weakness of the Byzantine Empire, and later, of Europe, at the time of Ottoman expansion; the absence of a hereditary feudal aristocracy to inhibit the rise of other talent;

and the undoctrinaire capacity of the early Ottomans to absorb into their system enemies and potential enemies living under less accommodating regimes.

The Ottoman state was highly centralized and worked well whilst there were lucrative areas to conquer and vigorous leadership existed to keep the military and administrative institutions in good order. Once deprived of fresh lands to conquer by stiffening European resistance, and weakened by the running sore of Persian opposition, the Ottomans seems to turn their exploitative genius onto themselves. Agonized by their decline, thoughtful Ottomans sought salvation in moral exhortation and in demands for a return to those Islamic traditions of social and political order which they believed had guaranteed success in the past.

Social and political order was not only disrupted by the effects of military failure, however; there were also other influences at work whose nature the Ottomans were not in a position properly to comprehend. These influences derived *inter alia* from a sixteenth century population explosion, declining trade, and a period of gross inflation which had its origins in the New World. Add to these subterranean changes the largely ineffectual leadership of the later Ottoman sultans and the impossibility of breaking away from centralized rule and it is little wonder that the Ottoman Empire began to break up. The Janissaries ceased to be the terror of Europe and became instead the terror of Istanbul.

The military defeats of the seventeenth century made the Ottomans realize that they had to pay some attention to European skills. Mildly inquisitive visits to France were followed by French help with military reform, truculently and arrogantly accepted. Further catastrophic military defeats in the eighteenth century made the Ottomans take up military reform in earnest. In 1826 the Sultan Mahmud II destroyed the Janissaries and created a new model army. He also defeated in the end a powerful group of notables who tried to limit his power and who had risen to a position of economic and social prominence through their leases of state lands and tax farming.

After the defeat of the Janissary and "baronial" opposition the gates were open to other than just military reform, despite religious opposition. Foreign embassies began to be opened in Europe and a few Turks began to acquire foreign languages, mainly French. To support military reforms more modern and efficient medical and supply services were necessary which in turn demanded more effective financial and administrative organization. The chief architects and supervisors of this reform in the middle of the last century were two famous grand vezirs, Ali and Fuad Pasha's. They were helped and cajoled by the Powers, notably by France and Great Britain as part of their policy of containing Russia. The powers also pressed hard for greater freedom and equality for the numerous Christian subjects of the Empire and for commercial privileges for themselves.

The reforms of Ali and Fuad and their disciples were not to the liking of a growing number of Ottoman intelligentsia. It was claimed that the reforms were too secularist, imitative of the West and ought not to be imposed without consultation. In conjunction with Western pressure, the liberal element in this critique gave rise to demands for forms of representative government and finally to the short-lived Constitution of 1876, whose principal architect, Ahmet Midhat Pasha, was nevertheless an established member of the Ottoman administrative elite. The collapse of the constitutional movement gave way to the despotic rule of Abdul Hamid II. His stifling but apprehensive and inefficient rule created just the right environment for the growth of liberal and patriotic revolutionary groups of intellectuals and conspirators—the original Young Turks. Some thrived in exile; others stuck it out at home, where they were to be found among lawyers, teachers, journalists, officials and, most ominous, among army officers. The Young Turks effected a revolution in 1908, restored the Constitution and deposed Abdul Hamid after an abortive counter-coup a year later. For all its initial liberalism the Young Turk regime became as authoritarian, and rather more severe in its treatment of its enemies than Abdul Hamid's government.

After defeat in the first world war the Young Turks were discredited. Yet some of their spirit, if not their leading personnel, lived on in the even more modernizing and notoriously secularist regime of Mustafa Kemal, later known as Atatürk (father Turk). He led the Turks to victory in their war of national liberation against the occupying Greek forces. His nationalist and secularist regime abolished the Sultanate and represented Turkey at the peace conference with the allied powers held in Lausanne in 1922, where Turkey's national independence was recognized. In the following year the new Turkish government declared that the state was a republic and did no less than proceed to abolish the Caliphate, which in the late nineteenth century had acquired a new significance with the development of a Pan-Islamic movement.

By these revolutionary acts the Atatürkists ostensibly rejected Ottoman authoritarian rule and its conservatism. The Ottoman dynasty was exiled forever, Islam was disestablished, if not completely destroyed; but authoritarianism persisted in a single party republican regime dominated by its President, Kemal Atatürk. The major institutional upheavals were followed by the abolition of religious schools and religious courts, strict state control of religious endowments, the dissolution of the dervish orders, the use of Turkish in the Muslim call to prayer and the enforced wearing of hats, which were the despised headgear of the Christians as well as being a symbol of modernity. New law codes of European inspiration were introduced. While the Ottomans had gone a long way in the adoption of European commercial and criminal law, the Atatürkists now introduced western civil law, thus removing all personal and family matters out of the domain of religion.

The new Turkey was to be both secularist and Turkish. Neither development was to the liking of the Kurds of Eastern Turkey. They broke out in rebellion in 1925, encouraged by the emergence in the Assembly of an opposition party and the appointment of a liberal to the premiership, Ali Fethi Okyar. They failed and were ruthlessly quashed. Then in 1926 an attempt was made on Atatürk's life in which numbers of his political opponents were said to be implicated and of whom fifteen were hanged. This discouraged opposition to further measures of "modernization", which included the purification of the language from its Arabic and Persian accretions, and a new emphasis on Turkish, in place of Ottoman, history.

Economic Development

During the nineteenth and early twentieth centuries political, administrative, military and educational reform proceeded apace. Newspapers, periodicals and books also began to make their appearance in some numbers, even surviving rigorous censorship under Abdul Hamid II. More concrete forms of communication were developed, too, in the form of railways and a telegraph service. These modes of communication were in fact promoted by the government with some energy, both being valuable aids to the maintenance of its control over the provinces. By contrast, road building and the postal service somewhat lagged behind, inhibited by the success, perhaps of the railways and the telegraph.

In the more strictly economic sphere progress was very slow, however, though the rate began to quicken a little towards the end of the nineteenth century. By 1915 there were only 282 industrial establishments in Turkey with over five workers each, the total number of workers being 14,060, a figure raised to 62,000 in 1933. A great deal of such Ottoman economic development as there was occurred in public utilities. Although the Young Turks realized far better than their predecessors the importance of economic development, and had some acquaintance with the subject of economics, the Atatürkists were the first to be really purposive about it, but found local capital scarce and foreign capital very hard to attract.[2] There was also some disinclination to accept foreign capital, though Turkey did obtain some foreign finance, including a loan from the USSR for development of the textile industry in Kayseri and another from Britain for military modernization and the Karabük iron works. Negative attitudes towards foreign capital where they existed were due to disastrous Ottoman experience with European commerce and finance, which made the Atatürkists generally rather cautious and suspicious. For European pressures for tariff concessions—not abolished until 1929—had helped destroy local Turkish industries, particularly the textile industry, by encouraging imports of cheaper and better mass manufactured goods. Ottoman exports were then much restricted—mainly to raw materials like tobacco and cotton. This was not desirable in itself, but is was rendered less so when foreign investment and partial control of the production of these

and other raw materials was accompanied by unrestricted export
of profits, despite some increased efficiency in this area of
production.

More dramatic than these economic developments, which were
not as clearly understood then as they are now, was the history of
European financing of the Ottoman government from the first
loan made in 1850. Vast sums were lent to the Ottoman government. Some of this support was undoubtedly used for purposes
of economic development even if much of it went into the
creation of public utilities, but resources were also devoted to
maintaining and modernizing the army and the bureaucracy and
to other non-productive functions. There also seems to have been
considerable waste and inefficiency. One loan led to another and
finally to a declaration of Ottoman bankruptcy in 1875. This
resulted in the appointment of a foreign "Council for the Administration of the Ottoman Public Debt" to supervise collection of
revenue to repay the debt. This was in fact much scaled down,
but by 1914 the Ottoman government was paying nearly one-
third of its income in debt and interest repayments. After the first
world war Atatürk's government assumed responsibility for the
debt—again much reduced by one means or another—and did not
complete its repayment until 1947. Not until after the second
world war did Turkey again experience significant importation of
foreign capital. The terms were generous, allowing foreign
investors to withdraw as capital in their own currency the value
of all that had been invested together with profits. This development enabled the Turkish government to play down the statist
economic policies which had been the rule since 1931 (three
years before the first Turkish five-year plan was announced)
and which had involved the state in the initiation and development
of major economic projects.

Turkey since Atatürk

One European aspect of Atatürk's make-up was a genuine,
and yet realistic, faith in liberal democracy. After Atatürk's death
in 1938 his shrewd and doughty lieutenant İsmet İnönü became
President. By controlling the Republican People's Party in what
was a single-party state he kept firm control of the national

destiny, which was in some peril during the second world war. Then in 1946 İnönü's government allowed other political parties to be formed and to compete for power in the general election of that year. One opposition party, the Democrat Party, won about one-seventh of the seats in the National Assembly. In the 1950 general election, the Democrats obtained a majority; an experiment with multi-party government was firmly under way.

The reasons for so momentous a move by İnönü are subject to some dispute, but it seems generally accepted that, in the first place, there was a demand for more economic freedom by the rising Turkish bourgeoisie. Atatürkist economic policy had been statist, but statist out of necessity; it had not sought to eliminate or even discourage private economic enterprise. With some industrialization in the 1930's, and with a high demand for Turkish products in wartime, a Turkish bourgeoisie had developed. Moreover this bourgeoisie and the wealthier landowners were also afraid of the incipient socialism of the People's Party, which began to emerge after the war. In addition, the particular interest in more economic freedom was reinforced by a very general desire for more governmental sympathy for religion, and a growing popular hostility towards the harsh, patronizing and didactic attitudes of the bureaucracy, backed as ever in the countryside by the unpopular gendarmerie. It was also important that these pressures for more freedom coincided with the victory and high prestige of the western liberal-democratic powers and Turkey's strongly-felt need to ally herself with the West in the face of post-war Russian hostility.

The change to a freer regime was important, but not revolutionary. Islam was not re-established. The economic system developed on mixed lines. The newly powerful Democrat Party government before long began to restrict various of the freedoms of its political opponents in questionable ways, but did not seek to abolish them. The real change was an emphasis on economic development with the assistance of foreign capital, particular attention being paid to agriculture, which advanced strikingly. Together with a relaxation in policies of enforced secularization and modernization, this emphasis ensured widespread support for the Democrat Party save from significant sections of the administrative, educational and military elite. They thought that the strict principles of Atatürkism were being corroded by the crude temptations of religiosity and materialism. When the government began seriously to threaten the much respected İnönü the military effected a coup in 1960 which in some respects constituted a revolution.

Whatever its long-term effects the 1960 revolution was a serious business. The Turkish mentality does not lend itself to light opera. The Democrat Party prime minister, Adnan Menderes, was hanged together with two of his ministers: there were twelve other commuted death sentences whilst over four hundred persons, including many deputies, received periods of imprisonment. The severity was in part occasioned by the general lack of popular enthusiasm for the revolution. A referendum on a new proposed constitution in 1961 was judged to be a vote of confidence on the revolution and its makers. The new constitution was voted in, but not with a large majority.

The new constitution sought to impose checks on the re-emergence of authoritarian government, and proclaimed social as well as individual rights—for instance, the right to strike. Under its provisions Turkey maintained a multi-party system but with devices designed to prevent the emergence of democratic tyranny. After a number of alarms signifying continuing military dissatisfaction, Turkey nevertheless settled down uneasily, first to a series of coalition governments of various mixes, and then to rule by the right-wing Justice Party under its moderate leader, Süleyman Demirel.

The Justice Party came to power in 1965 with a good majority, and returned again in 1969 with a slightly increased majority, thanks to changes made in the electoral system, and despite a smaller share of the vote. The party then suffered a defection of some forty deputies to a new more right-wing Democratic Party. Weakened by this, and by serious outbreaks of terrorism which they could not or would not control, the Justice Party government was eased out of power by the military in 1971. The military warned the government that they had failed to realize the reforms required by the 1961 constitution, and, more to the immediate point, that a strong and credible government had to be formed, or else the military would take over in order to prevent anarchy. The Justice Party fell, to the chagrin of Mr. Demirel, and coalitions successively held power under independent premiers until the 1973 general election. This period saw the imposition of martial law, severe measures against terrorists (three of whom were hanged) and the arrest and trial of over 2,000 persons variously charged, sometimes on scant evidence, to have assisted in word or deed attempts to overthrow the existing order by undemocratic means. The chairman of the Turkish Worker's Party, Behice Boran, was one of those convicted, as too was Professor Mümtaz Soysal, in his case for alleged communist propaganda contained in an introductory book on government. During this period military pressure resulted in the amendment of the constitution to restrict some individual and corporate freedoms. That liberty was not further restricted, was partly due to the influence of İsmet İnönü, still the leader of the Republican People's Party until his resignation in 1972, when he was succeeded by Bülent Ecevit. Subsequently the spirited opposition to the military evinced by leading politicians of all persuasions resulted in defeat for the military's favoured candidate for the presidency of the Republic, which fell vacant in 1973.

Most unfortunately, the 1973 general election did not produce a decisive result. The Republican People's Party gained ground winning most seats (185 out of 450), but the Justice Party was a strong runner-up (145). Two other parties with strong representation were the National Salvation Party, traditionalist and Islamic (48 seats), and the right-wing Democratic Party (45 seats). It took three months—until January 1974—before a coalition could be formed. Strange to relate, it was a coalition of the modernizing, secularist and now near socialist Republican People's Party and the traditionalist Islamic and conservative National Salvation Party. The coalition lasted until September, 1974, when it took the President just twice as long as before to find a government— despite off-stage promptings by the military. The governmental crisis was eventually resolved when the Justice Party leader, Mr. Demirel, succeeded in forming a government in which the National Salvation Party was the chief collaborator; the right-wing Democratic Party, by now weakened by defections, was not a participant. The solution was not ideal, but firm government was urgently necessary to cope with high unemployment, a thirty per cent inflation rate (in February, 1975), a faltering economy and delicate relations with the United States, shortly to be explained. A more definite mandate from the electorate was hoped for in the next elections to be held in 1977. The month was advanced from October to June, but hopes of a decisive result were not fulfilled. Both the major parties showed gains, whilst the People's Party obtained the largest number of seats. The National Action Party gained ground, but the National Salvation Party lost half its seats in the 450 member lower house of the Grand National Assembly. Its vote dropped from 11.9% to 8.6%. A coalition of right-wing parties was with difficulty formed by Demirel which lasted until January, 1978, when defections from the Justice Party allowed a government to be formed by Mr. Ecevit on a necessarily precarious basis. These defections partly arose from alarm at the increasing influence of the Justice Party's coalition partners.

The principal aim of the new government was declared to be the restoration of law and order in a worsening situation of political violence. This principally occurs between leftist and rightist militant groups, with the latter more to blame, but there have been violent incidents too involving Shi'ite Muslims and also Kurds. In Malatya in Eastern Anatolia there were three days of fighting in April, 1978, and serious strife, with hundreds of casualties, occurred in Maraş in December. According to the Minister of the Interior, from January to May, 1978, 159 persons altogether were killed in violent incidents as compared with 90 during the whole of 1976 and 262 in 1977, when nearly 2,750 persons were injured.

Foreign Affairs

Immediately after the second world war Turkey was seriously alarmed by the Soviet Union's demand for a Russian military base in the Straits and for certain territorial concessions. The Turks faced this threat alone at first and stood up to it. Later they were supported by the western powers. This stand denied to the Russians not just secure access to the Mediterranean, but what must have developed into a large measure of Soviet control over

Turkey. This indomitable resistance to great pressure laid the foundations for Turkey's subsequent policy of firm alliance with the West. That Turkey needed substantial western economic aid for development was also important in leading her to this commitment to the West in general and to the United States in particular. Not that the West was at all eager to extend membership of NATO to Turkey; on the contrary Turkey had to press her case with the utmost persistence. Opinion in Washington, and more especially in London, preferred to see Turkey as a leader of a middle eastern grouping which would be friendly towards the West. Nevertheless, Turkey was admitted to NATO in 1952, her participation in the Korean war having helped to dispose the western powers favourably towards her. This close alliance with the West did help to undermine the success of Turkish efforts to establish a defensive organization in the Middle East, however. The Baghdad Pact, a mutual security and defence agreement, was signed in 1955, between Turkey and Iraq. Accession was left open to other states, though Arab nationalists, including Nasser, regarded the action of Iraq as traitorous to the Arab cause. This could be asserted with even more conviction when Britain adhered to the Pact in 1955. The other states which joined were Persia and Pakistan. With the defection of Iraq, after the revolution of 1958, the Baghdad Pact became the Central Treaty Organization (CENTO) in 1959 with active American "observation". On the 5th March, 1959, the United States signed an Agreement of Cooperation with Turkey, as with Iran and Pakistan, to assist Turkey with "appropriate action including the use of armed forces" (Article 1) in case of aggression against that country. In the Arab world Turkey came to be regarded as an American satellite; Turkish-Egyptian relations were at a particularly low ebb. Yet despite full support for American policies during the decade 1950-1960 Turkey did not obtain as much as she hoped for from the United States. Even although financial and military help was substantial, over a quarter of the Turkish budget was still by the end of the decade being devoted to defence.

The overthrow of the Menderes government in 1960 made little difference to Turkish-American relations, despite a new Soviet overture of friendship. But the Cuba crisis of 1962 did so, for the United States was said to have bargained the Turkish missile bases against those in Cuba. This was denied in Washington, but widely believed in Turkey—even if they were becoming obsolete in the face of the development of the Polaris missile. The ill feelings engendered in Turkey by this incident developed during the rest of the decade. In June, 1964, President Johnson warned Turkey that unilateral action in Cyprus resulting in Soviet intervention would not entail NATO support and that military equipment supplied by the United States was not for use in Cyprus. When the Cyprus crisis blew up again in 1967 Turkey was once more on the brink of intervention. That she did not intervene was widely,if erroneously, thought to be due to American pressure. In 1974 Turkey did invade the island and established a large Turkish enclave, but in 1975 suffered an arms embargo by the United States. This was partially lifted the following October after Demirel's government threatened to close all but one of the twenty-seven military bases. The arms embargo, after many hopeful signs, is only partially lifted (1978). Principally its intention is said to be to make Turkey more conciliatory in negotiations with Greece over Cyprus and the Aegean, where rights to the sea bed are in dispute.

The American connection also came under fire when in 1971 the United States, after a long period of pressure, was promised that opium poppy cultivation would be restricted. This crop is valuable to the Turks and they did not see why they should be the ones to solve the American drug problem, especially when the compensation offered was regarded as inadequate. Nor in the late 1060's did the neo-Marxist intelligentsia understand why the United States and other "imperialist" powers should be allowed to continue to exploit Turkey under the guise of development aid. Moreover, as the large number of Americans in Turkey enjoyed privileges of various sorts, their presence reminded Turks of the capitulations of Ottoman times under which foreign subjects enjoyed economic and other privileges to the detriment of the Empire.

Yet underlying the emergence of these troubles affecting the special connection with the United States is the fact that in the last two decades the cold war has softened into *détente*. In 1967 even the leader of the rightist Justice Party, Mr. Demirel, visited Moscow, and the Soviet Union has assisted, and is preparing to assist, Turkey in various schemes of industrial development. Even if Turks sometimes declare that Turkey's defence posture is towards Greece rather than the Soviet Union, Turkey is too cautious, and the Soviet Union too diplomatic, to suggest arms deals. In fact Turkey has diversified her foreign policy in other directions, not least by looking towards Europe—where arms deals are also a possibility. As an Associate Member of the EEC since 1964 Turkey is for the most part looking forward to full membership in the course of time, but sometimes suspects that her membership of the EEC is not all that welcome, especially as she has the capacity to flood the community with workers.

For Turkey to turn to the Middle East is theoretically possible and is welcomed by the National Salvation Party, for whom Europe is either Christian or Godless. Turkey does already participate in a scheme of regional co-operation for development with Iran and Pakistan, an off-shoot of CENTO, but not with marked enthusiasm. To mend fences with the Arab world is often regarded as important on the grounds that the oil rich Arab states could provide a market for Turkish manufactures, though whether they could compete with those of Europe, Japan and the United States is doubtful indeed. Perhaps more fruitful are recent attempts to establish contacts with Romania and Yugoslavia, despite the obvious dangers of being sucked into that system.

Despite these attempts at diversification of foreign policy, Turkey, it has been said, "stands closer than ever before to the United States and Western Europe".[3] This is still true, especially if, as seems to be the case, conventional weapons are still important. In this case Turkey's role in the defence of the West is of more immediate significance to Europe than to the United States. The strength of Turkey is a vital European interest.

CONTEMPORARY SOCIETY

Turkey has a homogeneous population in two senses. In the first place, over 99% of Turks are Muslims. Secondly, the only really large linguistic minority is that of the Kurds (about 8%) who live mainly in the East. The next significant language spoken as a

mother tongue is Arabic (just over 1%) and large numbers of
both minorities can understand and speak some Turkish. The
Arabic speakers are concentrated in the South-East. These figures
appear to augur well for Turkish national unity, but they do not
quite tell all the story. The Muslim populace is actually divided,
up to one fifth, as an estimate, being Shi'ite (*Alevi* in Turkish)
whilst the majority is Sunnite. This may well be a division that is
declining in importance as a result of economic and social change,
but it is possible for it to be exploited politically. The Kurdish
minority can also provide more worries than its numbers warrant
because there are Kurds outside Turkey's borders in Iran and Iraq
to help keep alive nationalist ambitions. Fortunately for Turkish
unity, however, the religious and linguistic differences do not
coincide.

In fact it is arguable that the most important population
problem in Turkey is that of sheer growth and that there is little
to fear where homogeneity in concerned. In 1935 Turkey was a
thinly peopled country with a population of only 16 millions,
about one-fifth of whom were illiterate. By 1960 there were
some 28 millions and by 1965 about 31 millions. Now Turkey has
a population over 40 millions strong almost two-thirds of whom
are literate. The rate of population increase, at 2.5 per cent is
more than that of most European countries, but there is some
hope for the future since the birth-rate is beginning to decline. It
should do so for Turkey's development has been quite impressive.
In 1973 the *per capita* gross national product at current prices was
$952 and rose to $1,117 in 1977. This provides a somewhat unreal
picture due to inflation and overvaluation of the Turkish lira, but
there has been in recent years an annual real increase in *per capita*
GNP of some three and a half per cent at constant prices.

The single chief contributors to the Turkish gross domestic
product are agriculture and industry, the former now constituting
over a fifth and the latter about one quarter, miscellaneous
services providing about one half. The agricultural contribution
can vary a great deal according to climatic fortunes, but the part
played by industry, which is nearly all manufacturing, has
increased steadily over the past twenty years. The overall rate of
economic growth has in fact averaged some six to seven per cent

over the past decade. Nevertheless, Turks are less well off in comparison with Greeks, Spaniards or Italians than they were fifteen years ago. Among Turks who have greatly prospered have been those employed in Western Europe, notably in West Germany, whose numbers have been estimated at some 909,000 in 1975.[4] Their remittances home have substantially helped Turkey to cope with her balance of payments problems which, with increased imports (chiefly raw materials and investment goods) has become very serious. Earnings from tourism have also helped, even if the results have been disappointing, but the main burden must fall on exports, of which cotton, tobacco, vegetables and fruit form the bulk, with industrial goods amounting to just under a quarter.[5] As exports have not expanded at a sufficient rate, recent years have seen heavy trade deficits, which Turkey is trying to remove by means of a substantial currency devaluation (54% against the dollar in March, 1978) and by large foreign borrowings, mainly from international financial institutions. At this point it should be mentioned that foreign private investment in Turkey is low (less than one per cent of total investment) and that transfers of profit abroad under a quite liberal law amount to about half of foreign private capital inflow.

To add to her economic problems Turkey has suffered from gross inflation since 1963, and particularly in recent years. The annual wholesale price rise in the last five years has been of the order of forty per cent, with cost of living indices in Istanbul and Ankara, at least, going even higher. This has had the usual deleterious effects on salaries and savings.

To return to the Turkish people themselves, we find that in 1972 almost two-thirds of the economically active population were employed (or under-employed) in agriculture still, with 23% in services and only 11% in industry. In addition, about 12% of the employable population was recorded as unemployed, though the true rate was, and still is, probably higher.[6] The rate of industrialization has just not been fast enough. Moreover it has been highest in the production of consumer rather than investment goods, which is a cause for concern. Other countries at a similar level of economic development have better balanced industrial production.

As the numbers employed in agriculture have been declining so, too, have the numbers of the rural population—to some 58% of the whole in 1975. Nevertheless, whilst declining relatively, the rural population has been expanding absolutely by about one and a half per cent annually. With this continuing pressure on the land the way in which land is divided up is of particular significance both for economic and socio-political reasons. The problem is the familiar one of how to combine maximum production with a system of land ownership considered just by society at large, and in particular by those who manage and work the land. Turkey has lived with this problem for decades now.

Kemal Atatürk undoubtedly had the cause of the peasant at heart but his regime inaugurated quite modest reforms affecting only the re-distribution of state lands. (It is possible, then, though scarcely profitable, to criticize Atatürk for not being ahead of his time). A projected law of 1945 was more serious. This proposed that after using state and municipal land, the government should confiscate private land over 5,000 decares (1,250 acres), and then of 2,000 decares (500 acres), should this be insufficient. In addition, in densely populated areas confiscation could extend to holdings over 50 acres. Opposition to this bill was overwhelming in the Democrat Party, and support in the People's Republican Party was only lukewarm, with the result that only a tiny fraction of privately owned land was expropriated between 1945 and 1962.[7] The Democrat Party governments of the decade 1950—60 placed great emphasis on the need for technical improvements, not for re-distribution. The military junta, by contrast, when it assumed power in 1960, expressed deep concern over reform of land ownership. The new constitution of 1961 conferred authority on the government to expropriate land as necessary. A bill before the Grand National Assembly subsequently laid down upper limits on land holding ranging from 5,000 to 275 decares depending on the fertility of the land in question. İnönü failed to get such a measure accepted. Even when the bill was watered down to allow double the amount of privately owned land, and supported by Demirel when he was in power in the 1960's, a reform of land tenure could not be achieved. In June 1973, however, a bill was passed limiting irrigated land holdings to

1,000 decares and unirrigated to 2,000 decares, but has been implemented in only one province, the South-East (Urfa), and only in part.

The political importance of land reform to a number of those actively engaged in politics has prompted serious, but by no means easy, statistical investigation of the sizes of agricultural holdings. In the first place, landless families in settlements of less than 5,000 population, excluding tenants and sharecroppers, constitute 11.6% of the agricultural population. In this group about 10% are probably landless agricultural labourers. Of the farming families who actually farm their land 83.5% own all they farm, while another 12% own part of the land they farm. Only 4.5% of the farming families are either sharecroppers or tenants.[8] The prevalent pattern is one of small scale proprietorship, with 75% of the holdings being of less than 50 decares. Not surprisingly these small parcels of land together consitute only 30% of the cultivated area. These are the poor peasants. There is then a large group of middling farmers (22% of the holdings) farming land between 51 and 200 decares who occupy 45% of the cultivable land. Above this level some 3% of the holdings occupy as much as 25% of the cultivable area. These figures, deriving from a 1970 census, are broadly similar to those revealed by an earlier census made in 1963, save that the later figures show rather more land-holders with less than 30 decares and a small increase in the total area they absorb. There are also fewer large holdings, but this is almost certainly due to under-reporting by large landholders at the time of the 1970 census for obvious reasons. Indeed, the total area of agricultural land surveyed in 1963, and particularly in 1970, is well below that shown by agricultural statistics.

However, it is at least clear from these rather unsatisfactory figures that land is unequally distributed, if not remarkably so by international standards; but to offset the large landowners there is a solid group of middling farmers nearly all owning their own land. The most unequal distribution of the land occurs in the South-East of the country, the most equal division being in the Black Sea, Marmara and North-Central regions. But in considering these national statistics it is necessary to bear in mind that fifty decares of irrigated land can be worth a great deal more than the same amount of unirrigated land in a dryish region. So it is hazardous to attempt very many deductions from the national statistics.

Nevertheless it can safely be said that this unequal distribution of land is matched by an unequal national pattern of income distribution. Statistics for 1973 reveal that the top 2.6% of families enjoyed some 21% of national income whereas the lowest 30% had only about 7%. Those in between these two extremes earned between $714 and $7,143, but only 25% of the total number of families earned between $1,785 and $7,143, obtaining 44% of the total income.[9] These inequalities should provide an excellent opportunity for the propagation of socialist doctrines, especially the position of the poor, but global statistical analysis means more to social scientists than to those who are the object of their studies. Income in Turkey is distributed less equally than in many similar states, but we need to examine some of the facts of rural and urban life before reaching too many conclusions on the basis of broad statistical enquiry.

The Village

We must first begin on the village, however, with some more statistics. A study in 1968[10] of some 212 villages revealed *inter alia* that as many as half the villages provided emigrant labour, that far from being cut off from urban life about one-third of the villagers visited a town at least once a week, that they were in contact with the outside world through their quite numerous radio receivers (68% of the villages had twenty or more radios) and that 84% of the villagers would actually prefer to live in towns. Given the economic opportunities they could certainly reach them quickly enough; a quarter of the villages had all-weather roads while almost two-thirds were not more than ten kilometres from a main road. Life in the village has also changed. The extended family living under one roof was not the norm for two-thirds of the villagers. A large majority were in favour of more modernization, there was more accent on the importance of money than used to be the case and nearly 80% of the villagers wanted a higher education for their sons. To a man almost they were optimistic about the future and 60% thought they were better off than they had been.

Individual village studies have tended to confirm this general picture, whilst also adding significant detail and raising important questions. For instance, a study 'of four villages in the Çukurova plain north of Adana has shown how in the case of two of them marked agricultural development has led to an increase in the number of landless labourers and the draining away of wealth from the village to largely absentee landlords.[11] As a result these two "developed" villages do not enjoy a higher *per capita* income than the least developed of the four villages. In such a situation egalitarian reformers anxious to preserve technical efficiency would no doubt enthusiastically advocate co-operative or communal farming. Yet we need to be careful; another study suggests that co-operative enterprises are not that easily established against internal opposition by richer farmers and those loyal to them and that they also require outside funding.[12] Where there is large scale farming capitalist development is moving the surplus to the towns where to some extent it is being invested in industrial development. This means that it helps provide work for the many villagers who supplement their agricultural income with urban employment and helps take the edge off the small landholder's and the landless labourer's discontent. It is hardly an ideal situation, however, and schemes designed in times of over-population and unemployment to keep more villagers gainfully employed in the countryside have their appeal.

The availability of employment in towns varies from village to village. The villages of Sakaltutan and Elbaşı near Kayseri (Caesaria) in Central Anatolia are lucky in this respect. Since 1950 new agricultural techniques have greatly increased productivity. Consequently both villages have seen the emergence of sizeable holdings to make best economic use of the new techniques. There is growing division between the farmers and the rest in societies where not long ago almost everyone would regard himself as a farmer. But both villages are fortunate in that they have long supplied labour for the building industry. So many villagers, whilst retaining some land to fall back on, seek work all over Turkey, some becoming contractors and subcontractors in the building trades.

These individual village studies confirm more general observations to the effect that the family structure, for instance,
is changing. Extended families are giving way to those more
nuclear, though kinship connections are still important in helping
to assemble capital for small economic enterprises, and yet the
father is not so important now to the son as he used to be. The
latter is not only more independent economically with a job outside the village; he also knows his way about the world better.
Consequently parental authority has declined. Moreover, radio
plays, films and fiction are nearly all inclined to accept the norm
of the nuclear family. For this, and other reasons no doubt,
women are beginning to assert themselves in new directions,
even if they do not anywhere have much economic weight, in a
struggle for greater freedoms which will not be won overnight.
Religious practices are also on the decline—there seems to be less
and less concern with what is allowed or forbidden by religion and
certainly villagers are not at all fatalistic or inclined to turn away
from the solid satisfactions to be gained in this life for the sake
of a place in the next. Yet it can be reported from one village
that religion is booming, from others that mosques are being built
and repaired or that small societies spring up for the sake of
providing children with some religious education. There are also
as yet few signs of change in the rules governing relations
between the sexes. A young man still wants to marry a respectable
girl who will be a good mother and will preserve his and the
family's honour. Yet the changes which are occurring in the
countryside sometimes appear contradictory and are not all that
easy to explain. An increased attention to some aspects of
religious life may perhaps be a form of compensation for "back-
sliding" in other directions. Or again something of the confused
character of village life may be explained by the view that there
are two basic forms of change in operation. The first set of
changes stems from the processes of economic and social
modernization which accompanies the growth of a secular,
positivist, rational and, usually, individualist spirit. The second set
of changes are the structural changes occurring within the village,
like the creation of new means of livelihood or, say, the development of a co-operative enterprise. So a more or less psycho-

logically "modernized" villager may find himself in conflict not just with a traditional mentality, but with revised patterns of thought and behaviour emerging from the village itself and which are acquiring a new autonomy.[13]

As to those who are the most influential in the village in these changing times it is again difficult to generalize. For those who equate influence with economic power alone it is the large landowners and substantial enterpreneurs who have most influence. Obviously a large landlord in a village where most of the villagers are landless labourers must have a great deal of power over many aspects of their lives,[14] though this is not to say that the power is always abused, or that the responsibilities traditionally attached to the possession of wealth in Islamic society are necessarily forgotten. Yet sometimes even a schoolmaster may be influential if he is able to help pupils along the desired road to a higher education. Then there is the village headman, the *muhtar*, who can be powerful in his own right by virtue of his close connections with the outside world and particularly with government departments. He is also elected to office by the villagers, which is not always unimportant, even if in some villages he seems to be designated in fact by important village groups. There is at least one village where the *muhtar* has joined with the schoolmaster and others against the power of the landlord,[15] while in underdeveloped villages the traditional leadership groups continue to wield what has become a customary influence. The difficulty about locating power in the village is that, as we have seen, Turkish villagers are on the move both physically and psychologically, they can increasingly escape control, whether economic control by landlords, richer farmers or businessmen, or social control exerted by the kinship group. Sometimes the mechanisms of one system of control can work against those of the other to enlarge the areas of freedom, or they can combine—with just the opposite result.

Urbanization, the Gecekondu's[16] and the Towns

Urban migration and urban growth are as predominant in Turkey as they are in many other middle eastern and third world countries. The result in the Middle East is that many towns are superficially a cross between Manchester and Mecca, but it is a superficial resemblance if only because with the exception of a few, like Istanbul, they are not in fact very much industrialized. The new population which has swarmed to the towns for the most part works in small scale-crafts and in providing services. When they first arrive they find urban accommodation, but with its increasing scarcity such accommodation becomes too expensive. Consequently the newcomers then typically band together to move, often dramatically, as an organized body to occupy privately or publicly owned land, which overnight they crowd with shacks to serve as living accommodation.[17] For the most part in Turkey the authorities have wrung their hands and done nothing to halt this process. One way and another the new immigrants acquire a title to the land they have occupied (they have votes to buy after all) with the result that Turkish towns are now surrounded by shanty towns, often much to the annoyance of the urban residents who resent the "peasantization" of their environment. Certainly Turkish towns have become much shabbier in recent years, partly as a result of this migration.

The population of these *gecekondu*'s is between 3.5 and 4.5 million, or some 9–12% of the total Turkish population.[18] In the large towns from one-third to over half the population live in the new *gecekondu* suburbs. Their inhabitants are for the most part former peasants who have left the countryside because there are just too many people trying to get a living out of what is often poor quality land divided into uneconomically sized plots,[19] or mechanization, which accelerated in the 1960's has left them without work. Despite this experience they have not turned into rootless, resentful and alienated masses. For the most part they moved to a nearby town after reconnoitre and experiment and in the towns they tend to stick together in kinship and even regional groups. They are also still in contact with their home villages where a few sometimes still have some land, and family visits seem to occur quite frequently in both directions. The *gecekondu* suburbs may be poor, but they are not slums, with all the misery, crime and resignation to poverty that the word implies. The *gecekondu*'s are constantly being improved by the migrants, who nearly all manage to find some work, who are optimistic about the future and are very conscious of being better off than they were in the village. When they return to visit the village, perhaps to take a holiday there, or to work on their land, they are welcomed and esteemed. Indirectly they are a powerful force for modernization; to the villager their example is worth a hundred lessons from educated officials or teachers.

In the town the migrants take all sorts of jobs, including the unpleasant ones, but about a fifth of those who have migrated to Istanbul have set up small businesses of their own—the ideal for many migrants, whilst many others become skilled workers. Politically they are not discontented and certainly they are not enemies of the system. In fact, they use the multi-party system to obtain practical benefits, like sanitation and electricity for their settlements and educational facilities for their children so that they may rise to become professional persons or higher officials. The *gecekondu*'s are not the breeding places of revolution yet.

These migrants from the countryside often feel inferior to townspeople, but their social aim is not to oblige townspeople to treat them equally. They do not wish to be a species of urban peasants, but instead to become like townspeople themselves. They want to become civilized, just as Atatürk wanted all Turks to be, but civilization perhaps everywhere, and certainly in the Islamic tradition, is a thing of the town. Yet the effect of the rural migration to the towns is beginning to make them and all classes of their inhabitants seem less obviously European or American, and this Turkification is occurring despite the increasing numbers of cars, refrigerators, washing machines and the like. It is as if material progress is enabling an enchained Turkish culture to break free and assert itself with a fuller confidence than before.

What then of the towns themselves, and particularly of the smaller ones which have not been so subject to the invasion from the countryside? Unfortunately, information is scarce so generalization is as hazardous as ever in these matters. Patently, however, towns are going to differ quite a deal by reference simply to their size. Nearly all towns under 20,000, it can be said with some certainty, are likely to be market towns essentially, with minor commercial functions and some administrative ones if they happen to be provincial or sub-provincial capitals. Sometimes these small

towns have developed, or had developed for them, industrial enterprises, but neither these, nor indeed larger towns, always profit
from such enterprises as much as might be expected. This is
because industrial concerns in Turkey tend to be self-contained,
in accordance with   Turkish tradition in such matters. They
often provide accommodation for their workers as well as shop-
ping facilities and even schools. To some extent, and varying in
each case, the town is thereby by-passed.[20] Yet this should not
be exaggerated. Even the small towns, always held to be more
conservative than the villages, are changing under the influence
of education, commerce, easier transportation, the media, the
return of workers from the larger towns and from Europe and so
on. Consequently family patterns, as in the village, are becoming
more nuclear, and the population does not appear to be passive or
resigned to fate (they stress industriousness, determination, skill
and education as the requirements for success, not divine favour).
This is not to say that religion and tradition have disappeared as
effective determinants of behaviour. Apprentices, if far fewer,
still learn trades and are initiated into them with the traditional
ceremonies—and are said, at least, still to cherish the marks an
irate master's hand left upon them, spots where roses are said to
grow![21] Not all the graceful courtesies of Ottoman and Turkish
civilized life are reduced yet to mere ceremony and all the old
values are not yet completely eroded and perhaps never will
be. But more important than economic institutions like
apprenticeship, which will decline, most parents in towns as in
villages think it is important that their children should be brought
up in the values enshrined in Islam. In Susurluk in western
Anatolia, they obviously still do not like some of the modern
lycée teachers whom they regard as "itinerant invaders with
offensive ideologies and compare them unfavourably with the
teachers of the pre-Republican era, who participated fully in the
social and religious life of the community."[22]

Turkish society recognizes the need and inevitability of
economic and social change and welcomes it, provided some of the
traditionally hallowed norms of behaviour are preserved. Many
Turks, not least the women, want and value more freedom from
drudgery, boredom and tight social control. Individualism, and

certainly libertarianism, are not much in evidence, however. The desire for a cohesive society governed firmly by a paternalistic but responsive government is very deep-seated. Within such a framework Turks want their children, including the girls now, to acquire an education adequate to enable them to try for places among the elite. In the Turkish tradition there are no barriers, save that of education, to progress to the top. Those whom they regard as at the top are professional people, high governmental officials, landowners, and even perhaps businessmen now. Those skilled in practical techniques come somewhat lower down the scale, as in many old societies. Such a status scale is in a way unfortunate because Turkey, like many other old societies in Europe and Asia, needs educated but very practical leadership exerted among, not over, the people.

GOVERNMENT

Turkey is a unitary state. A degree of decentralization is admitted in the organization of local government, as will be described below, but all powers are essentially concentrated at the centre. The nature, extent and distribution of these powers is described in the lengthy Constitution of 1961 and its subsequent amendments. This Constitution differs from that of 1924 in some important respects. Individual liberties are expanded and legislative interference with their operation is restricted. New economic and social rights (like the right to strike and the right to medical care and land reform) are enunciated. Moreover, it is laid down that the legislature may not restrict the essence of any liberty and a Constitutional Court has been established. In addition, in order to amend the Constitution, it is now necessary to obtain a two-thirds majority of each of the two houses forming the Turkish parliament as compared with a bare majority of the single chamber parliament which existed under the previous Constitution. The principles which underlie the Constitution are contained in the statement in Article 2 of the Constitution that Turkey is a nationalist, democratic, secular and social (or welfare) state. This last principle is new. Secularism is not new. It is an Atatürkist principle which requires that religion should not be allowed to interfere in affairs of state or to influence education. Nationalism is also long hallowed, but the democratic principle receives new emphasis. It is intended that no political party will be formed that does not conform to "the principles of a democratic and secular republic based on human rights and liberties..." (Article 37). This doctrine "is not compatible with such contemporary distortions of the democratic theory as authoritarian democracy, guided democracy, tutelary democracy, or people's democracy."[23]

The Turkish parliament, the Grand National Assembly, consists of the totally elected National Assembly (450 members) and the Senate of the Republic, which consists of 150 elected members, 15 members appointed by the President and a small number of life members who are either former members of the National Unity Committee (the military junta of 1961) or former Presidents. The National Assembly and the 150 elected Senators are directly elected by universal suffrage. The National Assembly has a four year term. One third of the Senate's elected and appointed members retire every two years; by this means the Senate is maintained in perpetual existence. Nearly all Turkey's leading politicians are Deputies, not Senators.

The electoral system for both houses of parliament is one of proportional representation in which each elector gives his vote to the list of candidates in his constituency prepared by the party of his choice, or to an independent candidate. The system works against the interests of the very small parties. Being a list system, it also means that candidates at or towards the bottom of the list have little chance of election. In an attempt to ensure that the highest places in the list are not in the gift of the central party organization, primary elections for list candidates are held, though each central party organization may place five per cent of candidates where it wishes in the constituency lists. Voting in primary elections is limited to party members; it is not extended to the electorate, and the system is said to give an advantage to the candidate with "the time or personality required to spend his evenings in the pre-primary period cultivating the good will of a host of minor party officials in distant suburbs or villages."[24] Not surprisingly, many deputies spend a good amount of time, it appears, in attending to their constituents' affairs in the corridors of the ministries. Consequently it is claimed that deputies have to rely too much on the help and co-operation of the bureaucracy ever to be in a position of trying to fulfil one of the classic functions of parliament, namely to control the bureaucracy. Their being so closely oriented to local interests prevents them, it is said, from developing a broader and deeper understanding of their national responsibilities. However this may be, such evidence as exists suggests that parliament is not unpopular with the Turkish public.

Of the two houses forming the Grand National Assembly the lower is much more powerful. Legislative proposals are debated there first, and it makes the final decision with regard to amendments proposed by the Senate. However, a simple or a two-thirds' majority rejection of a bill by the Senate requires over-ruling by a similar majority in the National Assembly. In the case of bills involving political organization, a political parties' law for example, the powers of the Senate are a little greater. So, too, budget procedure accords a rather larger than normal place to the Senate, but again control is very firmly in the hands of the Assembly in the last resort.

The control of the executive is also in the hands of the lower, house, since government can stay in office only as long as it has the Deputies' confidence. Less drastic means of control are by parliamentary questions in either house and by parliamentary investigation. There is also the powerful weapon of interpellation, which may be used only by the lower house.

The executive is formally headed by the President, elected by both houses conjointly for a period of seven years. He is not allowed to be a member of parliament or to belong to a political party. The President's position is formal because it is the Prime Minister and the Ministers who are politically responsible. The President has used his power to delay implementation of legislation but his most significant political office has been in his selection of a prime minister able to sustain a majority in the Assembly. He has also, it appears acted as a channel for the transmission of the military's views to the political system. From 1961 to 1973 the military's voice in the selection of the prime candidate for election as President was the most influential. A factor that works against the dominance of executive power is the limitation

placed upon dissolution of the National Assembly. The Prime
Minister may advise the President to dissolve the National
Assembly only under very unusual conditions of repeated
governmental defeat.

The political parties which organize political opinion and
represent it in parliament are required to operate within a framework provided in the Political Parties' Law.[25] Political parties are
differentiated from associations, like chambers of commerce
or trade unions. Associations may express political views, but must
not directly assist, or be directly assisted by, political parties or
participate in their activities. This has acted as a brake on the
political ambitions of some associations, but political parties may
be formed without much difficulty and informal but close links
between associations and political parties in practice develop
easily enough. The Worker's Party and the Confederation of
Revolutionary Workers (known by the acronym DISK) became
very close, for instance. Political parties in Turkey closely inter-
twine with society and are principal actors on the Turkish political
scene, so it seems all the more important to Turks that an attempt
made to lay down what they should, and should not, do.
Consequently no party is allowed to deny republicanism or
nationalism. Nor may religion be exploited or any opposition be
shown to the principle of secularism. Not surprisingly, the achievements of both the Atatürkist and the 1960 revolutions are held
sacrosanct. The titles "communist", "anarchist", "fascist" or
"national socialist" may not be used. Nor must political parties
campaign against multi-partyism or against direct elections.
Internally, they have to be democratically organized and they may
not set up anything but a token organization below sub-province
level lest social disruption should ensue. Political parties are
assisted financially by the state on the basis of the degree of
success in previous elections—a device which does not encourage
new parties to emerge.

Elections are conducted under the administrative and judicial
control of the Supreme Electoral Council, but of Turkish judicial
institutions there are two which are of particular significance for
politics. Of first importance is the Constitutional Court,
established in 1961. The principal function of the Court is to

review the constitutionality of laws, decrees with the force of law, and the standing orders of the two legislative bodies, and annul all such rules if necessary. The Court does not, however, initiate action; this power is restricted to the President of the Republic, political parties with at least ten per cent of votes in the previous elections, the political parties represented in the Grand National Assembly, or one sixth of the members of either legislative body. In addition the prime judicial organs and the universities may initiate suits of unconstitutionality with regard to their own duties and welfare. Finally, an individual pleading in an ordinary court may have his case transferred to the Constitutional Court in cases of unconstitutionality.

The composition of the Constitutional Court was a difficult issue to decide. The question was whether it should be a legally constituted body—and likely therefore to be rigid, or whether it should be appointed by political institutions—and therefore be too pliable. A compromise was reached with regard to mode of appointment, but once appointed, judges serve until retirement. For this court and for other judicial institutions there are more safeguards for freedom from political pressures than under the previous constitution.

An effect of the 1961 Constitution was also to improve protection against administrative acts. Turkey has long had a system of administrative courts headed by the Council of State, but the problem before 1961 was that a government could simply declare that a measure was not subject to control by the administrative courts. This was remedied in the 1961 Constitution (Article 114) which declared that no act of administration could be excluded from the control of the judicial authorities. The independence of the Council of State itself was also enhanced in 1961. Whereas members were formerly appointed by the Grand National Assembly, they are now appointed by a commission formed from among members of the Constitutional Court on the nomination of the Council of Ministers (the Cabinet) and the Council of State itself. This greater freedom has enabled the Council of State—and the Constitutional Court to some extent—to take decisions which have not found favour with some recent governments. It was not altogether surprising that in 1971 constitutional changes were made to strengthen the hand of the government. The Constitution was amended to include the following:— "Judicial power cannot be exercised in such a manner as to restrain the fulfilment of the executive function carried out in conformity with the forms and principles prescribed by law. Judicial decisions cannot have the nature of administrative acts."[26]

Nevertheless both the Court and the Council of State play important roles in preserving the rule of law.[27] In fact the Constitutional Court annulled, if on technical grounds, the whole of a much contested law passed in 1973 under military pressure setting up State Security Courts specifically to deal with political offences. It was a victory for law over a measure ostensibly designed to maintain better order.[28]

Public Administration and Local Government

The Turkish system of public administration owes much to European, particularly French, models. Each ministry has a permanent secretary (müsteşar) who overlooks a number of usually quite powerful general directorates. Many ministries have provincial organizations whose work is co-ordinated by the Provincial Governor (Vali) who are officials of the Ministry of the the Interior. Other institutions performing public or quasi-public functions have varying degrees of autonomy. State Economic Enterprises are commercially autonomous and subject to private law, but are liable to considerable political and administrative control. Some institutions, notably the Turkish Radio and Television Authority and the Universities still enjoy a good measure of autonomy, even though restricted since 1971. Professional organizations are subject to considerable central control, though this has been eased in recent years. Although there is a state personnel office, each administrative organization largely recruits its own officials independently. One consequence of this is that "generalist" administrators are not much in evidence in the upper reaches of the bureaucracy; specialists with qualifications relating to the work of the organization mainly occupy the highest positions. Moreover, the need to recruit technically qualified personnel in demand in the private sector has entailed ad hoc arrangements for paying higher than normal salaries. This has produced a rather chaotic personnel system which is difficult to reform without creating shortages of required talent.

Local government in Turkey also follows closely the original French pattern. The Provincial Governor is both a representative of the central government and an executive officer of the elected Provincial Council, over which he also presides. He is much more powerful by virtue of his central authority than for his local representation. The most important locally elected person is the Mayor of each municipality, a municipality generally being established in towns of more than 2,000 inhabitants. Whilst in some ways subject to the tutelage of central authority and its prime representative, the Governor, a municipality enjoys a considerable degree of autonomy in the performance of its statutory duties. On the other hand finance is a real problem, municipalities being largely dependent on central government in this crucial respect. For this reason, as well as for reasons of available expertise, the decentralized administrative units of the central administration play a greater and greater part in local government. There actually seems to be little public inclination to develop an active interest in local affairs. Elections to local political office are political in the national, but not local, sense. To hold an elective office in the locality is a significant step in the development of a political career, it seems.

At the village level, however, as we have seen, national politics are regarded as socially disruptive, and political campaigning is not allowed. The village council (all adult members of the village) elects a Council of Elders and a Headman. This is democratic enough (though powerful village families tend to dominate the post of Headman), but the Headman, like the Governor, has a dual role. He is the representative of the central government as well as being responsible to the village. Often he is pulled in opposite directions. Subject to the tutelage of provincial Governor, or other representatives of the government, he is also at the beck and call of the village. There are also headmen in each quarter of a town, but they are nothing like as important as village headmen and have fewer responsibilities.

CHAPTER II

OTTOMAN LEGACIES

Classical Residues

Many modern states inherit political traditions from the past, political traditions evinced sometimes in continuing political institutions or sometimes in the less tangible and demonstrable form of political beliefs and attitudes towards politics and government. In between these two extremes there are often conventional and habitual ways of acting in politics which may well be quite informal and not at all institutionalized.

Even a non-traditional, or anti-traditional, state owes something to the past. For instance, Americans have a traditional distrust of government; they have therefore sought informally to make government responsive to groups and individuals and formally to weaken it by rigidly separating governmental powers and by restricting the growth of a cohesive career elite in public administration. By contrast the French have long relied on a highly organized, self-conscious administrative elite to man the state bureaucracy. They also show a marked tendency to check government by seeking legal redress after governmental action has been taken, rather than by encouraging prior pressure group activity. The British conservative and gradualist tradition is abundantly manifest in both the Conservative and Labour parties. West German politics is still much influenced by an authoritarian strand in German political culture.

Does modern Turkey inherit political traditions from the Ottoman past? This is a particularly difficult question to ask of modern Turkey for two reasons. First, if we are concerned with the heritage of the classical Ottoman period, Atatürk and his followers absolutely rejected it. The second difficulty in estimating the legacy of the past lies embedded in another—in that of separating classical from more modern Ottoman traditions, since the Ottoman Empire began to modernize in earnest nigh on two centuries ago. From the early nineteenth century until the time of Atatürk two traditions, both complex, lived side by side, one Ottoman, the other western. Sometimes they knitted together so well that the originals can hardly be discerned; sometimes they merely established a *modus vivendi*. In either event the classical Ottoman tradition was modified over a period of time. Moreover, it was refashioned, ignored, or attacked by the Turks themselves, not by foreigners in occupation. Although perhaps in some senses a disguised colony, the Ottoman Empire regarded itself as responsible for its own modernization. The classical tradition cannot therefore easily be resurrected by modern Turks to provide identity and protection against the influence of the West. Consequently, the classical tradition operates, where it does, without recognition; its existence cannot readily, if at all, be isolated, subjected to scrutiny and documented. The influence of this classical past in modern Turkish government and politics has to be felt; the best that can be done is to indicate to the student of Turkish politics the areas of political conduct where the tradition may break through—to alert him to possibilities of understanding and interpretation.

The first problem, however, is to establish some agreement on a fair description of the Ottoman past. The normal conceptualization, which has been under attack in recent years as we shall see, is that the classical Ottoman Empire constituted a patrimony, though possessing its own very singular characteristics. On this view, there was a most important line of division in Ottoman society between, on the one hand, the Ottoman Establishment, comprising the military, the palace entourage of high ranking persons close to the Sultan, the bureaucracy and the religious organization, and on the other, the rest of society—the peasants, craftsmen (in guilds) traders and merchants. The latter groups paid taxes but had no governmental functions. Although there were a few long-established families, there was in general only the semblance of a feudal system. Distinguished cavalry soldiers (*sipahi*'s) were granted fiefs, some of whose proceeds they were allowed to retain in return for military service, the numbers of men required varying with the size of the fief. But, in addition, they were also used as agents of government under the provincial governors in a quasi-military administrative system. The fief holders' sons normally inherited the fief, but not necessarily, since they had no accepted right to it.

This system went into decline when the feudal forces became inadequate to compete with European arms and the standing army had to be enlarged and financed. Since the *sipahi's* played an important part in tax collecting, their decline led to tax farming, with all its usual evils, and eventually, after much agrarian disburbance, to the emergence from tax farmers of a class of local landed notables situated between the bureaucracy and the peasantry. Whether this class 'exploited" the peasantry or defended them against the bureaucracy is difficult to decide. More important—and this is where some important differences of interpretation begin to appear—is whether these notables dominated the peasants as proprietors operating in a market, or as surrogate officials closely allied with the bureaucracy. The question is the fundamental one of whether the state or the economy was dominant in the Ottoman Empire and was responsible for Ottoman decline. Those who urge the latter argue the increasing involvement of the Empire in the world capitalist system, an involvement accompanied by the destruction of Ottoman industry through western imports, the rise of agricultural capitalists, the export of primary products (principally grain) and the subsequent proletarianization of the peasantry. In addition, through trading rights granted to foreigners under the capitulations a Levantine class of non-Muslim merchants and bankers is said to have arisen who possessed, through their privileges, advantages enough to drive Muslim Turks out of competition. This bourgeoisie, the argument goes, then provided a ready point of entry for foreign capital borrowed by the state for governmental purposes at exorbitant rates of interest. This led to the international capitalist exploitation of the Ottoman Empire.[1]

Whilst the influence of these factors cannot be denied, their overall significance is open to some doubt. Some advocates of the economic bases of Ottoman rule and decline are tempted to exaggerate the significance of economic factors on the basis of limited evidence and through an uncritical acceptance of some of the postulates of neo-marxist dependency theory. For instance, it has been pointed out that there were no self-generating peasant revolts in the Ottoman Empire directed against landlords; revolts of the peasantry were led by disaffected members of the official establishment against representatives of state authority.[2] It was the officials, on this view, not the local notables who were the main bogey of the masses, even in the later centuries. Then again, whilst merchants did arise, they did not do so from a solid burgher base in self-governing towns, as in Europe, and they were not able "to play anything like the financial, economic and political role of their European counter-parts."[3] Nor could they be so important. Not only did trade stagnate in a general period of decline, these merchants were nearly all Christians or Jews, "tolerated, but second-class subjects of the Muslim state."[4] Merchants were taxed when officials were not and this "was an aspect of Ottoman legitimacy; the wielders of political power, not the merchants, were the first citizens of the realm. The control established by the state over the economy was a further example of the primacy of politics in the Ottoman Empire."[5] In fact, officialdom constantly interfered with the economy to ensure, for instance, that supplies of foodstuffs were available in the towns, and that the export of certain goods was forbidden. Domestic trade and industry were strictly regulated, for "under the Islamic *hisba* rules, the community was to be protected from unjust practices in the market."[6] This did not mean that the guilds obtained undue prominence either, despite their informal connections with the Janissaries. Altogether the picture that emerges is of purposeful, if not always skilful direction of economic and other aspects of society by a generally powerful and sometimes corrupt and self-seeking bureaucracy.

Pending the emergence of substantial evidence to the contrary it does seem therefore to be closer to reality to accept that there was an Ottoman Establishment which was significant, an establishment which admittedly lived off the surplus provided by the other classes in society together with the proceeds of successful war and conquest. The highest posts under the Sultan, and the chief military commands, were filled by those who had been selected early for high office, though like all Janissaries, they were of slave status, bound subjects allowed neither property nor family. The religious organization, headed by the Chief Mufti, the *Şeyh-ül-Islam*, provided judges, religious functionaries and, in the early days, scribes for the bureaucracy, though officials were also recruited from among free-born Muslims as well.

Within this Establishment the military element was dominant, but not isolated. Governmental administration was a co-operative and well organized affair in which the slave elite, fief holders, religious judges and bureaucrats interacted in complex ways. The *Şeyh-ül-Islam* was important in government. He had to confirm that new legislation was in accord with the rules of Islam; he also had the power to issue a legal ruling that could sanction the deposition of the Sultan. This power was, however, balanced by the fact that the Sultan could dismiss the *Şeyh*. Clearly much depended on the general strength of religious feeling in the Islamic community, but more particularly on the support accorded to the *Şeyh* by the military. This was the nearest the Ottomans reached to any sort of constitutional control.

Consitutional control was hardly an overt Ottoman concern, of course. The Establishment, under the Sultan, sought to maintain the maximum control over society, justifying this by reference to *hisba*, (its duty to protect the general populace) and by *adalet*, (justice), which was interpreted as the need to maintain the supposedly traditional social order of separate, but interacting, social classes. Everyone had to be kept in his proper place for the health of society, and movement into the Establishment was greatly discouraged. As we have seen, when the Empire began to decay, the Establishment could not prevent the emergence of powerful notables. Yet is is significant that these notables did not seek to change the system; they tended to set themselves up as mini-Sultans, with provincial courts on the Istanbul model, not as economically motivated landlords. Not until the later nineteenth century, when ownership rights became accepted did any stable landlord class emerge from these depredations of the central bureaucracy.[7] Yet this class has always sought, out of habit or circumspection, to work with the government in power, not against it.

What political traditions did then the classical Ottoman Empire hand down to the subsequent, nineteenth century, period of modernization and what has survived to the present day?

The first and perhaps most crucial survival, even almost to the present day, has been the continued predominance of officialdom.

During and well past the nineteenth century modernization was led solely by the bureaucracy and in some important senses this still is the case. The western powers generally favoured liberal attitudes, constitutionalism, a measure of local self-government and a market economy, but as we have seen there were no established social or economic groups in Ottoman society strong enough to accept these new doctrines and strengthen their position in the state and society by means of them. Not until 1950 was the bureaucracy really displaced from the centre of the stage.

In their hey-day the Ottomans were concerned with the welfare of the general populace but this concern was anything but intimate. The subjects were always away out there in the countryside, on the periphery as it were, to be regarded and dealt with from afar. This rather distant attitude persisted into Young Turk and Atatürkist times, as Turks themselves are well aware, and has not died out yet; it exhibits itself these days, it is often claimed, in the didactic manner of "we know your *real* needs" radical reformers. By contrast, after the second world war the Democrat Party showed a new capacity, for Turkey, of *mobilizing* the populace, not just *improving* it by exhoration and regulation.

An inheritance from Ottoman times, half tradition, half myth, has been that of the official career open to the talents. The pantry boy to Grand Vezir tradition goes back at least as far as the recruitment of the sons of Christian subjects for Ottoman service, but perhaps even further than that to Turkic traditions. There is another side to the tradition however—the rapid demotion from Grand Vezir to pantry boy or worse. All this implies a fluidity, if not indeed instability, in bureaucratic relationships. A mitigating factor, however, and perhaps also of Ottoman origin, is the apparent capacity of Turks to shrug off the misfortune of a fall from favour and to wait philosophically for fortune's wheel to turn. Connected with this is a sense of social equality among the educated elite in the higher realms of the bureaucracy. Within the bureaucracy no-one seems to earn much esteem by virtue of his social provenance. Educational or cultural achievement may count for something, but esteem seems mainly to come simply from holding a powerful place in the governmental structure. It is not the case, however, that tenure of high office confers the ultimate political *desideratum*, namely, authority; it seems rather to provide an opportunity for the exercise of power. A holder of high office does not seem to earn any marked degree of respect for holding the office as such.

These and other nuances of political behaviour underlie the fact that the Ottoman Empire was a state of rich political complexity, though operating within a restricted compass. Those involved in politics beside the Sultan were the Palace, the military, the bureaucracy, the divines and the local magnates. We have seen that these groups did not much participate in resolving disputes through specific institutions. But they struggled for positions and power within a broad framework of Ottoman and Islamic norms.

The task of the Sultan was not so much to reconcile contendants, as to manipulate and control them. If in the process the Sultan further consolidated his own wealth and power that too was to be expected, yet not at the expense of accepted values. So the Turkish tradition is to govern very firmly against a background of an accepted and coherent social philosophy. If such a philosophy is missing government will seek to provide it. This tradition can be fitted into a broad category labelled authoritarian, but at the expense, it has always to be remembered, of the subtle realities of the unique "Ottoman way."

The Growth of Modern Political Institutions

During the nineteenth century the political elite of the Ottoman Empire was divided into three groups. There were those who wanted simply to put the clock back—chiefly those with deep religious convictions, though not all of them. Then there were two groups of modernizers—those who developed liberal and democratic ideas largely under the influence of the British and French example, and those who preferred an authoritarian road to modernization under the influence both of Ottoman tradition, and that of the authoritarian central European powers, whose example exerted an influence over Turkish minds in the later Ottoman period. The impetus towards the creation of the modern Turkish state has not, therefore, always been liberal and democratic in nature. In discussing the political reform of the Ottoman

Empire we undoubtedly have to give first place to the transition to popular sovereignty, the growth of representation, individual rights and constitutional forms of government. Yet we cannot ignore the development of authoritarian leadership and centralized control by the political elite, whether exercised through the bureaucracy, the military or, later through the mechanisms of single-party rule. This desire to centralize and control was a response in part to the fact that the adoption of the device of ownership from the West permitted in a developing mixed economy the acquisition of wealth and power by industrial, commercial and landlord groups outside the central bureaucracy, who have thus been enabled to establish over sections of society a form of control quite often traditional in style. There has not simply been a steady development towards the norms of liberal-democracy. In fact some liberal and democratic reforms may be advocated for what may turn out on examination to be quite undemocratic reasons. For example, the motives behind the establishment in 1840 of part-elected administrative councils were very mixed. The government wanted the new councils not just in order to advance democracy but also to weaken the local influence of notables and strengthen central control. This reflects the fact that during the nineteenth century the Ottoman Empire slowly but surely began to exchange an Islamic autocracy for a more pervasive and centralizing despotism. Liberals and democrats were fighting this later development rather than the loose auto-cracy of the classical empire.

Perhaps the most significant of all changes in the development of the Ottoman state and modern Turkey since the beginning of the last century has been a shift in ideas regarding the proper location of political power. In Islam, God is sovereign. All essential legislation for Muslims, covering all aspects of life is contained in the Holy Law, which is constructed chiefly from the Koran, the traditions relating to the practice of Muhammad and the Companions, and from the generally accepted custom of the Islamic community. This early formula proved too rigid for the conditions of later Islamic and Ottoman times. Under the influence of Perso-Turkish traditions, the practice therefore grew up, and was condoned, whereby a temporal ruler in Muslim lands

could make rules for matters unclear in, or omitted from, the Holy
Law. These rules, known as *kanun*'s in the Ottoman Empire were
intended to embody approved local custom or to give written
form to the temporal ruler's day-to-day commands. As we have
seen, this legislation had to be approved by the chief jurisconsult,
the *Şeyh-ül-Islam*, as not in conflict with the Holy Law. This
would not appear to leave much power to the Sultan, since he was
in theory obliged to operate within the confines of the Holy Law.
But there were large areas of governmental activity not envisaged
in the Holy Law, and even within it there were many imprecise
provisions governing the exercise of political power. (In the early
and less complex Islamic community this was not a very pressing
problem). Consequently, the Ottoman Sultan had potential power
which, with a dedicated "slave" army and a largely co-operative
religious institution, he was well able to realize. Significantly the
Sultan was more often referred to as *Padişah* (King) and *Hünkâr*
(World Creator) than as Caliph, the Islamic title for the executive
and judicial successor to Muhammad. Provided he recognized the
claims of Islam, the Sultan's power was regarded by the Muslim
populace of all ranks as legitimate—as constituting a true caliphate
in fact.

   During the nineteenth century the Sultan's authority was
eroded in the minds of many of the increasingly westernized and
increasingly secularist educated elite. By contrast, the allegiance
of the general Muslim populace was augmented by their dislike
of the westernizing trends in society. Moreover, the challenge of
the notables who obliged Mahmud 11 in 1808 to ratify a charter
of liberties for themselves was much less significant than the
gradual defection of the educated elite, many of whom were in
the bureaucracy. The notables' charter was soon rescinded; they
had only attacked the Sultan's power, not his authority and were
soon brought under central control again. The case with the
bureaucratic elite was altogether different. Beginning with the
bureaucratic prominence of Ali and Fuad Pasha's this elite was at
first content to use the Sultan's power, whenever possible, to
modernize and defend the Empire. Eventually, however, they
sought to undermine his political authority, especially when
Sultan Abdul Hamid stressed the personal nature of his rule and

emphasized his caliphal role at a time when Pan-Islamic ideas were in vogue. The later Ottoman bureaucratic and intellectual elite opposed this trend by asserting either the Islamic principle of consultation, or the western principle of popular sovereignty until eventually, in the Young Turk era, they came to wield power themselves behind something of a smokescreen of constitutional reforms. The Young Turk revolution was in part a victory for the modern bureaucratic intelligentsia over the palace.

During the whole of the preceding century the new reformers were unable to challenge successfully the principle of the Sultan's sovereignty, but they made attempts to limit it practically. For instance, a Supreme Council for Judicial Ordinances was set up to establish, discuss and elaborate the specific proposals for reform set out in an important reform edict of 1839 (the Illustrious Rescript of the Rose Chamber). The Sultan actually promised to be bound by a majority vote in working out these specific measures though this intrusion into his sovereignty did not proceed further. The 1839 edict had, however, declared for all subjects security of life, honour and property, these promises being repeated in a further edict, the Imperial Rescript of 1856. As some practical measures to guarantee these rights were slowly developed the arbitrary power of the Sultan was gradually curtailed. Of particular importance for ministers was the ending of the Sultan's power to confiscate the fortunes of officials, a measure which now made the bureaucratic career less hazardous and more rewarding. Even more important, perhaps, was the 1858 Land Law which, by allowing the development of freehold right to land, established a security of property which it had not been in the nature of the patrimonial classical Empire to recognize.

The Constitution of 1876 was the closest formal approach to limiting the Sultan's power in the nineteenth century; it is the summation of the efforts of the liberal modernizers—not a statement of their ultimate aims, but a revealing account of how far they could go in the face of opposition from an entrenched autocracy despite the very spirited parliament which emerged. Its members included representatives of the new monied groups, both Muslim and Christian, which were beginning to arise with economic and social development.

The 1876 Constitution sought, in the first place, to limit
the Sultan's powers, but in fact only enumerated them without
stipulating that these were all the powers he possessed. Parliament
had the right to legislate, but no right to initiate legislation and no
possibility of circumventing the Sultan's veto. Nor did Parliament
alone possess the right to legislate; the Sultan was empowered to
legislate by decree—and did so. Then there was the notorious
Article 113 which allowed the Sultan to exile any person deemed
(by him) to be dangerous to the state. (Ironically the author of
the Constitution was later exiled under this very provision). Nor
was collective or individual responsibility to Parliament achieved.
The Sultan appointed his ministers and had the means to defend
them from parliamentary attack. Nor need the minister come to
explain his policies or actions to Parliament on demand; he could
postpone his appearance indefinitely. Parliament did have the
power of financial control, but there were effective ways round
this too in practice. Individual rights were also laid down, but
none too precisely and subject to regulation by law. Finally
Parliament could be prorogued for as long as the Sultan wished; it
was so prorogued in 1878.

It was not until 1909, during the Young Turk era, that the
vital step was taken of requiring the Sultan to swear fidelity to
the nation. Abdul Hamid's successor, the pliant Mehmet V,
hastened to affirm that he would not deviate one jot from the
nation's wishes. This was a period of transition. The sovereignty
of the nation was not accorded its full recognition in a constitutional document until 1921, when the new Grand National
Assembly summoned by Mustafa Kemal passed a law of Fundamental Organization in which the nation unequivocally asserted its
own sovereignty, though it was to be "represented" by the Grand
National Assembly.

Representation is also a feature of modern Turkish government which has a late Ottoman background. Being a less dramatic
concept than sovereignty, it could be developed in a more piece-
meal way. It first appeared in 1840 when it was deemed that
representatives were to be elected to form part of the membership
of administrative councils set up in the provinces. These representatives were usually provincial notables and were elected to

represent their religious communities (*millet*'s) so their representation was corporate, not individual. Then in 1845, reviving an old tradition, the government required the provinces to send delegates to the capital in a consultative capacity to express rural needs. They did not in fact perform their representative function with distinction; they were very overawed and unforthcoming.

Other more promising instances of representation occurred, however. In 1868, for example, a Council of State was established, for pre-legislative functions.[8] It was required to meet every year four delegates from each provincial General Assembly, a system which continued until Abdul Hamid's reign. These assemblies had been set up as part of a scheme of provincial and local government established in 1864, after the French model, and equipped with part-elected administrative councils at various levels. For the first Ottoman parliament in 1876 the electoral law required the elected members of the councils just mentioned to act as electors in an indirect electoral system. A new but still indirect, electoral law was passed by the lower house of the 1876 parliament; it was resurrected in 1908 and then used, with some amendments right up to 1939. Only in 1946 were parliamentary elections made direct, allowing for more immediate impact by the electorate on the government.

The Islamic and Ottoman political tradition did not accord any importance to the principle of separation of powers. Unity, not division, had always been the aim. Not surprisingly then, the trend in Ottoman and Turkish reforms was not to divide power, but to capture it intact in the name of the people. Characteristically, the Atatürkists' first attempt at constitution-making was to set up "Assembly" government, incorporating legislative and executive power in one body. During the nineteenth century progress was made, however, towards a greater separation of governmental functions, an important and less obtrusive preliminary to the separation of political powers many reformers considered vital. For instance, the Supreme Council of Judicial Ordinances, set up in 1838, was regarded by some would-be Ottoman reformers as an incipient legislative chamber. It never became such, though it had more power than its eventual successor, the Council of State, even although the latter was given legislative as well as administrative functions. These were increasingly distinguished from judicial functions, which in 1867 were given to a Council of Judicial Regulations, whose prime role came to be that of a supreme court of appeal. None of this amounted to a division of powers, but it accustomed Ottoman Turks to discussion and resolution of a large range of legislative administrative and judicial problems within the framework of imported western institutions; the Council of State, for instance, inevitably operated where it could by reference to French rather than Ottoman norms.

A new state was being created under the umbrella of the old, though change in other parts of the governmental machine came slowly. For instance, the Grand Vezir had great difficulty throughout the nineteenth century in establishing his control over the Council of Ministers, since all ministers were individually responsible to the Sultan. In fact, Grand Vezirial control was not formally achieved until Young Turk times, after the Sultan had ceased to wield supreme power. Nor was the collective responsibility of the Council of Ministers established until 1909; even so it had to be reasserted, with difficulty, in 1923 in the face of opposition from the new Grand National Assembly, full of its own importance after the successful struggle for national liberation. Yet there was a constant pressure in Ottoman times for a co-ordinated and mutually supportive Council of Ministers, both under the influence of the example of western European political systems, and as a practical response to the growing complexities of government in times of great social and some economic development.

Not all the political and governmental reforms promoted by the new modernizing elite were directed to limiting or capturing the growing power of the Sultan, however. Many of the reformers saw organized religion as the great force for reaction acting behind the Sultan in the later years of the Empire, and very likely to impede the modernization they thought was essential if the Empire was to survive in a powerful and hostile world. In the early nineteenth century, however, the Sultans had attacked religion, if partly for financial reasons. In 1837, Mahmud 11 reduced the power of the *Şeyh-ül-Islam* and the jurisconsults, the *ulema*, by bringing under governmental control the pious foundations from whose revenues the *ulema* class was substantially supported. The *Şeyh-ül-Islam* was also housed in a government office, thus losing much of his former independence. Within government the *Şeyh* still maintained a great deal of influence during the nineteenth century; even as late as the Young Turk period he could claim that by virtue of his office the Chamber of Deputies had no right to interpellate him. Yet the right of the Sultan to appoint the *Şeyh* went a long way to ensure that those appointed were acquiescent enough.

In some ways the *Şeyh* compensated for his decline in political significance by strengthening his control over the religious establishment during the period of modernization, but it was an extension of control over a diminishing area. This was because religious control over the administration of law and over education was eroded in the interests of a modernizing state for which neither Islamic law nor Islamic education was perceived to be adequate. Despite protests the *ulema* had to stomach, during the middle years of the century, the establishment of criminal and commercial codes of direct western inspiration. They were saved for the time being the wholesale importation of the French Code Civil by a massive compilation of Islamic law, arranged in modern form, and completed in 1876. It was to last until 1926 when it was swept away in favour of a European code. For the new western inspired codes appropriately educated judges were necessary—another blow at the *ulema*, from among whom the judges had always been recruited. So, too, in the field of education a system of schools grew up alongside those manned by the religious institution, which provided a classical Islamic education. The government made a start with state primary schools as early as 1847, though secondary education did not get under way until late in the century. Nevertheless two secondary schools, Galatasaray and Darüşşafaka, were of importance in the training of a new western educated elite. Despite a period of Pan-Islamic sentiment during the last decades of the Ottoman Empire, the secularization of Ottoman political and social life proceeded apace. The Young Turks removed the administration of the Holy Law Courts, the religious schools (the *medrese*'s) and the religious

foundations from the office of the Şeyh-ül-Islam, who was left
only with religious consultative functions. He was also deprived of
his seat in the Council of Ministers. In fact, a new government
department, subordinated to the Ministry of Finance, was set up
to manage the finances of religious foundations and to direct
surplus revenue to the Treasury. In 1917 a law on family rights
made a direct assault on the hegemony of Holy Law by restricting
polygamy and granting women the right to initiate divorce
proceedings. By this law religious marriage contracts were under-
written by the secular state. So it might be argued that in
restricting the influence of religion and abolishing the Caliphate
Mustafa Kemal was simply completing a historical development,
but most Ottomans wanted to reform Islam and not to abolish it
from political life.

It should not be assumed, however, that religion was completely eradicated in Turkey by the Atatürk government. It has
had social—and political—consequences despite the abolition of
most of its formal structure. This is because there lived alongside
the religious institution of orthodox learned divines a more popular Islam not much dependent on the formal structure, and located
in the dervish orders. These brotherhoods provided a less stark
religious solace than that offered by orthodox Islam—through
personal guides, revered saints or divine and enraptured mystics.
It was they who brought Islam to unsophisticated village folk.
The brotherhoods were dissolved by Kemal, and this was a sudden
break, for nothing had been done to reduce their influence in
Ottoman times. Political life in Turkey has been secularized, but
there has been a groundswell of religious feeling among the
populace, as a "legacy" from the Ottoman past. Centre and right
wing political parties in Turkey are still sometimes accused by
their opponents of exploiting peasant religious feeling in their
election campaigns.

A discussion of sovereignty, representation or secularism
should not, however, lead us to overemphasize the liberal and
democratic elements of nineteenth century modernization. For
two authoritarian institutions—the bureaucracy and the military—
developed during the late Ottoman period to become instruments
of the strong and purposive government of the Young Turks and

the Atatürkists. On a not altogether unprepared foundation the nineteenth century reformers used a French blueprint to construct a cohesive, if somewhat rickety, administrative structure, quasi-modern and fitted to the quasi-modern tasks it had to perform.

To prepare new recruits to manage state affairs, a number of training schools were set up, one in Paris, even, in 1855, but of which the one which had the greatest potential was the Civil Service School (*Mekteb-i Mülkiye*) set up in 1859 and forbear of the present Faculty of Political Science of Ankara University. Perhaps the most sought-after qualification obtainable in the schools was knowledge of a foreign language, usually French— a remarkable new passion for the offspring of the self-sufficient and arrogant Ottomans of former generations. Further administrative reforms relating to the organization of functions and personnel were carried out during the remaining years of the Ottoman Empire and included even a major restructuring of local government in 1913. These reforms bequeathed a more or less efficient administrative system to the Atatürk regime. Yet neither westernization, nor the amalgam of East and West, produced an altogether happy result. "In Anatolia", it has been said, "official arrogance was still modified by the innate courtesy of the old Turkish tradition. In Istanbul westernization all too often resulted only in superimposing the morose fussiness of the French fonctionnaire on the alternating indolence and insolence of the Ottoman bureaucrat."[9] With the expansion of education the highest officials of the late years of the Ottoman Empire came to be recruited from a broader field, in particular from the lower echelons of the public service. This was a slow process; nor were the newcomers markedly different from those they replaced. Indeed the later officials of the Ottoman Empire were not recruited from so wide a background as the military officer class, more of whom, it seems came from a non-official and more modest social background. Yet wherever military officer recruits came from, they were nevertheless socialized into the norms of the officer corps. These norms dangerously included by the end of the nineteenth century a determination not only to save the

Empire but by whatever means were deemed necessary. The officers were by consequence vitally interested in politics; the education through the military schools provided them with a means to articulate their political feelings.

The instruction of the Ottoman military in western techniques began in the years of Ottoman decline before the nineteenth century, but relied on the occasional visits of Turks abroad and the use of individual European instructors like the Comte de Bonneval (1675-1742) or the French artillery officer, the Baron de Tott, and his associates at the end of the eighteenth century. The first major European impact, however, occurred just after the French Revolution when a substantial French military mission set to work. A number of military schools began to be established, leading eventually to a general staff college in 1849. In these schools officer recruits were taught not only tactics and strategy, but also mathematics, french and history. More important, deriving intellectual inspiration from their often quite distinguished teachers, they had the opportunity to discuss politics. In addition they were learning and working in institutions which stressed such qualities as efficiency and promotion by merit much more than was usual in the official institutions of the Empire at that period. Deeply influenced by liberal ideas on politics and government, isolated from the realities of political life, decisive and efficient by training and temperament, the officer class often did not realize the incompatibility of their liberal ideas and their authoritarian mentality. The native authoritarian strand was reinforced in the latter part of the nineteenth century when German influence became predominant in their military education. Yet at the back of the authoritarianism of the Turkish military mind has lain something of a feeling for forms of political organization encompassing respect for some basic liberal values, even when the authoritarian element was immediately uppermost as in 1908, 1922, 1960 and 1971.

It is hazardous to attempt any firm conclusions with regard to historical legacies, but a few features call for comment. In the first place, most educated Turks have rejected their Ottoman past, which was at least as Turkish in inspiration and drive as it was Islamic in structure. In Atatürk's Turkey the vision of most Turks was deliberately directed beyond the Ottoman Empire to a purer Turkish past for the sake of finding a historical under-pinning for modern Turkish nationalism. For a nation to reject so much of its past is remarkable, but it was the decline, not the expansion, of the Ottoman Empire that weighed heavily on the minds of most Turks in the two decades following the Atatürkist revolution. This decline was interpreted by many Turks as due to failures of morale, character and energy on the part of the Ottomans. This attribution of failure to cope with the challenges of the modern world to Ottoman defects was the chief message of historians, both non-Turkish and Turkish. It was therefore natural and even psychologically necessary for the Atatürkist Turks to try to account for these Ottoman shortcomings by stressing Turkish corruption by Islamic and Persian influences. In this regard it is interesting that there is now a trend, as we have seen, to stress the baleful influences of European economic penetration of the Ottoman Empire as the principal cause of Ottoman decline. This interpretation naturally allows for a more sympathetic regard for the Ottoman Turks to emerge, especially if, as in most neo-Marxist orientated economic history the blame for Ottoman failure falls squarely on the evils of international capitalism. But it is probably much too fanciful and paradoxical to suggest that Marxism may serve to liberate a conservative tradition.

The rejection of the Ottoman past as exemplar by the Atatürkists was certainly revolutionary, but this revolution was based on a long tradition of reform, as we have seen. Despite the revolution many Turks seem to have inherited a reforming rather than a revolutionary tradition from the nineteenth century. This reform was in part genuinely liberal in origin and justified itself in the language of nineteenth century liberalism or Islamic modernism, but it inherited too, much of the authoritarianism of classical Ottoman rule. This was often paternalistic and watchful of the rise of other groups in society, but it was not heedless of the law of the Islamic community. Perhaps it is significant that this law was not subject to frontal attack save in Atatürkist times. During the earlier long period of reform it was mainly bypassed on the grounds of its inapplicability to modern problems. Law was always respected as a vital part of the life of the Islamic community. There have since been great legal changes, but the permanence of their success must owe something to the general respect for law itself which derives from the Ottoman past.

CHAPTER III

POLITICAL ELITES

To qualify as a political elite a group of persons must obviously be those who make, or are most influential in making, political decisions about those matters of general concern considered most crucial for the society in question. The criteria sometimes seen as signifying the presence of such an elite are group consciousness, cohesion and conspiracy, in the sense of having a common will to action.[1] An elite is a minority governing a majority; and for convinced elitists the devices of selection by the majority or accountability to the public, by whatever means, can never be adequate to stop the minority from dominating the majority, or the 'mass' as those in the majority are typically dubbed. Moreover, it is claimed, one man can never rule; government of almost any but the simplest society requires that the ruler shall have at his side a group of persons with political and governmental abilities, who rely upon one another and who are aware of that important fact. Well organized, such a minority is clearly powerful over isolated individuals; it is also able to manipulate the majority. This can be done at a very practical level by restraining individuals from raising unwelcome issues. More fundamentally, a political elite is said to be able, by control of the media, education and the like, to direct public political action in ways beneficial to itself by establishing what the key issues of politics shall be. It does this through the propagation of political myths, like the divine right of kings, equality or democracy. Such popular beliefs are ostensibly accepted by the political elite, and incorprated into its political ideology, and then used to justify what may well be anything but divine, egalitarian or democratic rule in the certainlty that the masses, only too anxious to believe in such great principles, will not notice the imperfections in their realization.

How far Turkish political elites have acted in the ways that the great elitist theorists have described is open to question, particularly as the detailed information with which to test their claims is not much available. Given the existence, by general agreement, of the importance of political elites in Turkish politics some attempt at assessing answers to these important questions must be attempted, but there is in the meantime at least one more prosaic, but still difficult, question to settle.

This is that the political elite has in the first place actually to be identified. How is this to be done? For those of a Marxist persuasion it almost suffices that they are those who occupy the significant economic positions in society. Followers of C. Wright-Mills,[2] would locate the political elite among those who occupy the top positions in key institutions, economic, social and political, the institutional network being very significant. James Burnham[3] stresses the political elite role of the managerial elite, which is seen to replace the classical capitalist elite as the repository of economic and, therefore, political power. These proposals all look for the source of elite power in factors outside the elite, and play down either the organizational, or the psychological skills required for political elite domination which are stressed, respectively, by Mosca and Pareto.[4] To find a way through these difficulties of political elite identification modern students of elites have used two methods. The first is the "reputational" method of asking key politicians and students of politics who they think really are the politically powerful and influential; the other is actually to examine key decisions in a political system to see who were in fact most influential. In combination these methods have been most valuable in studying small scale, and therefore manageable, political structures. Their application, particularly that of major decision-making analysis, to a large political system like that of Turkey is well nigh impossible. Consequently, the existence of political elites has largely to be deduced from historical and political studies supplemented where possible by the "reputational" method.[5]

If we locate a political elite our next task is to discover who they are, and where they come from. Have they come from rich or poor families, from town or country? How have they been educated? By what career routes have they arrived at the top? These sorts of questions are interesting in themselves when asked of influential people. The answers also throw some light on their basic attitudes and their particular political aims and beliefs, though study of their economic, social and psychological experience does not dispense with the need to study what politcal actors do and the rational basis for their actions.

The Bureaucratic Elites

We have seen how in the heyday of the Ottoman Empire political control under the Sultan was in the hands of the upper-most military and civil officers recruited from the Balkan Christian population as boys and trained—the best of them—to take on the major tasks of military and civil command. In this they were supported by the religious institution under the Muslim *ulema* who both participated in judicial administration and constantly reaffirmed the social and political formulae by reference to which the society was governed. These formulae, which were part myths, stressed first, the essentially Islamic character of Ottoman society and second, an ancient vision of society as composed of classes with interlocking functions, a society in which it was imperative that everyone knew his place. These two rather conflicting "myths" could not altogether be reconciled, but both may be presumed to have appealed to deep-felt instincts, in the Ottoman populace.

As we have seen, the Ottoman urge to modernize the state along European lines found firm expression in the early nine-teenth century when the Janisseries were finally abolished, the influence of the *ulema* curtailed, and when the ambitions of the provincial notables were frustrated and bureaucratic and military reform was initiated along Western lines. The effects of these changes for the Ottoman political elite were very great. With the military coming to adopt Western norms, which excluded any natural right to their exercise of political power, with a religious institution of diminished influence, and with the emergence of a need for efficient managers of modernization, a class of high ranking bureaucrats came into power.

Recruitment to this mid-century bureaucratic elite, it has been noted earlier, broadened in the later years of the Empire. This did not occur without friction, however. Officials of lower status, often educated and with high expectations, frequently found the higher posts banned to them by appointments of dubious legitimacy made by the highest officials. This frustration helped give birth to a critique, both liberal and traditionalist, of the superficial westernism of grand vezirs like Ali and Fuad Pasha's. This critique, with which certain elements of the new military and the demoted *ulema* class associated themselves, eventually helped widen recruitment. Consequently, in the later years of the Ottoman Empire the bureaucratic elite began to draw its recruits from a wider field. Until and including the Hamidian period (1876-1909) the political elite was still a small circle of persons known to one another, but by Young Turk times recruitment was from a broader range of intelligentsia—from among lawyers, journalists, teachers and not least, army officers, as well as from the broader reaches of the bureaucracy. Recruitment to the bureaucracy from bureaucratic and military families reached a high peak (almost 75%) in the Young Turk period, declining to 50% between 1921 and 1939. This self-recruitment when further examined reveals, however, a pronounced trend towards increased recruitment from military families in the provinces rather than from families located in Istanbul. In fact the Hamidian administrative elite families tended not to encourage their offspring to follow them, probably seeing a better opportunity for them in the professions. Some of the older administrative elite families did nevertheless choose the bureaucracy as a career, mixing with new recruits from a variety of official and other backgrounds. For the influential ministries of Internal affairs and Finance, at least, the development of the Mülkiye (Civil Service School) notably in Young Turk era, did lead to a greater breadth in recruitment. Consequently the Atatürk regime inherited a bureaucracy with attitudes attuned to its own, and all the more pliable perhaps by virtue of the fact that the Civil Service School had not been allowed by Abdul Hamid to become a hotbed of sedition.[6] During the Atatürk period there was a decline in recruitment to the *Mülkiye* of students whose fathers were officials, though together with the sons of military officers they made up 50% of the intake,[7] divided about equally.

A study of the social background of provincial governors and deputy provincial governors carried out in 1957 revealed a substantial offical and military background for the governors (nearly

50%), but not so for the deputy governors many of whom will since have become governors, and who came from a varied background, the largest single category (nearly 22%) being from farmer and peasant families.[8] A study of higher officials in 1964[9] showed almost half recruited from an official/military background in roughly equal proportions. If to this figure were added those with a professional background, chiefly judges and teachers, who would also rank formally as officials, then it could be said that some 60% of the highest officals came from a public service background. Of these officials only 12% had paternal grandfathers who had been officials and 8% who had followed military careers. Over half the grandfathers had been farmers, traders and shopkeepers. If there is a tradition of son following father in the higher bureaucracy in Turkey it has been diluted by the influence of other factors, if only by that of bureaucratic growth. There is a firm bureau-cratic-cum-military element in the social background of higher officials, but the door has not been closed to recruitment from other areas of society, always provided that other aspirants first acquire a higher education, a *sine-qua-non* for membership of higher officialdom.

As to the power and prestige of the higher bureaucracy it reached its highest peak under the Atatürk single party regime. The graduates of the School of Political Science in Ankara, as the Civil Service School had by then become, really came into their own in this period with regard to their occupancy of high administrative posts; fifteen out of the twenty seven graduates in 1921 subsequently occupied important administrative positions.[10] The senior administrators had the task of both carrying through Atatürkist reforms and of leading economic development through the state economic enterprises set up in the 1930's. The difficulty of these tasks required that all forces should be mustered to ensure their fulfilment. Not surprisingly then, the administrative and political were in certain instances combined. Graduates of the School of Political Sciences provided many deputies for the Grand National Assembly during the 1920-46 period (21%) and an even greater number of cabinet ministers (28%). These graduates have been said therefore with justification to represent an elite within an elite. The period of greatest bureaucratic political power, was just before the second world war "when fully 61% of the cabinet members were former bureaucrats or officers."[11]

As measured by its prestige, the influence of the bureaucracy as a whole has declined steadily since those halcyon days. When in 1965 graduates of the Political Science Faculty were questioned on the prestige of different occupations they ranked the professions (e.g. doctor, engineer, judge) most highly, with public administration and business lower down.[12] This confirmed earlier studies of the attitudes of *lycée* students on the same subject. For them the free professions came out by far the most respected with the profession of diplomat second. A government official ranked very low.[13] The 1965 Political Science Faculty graduates, on the other hand, thought that the businessman was the one who could make the greatest contribution to the country's welfare. Next came the politicians and then the public officials, followed, rather surprisingly perhaps, considering their prestige, by those in professional occupations. The utility of the military in this regard was rated very low. As for the actual influence of the graduates of the Political Science Faculty, that may well have diminished as they have sought for new opportunities in a period of economic expansion in other ministries and departments than those traditionally associated with power and influence, namely the ministries of the Interior, Finance, and Foreign Affairs. This elite within the elite has been watered down, as we shall see below.[14]

The Military Elite

As to the character of the military elite, that is as open to question now as ever given the lack of opportunity to study the military at close hand. It probably still is the case that the Turkish officer corps is mainly recruited from the lower middle and salaried middle classes "for whom the military profession represents one of the few available channels of upward mobility."[15] No doubt many army officers have obtained their education in military schools and come from families who could not afford to keep their sons at *lycée* and university. Certainly they do not come from well-off families, but whether this lowly background makes them socialist in outlook is doubtful, given their long period of acculturation to the military mentality. With this background officers tend to look for order and good clean administration in civilian society. They probably welcome it more, too, from the right than from the left, since in leftist ideologies there are dangers to the notion of authority.

One factor disinclining families with the highest incomes and/or status from placing their sons in the military is that the military profession does not now enjoy the high status of early republican days. Their decline in public esteem is of longer standing than that of the bureaucracy. In the first place Atatürk took every step to ensure that the army returned to its barracks after the War of Liberation; he had always been opposed to military interference in politics. Secondly, the image of the military as leaders of modernization has faded in the public mind since Hamidian and Young Turk times. The military had for long been the most modernized Turkish institution and derived prestige from this fact. True it continued to be modernized after the second world war, largely under American influence, but in a rapidly developing society it was not in the van in this respect. Moreover, officers suffered badly in the Democrat Party era. That regime was careless of the military and the effects of inflation both depressed and inflamed them. They also made mistakes when in power after the 1960 revolution, which endeared them to no-one, but their unpopularity with the educated elite is a little surprising seeing that the 1960 revolution was sometimes hailed as a re-forging of an Ottoman alliance between the "men of the sword and the men of the pen." If we interpret the latter expression to include academics as well as bureaucrats, there certainly was a very close liaison in 1960. Academics were brought in by the military, with a touch of naivety perhaps, to advise them on how to get the country to rights. The university intelligentsia rose to the occasion fulfilling the Ottoman role of the *ulema*, the learned men of good intent who counselled on how to keep the community moving along a godly path and who could rise above the fury of petty squabbles in their larger concern with the health of society. The comparison with the ulema is apt; but it is from its very aptness that difficulties arise.

The Intellectual Elite

The aptness of the comparison between Ottoman divines and the modern intelligentsia derives from the fact that Atatürk fostered the development of an intellectual elite more or less dedicated to the principles of the Atatürk revolution. This intellectual elite worked in a tutelary capacity to society at large and to the youthful intelligentsia in particular. As with the *ulema*, their influence did not penetrate to the countryside much; moreover this new intelligentsia had no dervishes working among the peasantry, no colourful or popular religious orders to catch the imagination of the unlettered, who on account of that disability cannot easily be tutored. More so than the *ulema* they were at odds with large areas of society, or at least did not understand it very well. On that account they were not, even by 1960, very perceptive guides for the military, though their knowledge of their own country has greatly advanced since those days as a result of noteworthy work in social anthropology and sociology and an awakened social conscience.

The fact that the intelligentsia was in 1960 a sort of latter-day *ulema* had also the tremendous disadvantage that they were too involved with the contemporary predicaments of their society. Turkish intellectuals do not find it easy to reach out for the, now unfashionable, ideal of impartiality. This is not an ideal much realized elsewhere, but there are still many who take a pride in striving to be intelligent observers rather than participants. This is immensely difficult in Turkey—for intellectuals in the social sciences and some humanities, at least. It has always been regarded as a duty for intellectuals to guide and assist state and society. This deep-seated attitude emerged after 1960 with renewed force. "It was abundantly clear," writes one distingushed Turkish scholar "that one's intellectual achievement lay not in pompous titles and symbolic diplomas but in concrete practical deeds."[16] The assumption that academic titles are pompous and diplomas symbolic lies at the crux of the matter. It is argued that under certain conditions the academic intelligentsia should serve the state in certain ways. But when the intellectual elite is not only deeply divided as to basic political values, but also partly involved in politics, it is an altogether different matter. In 1960 the military received much help from the academic intelligentsia in the making of a new Constitution and the trial of the Democrat Party deputies. This help was very valuable, but it was necessarily marred by the fact that many of those consulted did have strong political convictions.

The academic intelligentsia in Turkey is not now generally as important in politics as it used to be. Under the Atatürk regime they constituted a nationalist group which powerfully supported, *inter alia* secularism, modernism, populism, a degree of private enterprise and democracy. Since the end of the second world war, however, the intellectual elite has tended to move in a variety of directions—from populism to socialism, from secularism to a search for spiritual nourishment and from self-confident tutelage to a rather agonized self-examination now that the voice of the people is being heard! Moreover, the ranks of the academic intel-ligentsia are increasingly filled with larger numbers of persons highly educated in the professions of engineering, medicine, architecture and the like. Important though their contribution is to society, this newer brand of intellectual tends to get deeply involved in society not through his opinions, but through his interests, which can be even more compelling. According to Karpat "Many of these professionals became identified in interest and thought with various economic groups and formed in fact their upper intellectual stratum."[17] There seems to be even less chance for the emergence of impartial informed opinion.

The social and political consequences of intellectual specialism, the development of a variety of ideological trends in politics, and a tradition of intellectual involvement in state affairs combine now to fragment the political influence of the intellectual elite as such. It is no longer united enough to inculcate a set of common values; and to strike out now for the autonomy of intellectual endeavour would be not just untypical for Turkish academics, but immensely difficult given the intellectual climate of the modern world.

Political Elites

There have been political elites, as distinct from governmental or bureaucratic elites in Turkey since the Young Turk revolution.

The Young Turks were engaged in a variety of professional occupations, being army officers, journalists, teachers and lawyers among others. Their social origins were modest; they appear generally to have been the sons of lowly situated officials,[18] who had attended the new state schools.

As we have seen, the Young Turk era was crucial for the development of a new western educated elite of rather wider and lowlier origins than their Ottoman forbears. Atatürk himself was the son of a customs officer of low rank, later turned lumber merchant in Salonica, and had a mother of peasant stock. He disliked the Young Turks, among whom he had cut a modest figure, not so much for their origins but for their parvenu style, and their taste for politics. He himself rose to become an Ottoman general during the first world war through regular promotion based on military still, not political advancement. His immediate associates during and after the War of Liberation were persons of high rank and established family. This did not imply any love for Ottomanism, which he sought to abolish, not just to reform after the fashion of the Young Turks of the Committee of Union and Progress. Yet he did greatly approve of a respect for law, order and regular procedures, especially when he found this quality in others, though he was himself careful to use legal means and established procedures when they would serve. When they would not, he used charisma, of which he had plenty, with or without force as the situation might require. It was not therefore in his character deliberately to create a new political elite. Moreover there was no need to do so. He had a band of willing followers available to support his aims, which were close to those of many Young Turks. So long as they had not been members of the Union and Progress organization they were acceptable, but Atatürk gave a more specifically political orientation to the educated sons (and daughters) of the modern widening elite which had appeared in Young Turk times. He had perforce to work at first with the provincial notables, the military, and with those men of religion he had attracted from the Sultan's side during the War of Liberation. As the opportunity arose, however, he removed them from influence. The disestablishment of Islam and the abolition of the Caliphate removed the *ulema*. The military he persuaded and cajoled out of power.

As to the notables in the countryside, who had helped Atatürk in the War of Liberation for nationalist reasons, they continued as a separate supportive group. They did not seek influence at the centre and by way of return, perhaps, they were not much molested by the bureaucratic elite. The reasons for this unlikely alliance are not easy to understand. Yet it should be remembered that the philosophy of the Atatürkist elite was political not social, that this elite inherited the rather didactic and patronizing Ottoman attitudes towards the peasantry and that in their ignorance of the countryside their only contacts would be the partly educated notables. Moreover, with the exception of Atatürk, and perhaps İnönü, renowned military leaders, the peasants had no respect for an elite that reminded them of tax collectors and similar rapacious officials who used the hated gendarmerie to suppress disaffection. But the new elite made a start in the mobilization of peasant support when in 1932 the Republican People's Party established People's Houses (and in 1940 People's Rooms) in towns and villages in order to bring the revolution to the people. The People's Houses replaced the religiously orientated "Turkish Hearths" founded by the Young Turks. By 1950 there were 500 People's Houses and 4,000 rooms. Perhaps more important were the Village Institutes set up in 1940 to teach practical agricultural and allied skills to village boys and girls destined to become teachers. By 1948 there were some 15,000 students in some twenty institutes.[19] They were abolished in 1954, on the grounds that they were hotbeds of political and social radicalism. In 1951 the Democrat Party Government also closed the People's Houses; it was claimed that they were too closely associated with the Republican People's Party and its philosophy.

It has been observed as a "characteristic of Turkey's gradualist pattern of political development that its political elite changed most drastically at times when political institutions underwent little change (e.g. 1908–18 and since 1950) and that its political institutions were extensively recast (in 1919–25) when the composition of the elite remained essentially unchanged."[20] Against this view it might be argued that the period 1908–18 was crucial for political development generally if not just for institutions, since, for instance, the populace began in those years to be mobilized into political participation through political party activity and the press. Nevertheless, the observation is broadly correct, even if the reasons for its being so are so difficult to assert with any confidence.

Certainly the nature of the Turkish political elite began to change after 1950 and this change is seen by Professor Frey to have led in the following decades to "the resurrection of severe intra-elite conflict. The Kemalist unity which itself resolved a bitter and debilitating dogfight within the Turkish elite, has been fractured. No integrated elite offers discipline and direction to Turkish society today. Warring elite elements engage in the intense infighting that produces in Turkey, as in many other nations, simultaneous stagnation and instability."[21] According to Frey, the key conflict in Turkish politics in the 1960's was "between the residual national elite, basically found within, or in support of, the People's Party and the new breed of local politicians basically found in the Democrat Party and its successors."[22]

The principal changes observed by Frey between Atatürkist and Democrat Party government times are, first, that the largest single occupational group among the deputies (27 per cent) had come by the 1954 parliament to be composed of those who were otherwise lawyers—and in this had come to resemble western parliaments. The deputies of other professional, economic and agricultural occupations also increased markedly. Secondly, and by contrast, the previously large official and military group of deputies had declined substantially—from 38 per cent in 1920 to 13 per cent in 1954.

In his study of the political elite Frey also discusses a trend since Kemalist days towards "localism"—the election of members born in the constituency they represented. In 1957 localism reached 66 per cent, as compared with only 34 per cent in the fifth assembly, 1935—39, when under the single party regime central designation of candidates for election was more usual. It is curious, in this regard, that relatively few deputies have ever held a local party office or have been successful in local elections. Those who arrive at the top have not come by this allegedly important route, though they do take care to be influential in provincial party organizations "through supporters, clients, or hangers-on upon whom they rely to protect and enhance their political careers."[25] There are therefore grounds for the claim that "the deputies have changed from being primarily a national elite group, oriented towards the tutelary development of the country, to being primarily an assemblage of local politicians oriented toward more immediate local and political advantages."[24]

The first question that arises is whether these trends are continuing. The situation as regards the occupational background of members of the National Assembly is that there has in fact been little significant overall change since the position in the 1950's, with the official element showing an increase to 18.5%. It is the case that members of parliament have continued to become rather more localist since those days with three-quarters of deputies being born in the constituency represented in both 1969 and 1973. The second, and more important question, perhaps, is whether the differences between major parties have continued. In fact they have not. The major parties have converged with regard to the sorts of occupations and the rising degree of localism of their deputies, who are also alike as to education and average age. The Justice Party deputies are just a little older, but in 1973 revealed a more pronounced civil service background than the People's Party deputies, among whom teachers and lecturers figure significantly. The People's Party may look schoolmasterly, but its close involvement with the bureaucracy is not now so apparent. Finally it may be observed that there has been considerable turnover in parliamentary membership; less than half the deputies have generally been re-elected to a subsequent parliament, with neither major party being unusual in this regard. There seems to have been a marked circulation of this particular elite.[25]

But does this position obtain at the highest level, that of the Council of Ministers? Is Turkey in the same position as, say, France of the Third Republic when governments fell only to be replaced from a re-shuffled pack? If we look at the lists of those who have occupied ministerial office since 1961 we find that there has in fact been a high rate of turn-over of persons, if somewhat reduced in more recent years.[26] For instance, only one-fifth of the 1965 Justice Party cabinet had previously served either in the 1961 or 1965 coalitions. The 1969 Demirel cabinet included fifteen new members, about three-quarters of the membership. Subsequently, the period of coalition governments during the critical period between 1971 and 1973 produced four coalitions which leaned heavily on independent deputies and senators and on appointments from outside parliament, which the Constitution allows. There were some Justice Party members of these coalitions, but they did not appear in the Justice Party contingent to the 1975 National Front government, whose fifteen Justice Party members did, however, include five (including Demirel) who had served in 1969. In the July, 1977, government, in which the Justice Party was the major participant, ten of the sixteen Justice Party members had been members of the cabinet for some period over the preceding decade, eight (including Demirel) having belonged to the 1975 government. Recently in this party there has been a greater measure of continuity at the top, after a high rate of turnover brought about by the selection of Justice Party ministers during the period 1971 to 1973 by non-party prime ministers.

In the People's Party we can compare membership of its contingent to the 1973 coalition with the National Salvation Party with that of the government formed by Ecevit in January, 1978. It may first be noted, however, that when Ecevit tried, unsuccessfully, in 1977 to form a minority government seven out of the seventeen 1973 cabinet members were chosen as part of what would have been a cabinet of twenty-five members. In 1978, when Ecevit did succeed in forming a minority government, in fact he chose only four members of the 1973 government out of the nineteen People's Party members besides himself.

By way of conclusion it can safely be asserted that Turkey is not governed by a small group of persons conscious of their separate identity, acting in concert in some conspiratorial fashion to exert power over the majority. There are small groups who from time to time dominate important sections of the political system, but they have been replaced frequently. At the very top this is partly due to the intervention of the military, which disturbed in 1960 and 1971 any processes of consolidation. The main influence at work in breaking up top elites is undoubtedly, however, the operation of the multi-party system, especially when the smaller parties are strongly represented in parliament and, by forcing their way into government, restrict processes of re-selection by the leadership of the major parties. Even so, it is still probably more important that parliament itself has shown a considerable turn-over in membership; also it is not by-passed when it comes to the selection of cabinet members, even although the government does not necessarily have to be formed from among members of parliament. The constant renewal of parliament is itself indicative of the fluidity and impermanence of positions of power and influence. There has also been a good deal of upward social mobility, due to the operation of the educational system and the lack of entrenched classes maintaining a hold over the power positions in Turkish society. In this regard it could not be denied, however, and with some justice, that the political and administrative elite is very broadly middle class. Certainly it contains almost no-one fresh from field or factory floor; to get to the top requires higher education. But with more variety in higher education now available, and with recruitment into the system from still wide, or wider, backgrounds—and often more directly from the provinces—the Turkish political and administrative elite is being broadened as well as renewed.

It is reasonably clear, therefore, that the major problem with regard to the Turkish political elite is not, in fact, that of having to guard society against the potentially conspiratorial and exploitative inclinations of an interlocking group. To some extent in Atatürk times the political elite was united and collectively dominated society, but even then there was substantial discord behind the scenes which called out for the forceful leadership which is so very much part of the Turkish scene. Since the advent of multi-party politics this discord among elite groups has had ample opportunity to reveal itself. It is shown in the tendency of each group, or usually now, for each party to accuse its opponents of harbouring evil designs, like wanting to disrupt society, being out to destroy its opponents and so on. Opposition is taken very seriously in Turkey in general and among its political elite in particular.[27] Emotional group solidarity is sometimes so intense, in fact, that it is almost treasonable to one's side to listen to an opponent's point of view, let alone understand it. On the other hand there is the greatly redeeming feature of Turkish culture and civilization that a defeated opponent is not treated in grossly inhuman ways; behind the furore there is a fundamental moderation.

As we have seen, an attempt has been made by Frey to relate this conflict between the elites of different political parties to differences in socio-economic background and experience. This has only been partly successful because in recent years these differences have declined whereas intra-elite conflict has if anything intensified. To some degree this must be due to ideological differences between the major parties, to be considered later, but very much more must be left unexplained and attributed to the persistence of a tradition of intra-elite hostility with deep-seated historical and social origins.

CHAPTER IV

POLITICAL CULTURE AND POLITICAL IDEAS

POLITICAL CULTURE

"The political culture of a nation," say G.A. Almond and
S. Verba, "is the particular distribution of patterns of orientation
toward political objects among the members of the nation."[1]
Orientation includes knowledge and beliefs about the nation's
political system, feelings about it and judgements on it. In this
chapter we are concerned with attitudes and beliefs of various
categories of Turks; this subject lies close to the enterprise of
teasing out the political legacies of the past which was our concern
earlier, but seeks to establish the nature of basic attitudes to
politics by more contemporary references.

Before proceeding, however, with an attempt to describe
Turkish political culture there are first three points to be made
about the subject of political culture in general. The first is that
those of Marxist persuasion believe, with greater or lesser refinement, that there is only one political culture—that imposed on
society as a whole by those in the strategic socio-economic
positions. In this study this is not regarded as axiomatic. Secondly,
studies of political culture tend to stress   attitudes equally,
neglecting that some persons and groups think and feel more
intensely than others about the politics of their society, with the
result that the numerically averaged conclusion may be a completely unrealistic portrayal of a complex reality. However
precisely formulated such statistical generalizations may be they
are better regarded as a guide. Thirdly, knowledge of a society's
political culture is not necessarily an exact indication of the nature
of its politics. Societies with democratic governments but authoritarian political cultures, and vice versa, are not uncommon.
Weimar Germany is often cited as an example of the former,
Gaullist France of the latter. Nevertheless these disparities suggest
the value of the concept which, in the form of national character,
is hardly new. After all, it is politically important for a government to know whether its policies and personalities are going to

meet with a ready response by their concordance with political attitudes. Whether the populace has to be persuaded or coerced into acceptance is an important matter.

Granted that political culture is important enough a subject of study, the difficulty that now arises is that it is not much studied, and certainly not in Turkey. Consequently it is necessary to glean what can be gleaned from a meagre number of studies and fill in the gaps in a more impressionistic way.

To begin at the cradle, or as near as we can get, a study of Turkish and Iranian national character and economic growth, based on a content analysis of children's stories, finds a few themes stressed which have political relevance.[2]Bravery, particularly in battle, charity to others to the extent of serious self-sacrifice, and loyalty to one's master, even unto death, are popular themes. Yet trickery and intrigue form part of this type of socialization, particularly the capacity to outwit an opponent, including government officials. Save when a stranger is in difficulty or needs hospitality, he is not to be trusted, but when a relationship exists attitudes are radically different, it appears.

The state is regarded as having a relationship with ordinary humble subjects, but this relationship does not extend to the servants of the state, who are feared or despised. The state is known as *devlet baba* (father state) and is expected to provide for, look after, and protect the common man, to be accessible, to dispense justice and to maintain an orderly society. Government is unquestionably regarded as vital for holding together the community; it is not just a device for holding the ring. Ottoman officials hardly fulfilled all these expectations—they were often rapacious, uncaring and extremely severe in their treatment of plain folk—but the notion of the importance of government itself does not seem to have suffered much from the defects of its servants. Moreover, there is in certain respects a strong strain of egalitarianism running through Turkish society. In the face of high officialdom a lowly peasant is humble, but dignified and not at all servile. In his study of migrants from the countryside to Istanbul Professor Karpat found widespread among them the belief that "the wish of the humblest peasant and the will of the Government were somehow congruent" and concluded that this, together with egalitarianism, "appeared to be among the outstanding features of the migrants' political culture." Karpat quotes a migrant squatter as saying "We have built our dwelling on the land of our father, the state. We took it and built it . . . Is this a crime?"[3]

Despite these lingerings of tradition it would be wrong, however, to see attachment by the uneducated Turk to any mystique of government. From government he wants practical benefits. Consequently, it is quite natural for him to support political parties which provide these, including even modern innovations. The Turk has a lively appreciation of material benefits since "God has promised to the righteous prosperity on earth and eternal bliss in the hereafter" and there is consequently no real criticism of those who seek after power and wealth even if they use it for high living. Who would not? "For the peasant knows that women and easy living are the tangible rewards that would send him to the distant city in quest of power and glory if he had the chance."[4]

Other stories throw light on various characteristics of the political culture of the general populace. For instance a study of Elite-Mass Relationships in Turkish Village Development[5] in 1962 showed that villages want practical improvements rather than educational or cultural change. Moreover all villagers, including the headmen, saw the village as egalitarian in structure and they nearly all thought a good headman was one who consulted the villagers. A large number felt, however, that they could do little or nothing in response to harmful or unjust action by the central government. By contrast migrants to Istanbul living in *gecekondu*'s seem, by virtue of their predilection for voting and for their belief in political parties, to believe that they can affect the actions of central government. In fact they have been wooed by the political parties and have achieved solid benefits through political action— which is all the more reason perhaps for their generally believing "that their association with the political parties was motivated by a moral obligation towards the country and the government rather than by personal gain."[6] This is because, continues Professor Karpat, "the Turkish political culture developed by the elite in the past remains encumbered with rigid, stereotyped ideals of perfection, morality, abnegation and sacrifice, which many

politicians brandish in their public speeches, but few adhere to."
Actually, the demand for moral standards, and for self sacrifice
may appeal, as we have seen, to something more remote in the
Turkish past. Modern moralistic politicians seem to use these
ancient appeals for subtly different systems of morality, such as
for instance the condemnation of the Prime Minister, Adnan
Menderes in 1960 for loose living. This particular moralizing did
not seem to evoke much response from the less educated (or
modernized) sections of the community in 1960.

Karpat's study is of migrants from villages who wish to partake
of city culture. With immediately pressing problems of residence,
public recognition, and the like to solve they have developed very
pragmatic attitudes towards politics. What then of those who
remain in the villages? Clearly they are affected by the migrants,
who make frequent return visits to their villages and who maintain close contacts in other ways. Yet much earlier studies than
that of the migrants to Istanbul have demonstrated that the
peasants have long wanted schools, roads and water—as reported,
for example, for Erdemli in the late 1950's. "The extent to which
villagers were concerned with their own immediate problems
cannot be overstressed, although it is to be expected. Many
peasants were either unaware or uninterested in anything beyond
their immediate environment."[7] Nevertheless some of these
villagers disliked the stiff authoritarianism of the People's Party
government and had begun to realize their own importance when
political parties went out after their votes.

A massive survey of peasant attitudes[8] in 1962 confirmed and
filled out this picture for the country as a whole. For instance
only 16% of the villagers in this survey named Atatürk, the prime
symbol of national awareness, as the person most admired, and
even less than a quarter of the men did so. Half the respondents
significantly responded to the question by naming members of
their family! Another 15% gave pride of place to religious personages, with half of those questioned just not knowing.[9] Another
study of married couples showed a higher national awareness in
the towns,[10] a finding corroborated by the results of a survey of
political attitudes in a small town in the early 1970's. In this
study 40% named Atatürk as the most admired person, with

President Kennedy and Adnan Menderes obtaining 16% and 12%, respectively, but the sample seems heavily weighted towards the educated and the skilled.[11] A detailed survey of four villages in the late 1960's by Dr. Ozankaya found that between 30% and 40% of the men (according to village) chose Atatürk as their most preferred personage, with preferences for other national Turkish leaders ranging between about 40% and 55%.[12] Significantly, perhaps, there was very little mention of family figures or friends. Most of the women did not find any person to admire! National awareness in the villages obviously varies greatly. The four studied by Ozankaya do not in this respect quite match the national picture. At best, and restricting the national study only to married men, about 36% of the men most admire Atatürk and political and military figures.[13] For Ozankaya's four villages, the male respondent percentages for all political figures (there is no mention of millitary figures) range from 77% to 93%. The 1962 survey figures shown that literate villagers are significantly more nationally aware than illiterate,[14] and as the male literacy rate in three of the villages studied by Ozankaya is very high (60%—80%) this may well be one explanation of the differences.[15]

Another pointer to the degree of national orientation could derive from the general opinion of the Turkish populace regarding its own principal characteristics. In the 1962 national study the villagers were, rather quaintly, asked to name "the two main characteristics of Turks as people." Unfortunately most of them by far simply had no idea. But those between 16 and 19 years of age showed some inkling provided they were literate. They stressed "strength and heroism", "religion", "morals and ethics" and "nationalism", in that order. This assessment corresponds in part with that of the townsmen of Susurluk, who listed strength and heroism, religion, hospitality and patriotism in that order, with not much difference between the first three attributes. Since heroism is usually depicted as heroism in war in service to the country, the link with patriotism is close. When asked what two values they most wanted to transmit to their children these townsmen emphasized religion, patriotism, morality and the importance of the family, whilst more opted for loyalty to religion (44%) than to nation (35%) or to kin (10%) as the loyalties they thought most important for children.[16]

These are very general aspects of Turkish political culture, but it is possible to obtain some expressions of opinion concerning more concrete political matters by comparing, where it is possible, some features of Karpat's study of migrants to Istanbul in the *gecekondu*'s with that carried out by Ozankaya on the four Anatolian villages.[17]

In the first place it appears that both the migrants and the villagers believe overwhelmingly in the importance of voting or (in the villages' study) in the importance of elections for the future of the country. The Istanbul migrants claimed they voted for various reasons—loyalty to the chosen party, to elect national leaders, to fulfil a citizenship duty, or to secure national gains. The villagers apparently reacted rather differently. They did not see elections as an expression of national sovereignty, or as a means to reach positions of power, or to have a representative there in order to protect their interests. Rather they saw political competition as a game from which they could derive immediate and solid benefit. Yet, secondly, when asked the meaning of democracy a good proportion of both sets of respondents gave replies which emphasized freedom, or in the case of the villagers, efficient government too. However, according to Karpat, "The respondents seemed to regard equality as the chief characteristic of democracy. Emphasis on freedom, self-government, economic opportunity and proper service by government officials implied a conception of democracy as a means to end the inequality between the elite and the masses . . ."[18] The villagers seemed rather less confident, a large number returning "wrong" replies.[19] Of those who did have some notion of the meaning of democracy they regarded it as something given by the state, not something to be fought for. The villagers still feel strongly that the state is father-state, the provider. Thirdly, both migrants and villagers, about 70% of them, thought that political parties were useful, but with about one fifth believing in one-party government. The migrants saw the essential functions of parties as the control of government, including the prevention of dictatorship, the selection of the most appropriate policies, and economic development. The villagers said that "without party competition we shall be back to rope sandals again."[19] But they often did not want more than two or three parties, in order to avoid excessive disruption, a sentiment echoed by the Istanbul migrants. Finally, when it came to selection as among parties, the Istanbul migrants mostly gave benefit to the country, to the *gecekondu*, the capacity to provide employment, and sympathy with migrants as the principal reasons governing their choice. The villagers seemed to determine their choice by local economic criteria, and like the migrants studied, they happened also mainly to vote for the Justice Party.

On the face of it migrants and villagers have much in common. For different reasons both groups support the system though the migrants seem to use it more to satisfy their longer term needs. Although precise comparison is not possible in this respect, the migrants appear to be more active politically, more conscious of their significance and of their role in the larger scheme of things. According to Ozankaya's study the villagers are very parochial, especially in those villages where agriculture is the only occupation, this feature being a better indicator of parochialism than lack of exposure to the outside world. The villagers are both fearful of the state as well as dependent upon it. They do not much discuss national politics, to become involved in which is in their view a dangerous business; they nearly all feel it is necessary to give absolute obedience to the state. The peasants' political beliefs and values, Ozankaya concludes, are influenced by the *ağa*'s (village notables) whose active political roles and social power greatly influence villagers' ideas, which do not therefore come to them direct through the media,—though those villagers who began to interest themselves in politics did so when party competition began, or when the village came into touch with the outside world. The party members in the two agricultural villages belonged to the notables' families; and only in the two villages with diversified economies did villagers belong to political parties different from those of the power holders. In the Istanbul *gecekondu*'s, by contrast, there seem to be many active party members of various sorts. "The belief that higher economic and social status can be achieved by political action coupled with ability and effort indicates that the old belief in the immutability of the social arrangements and ascribed social positions prevailing among the lower classes in Turkey has been drastically undermined."[20] The immutability prevails to some extent in some villages. Certainly it is mistaken to assume that party competition is going overnight to revolutionize political attitudes. The peasant—and the migrant to some extent—have local economic and social, not national and political, concerns at heart. They are pro-democratic because they have prospered materially and are now freer, particularly from the state, than they used to be. They are nationally conscious, though not excessively nationalistic; and there is a strongly developed social consciousness which owes much to Islam and is still often expressed religiously. Both these sentiments are strong enough to be open to exploitation by ruthless national political leaders. So too could the general spirit of egalitarianism that is hidden underneath the social and economic inequalities. It is, however, to hazard a personal impression, a limited egalitarianism which does not resent riches, power or social advantages provided some obligations to society are not neglected.

POLITICAL IDEAS

Islam and Politics

From such relatively meagre studies of social and political attitudes as exist it is at least clear that religion in Turkey is not dead, despite the massive secularization of the Atatürk revolution. In particular, since the inauguration of the multi-party system after the last war there have been many and repeated manifestations of the persistence of popular religion even although overt participation by Islam in politics and government is banned. Unlike say, the Soviet Union, where religion may be practised, but only preached in the recognized churches, Turkey has always allowed Islam to use what means it can to spread itself, always provided the Islamic institution is not recreated outside and apart from the State. In 1950 the new Democratic government allowed the call to prayer to be delivered in Arabic; a little later mosques began to appear, or old ones to be repaired. In addition State radio introduced religious broadcasts, and even the higher secondary schools began in 1965 to provide religious instruction, though only in Islam as, *a* not *the,* religion for their pupils. In the villages there has been a strong demand for courses in the Koran, especially, and, surprisingly, in the more developed western and north-western regions of the country.

Another development of great potential significance for the future was the support during the Democrat Party government of schools for prayer leaders and preachers set up in many towns. The pupils in these senior secondary schools spend half their time in Islamic studies, including the study of Arabic.[21] Their better students graduate to Institutes for the Advanced Study of Islam in Ankara and Istanbul; these are more "traditionally and religiously committed than the Ankara University Faculty of Theology."[22]

The formal institutional position is unchanged since Atatürk's time, however. The organization of religion is under the control of the Department of Religious Affairs, which is attached to the Prime Ministry lest it develop into a separate institution. Since there is no religious hierarchy in Islam, but only religious personages with different functions, there is not much of a base from which to direct any moves for greater independence. In addition, the Constitution is brief on the role of religion. In it the state is described as secular and it is forbidden to exploit religious feelings for political or personal reasons. Nevertheless there has been something of a religious revival.

One important aspect of this revival is the appearance of a vast flood of Islamic literature on the Turkish market since the 1950's though this must be in part due to greater literacy.[23] Another is the persistent activity of a relatively new popular religious order, that of the disciples of a Kurdish Sheykh, Saidi Kürdi, or more popularly Saidi Nursi, after his birthplace, the village of Nurs.

To take the religious publications first, these include books providing simple explanations of Islamic rites and dogmas, textbooks for learning Koranic Arabic, collections of Friday sermons, books on Islamic history, Islamic classics translated into Turkish, and a great deal of apologetic literature, including some works designed to prove that Atatürk was a good Muslim![24] The message of these books is to stress, *inter alia,* that the decline of faith was a major cause of Ottoman decline, that enlightened secularism supports Islam, that Turkish nationalism and Islam are compatible, as too are Islam and Western civilization, and that Islam is progressive, and opposed to exploitation and fanaticism. All these points are highly debatable assertions, as will shortly be indicated. In addition to books a number of newspapers and periodicals have arisen which argue the Islamic point of view, frequently asserting the superiority of Islamic culture over Western materialism.

As for the new religious order, that of the *Nurcular,* which emphasizes its message and does not consider itself as a mystic way to God, it has been very active, despite prohibition of its activites, and the arrest of many of its members, especially after the 1971 military intervention. In their early years the Nurcular were careful not to attack secularism—and they still have to be cautious—but their doctrines are of a fundamentalist sort. All truth lies in the Koran; secularism is contrary to Islam, the head of state and the members of the National Assembly ought to be Turkish Muslims; the Holy Law of Islam should be restored; the Koran adequately lays down the principles of political organization. All these assertions, hardly at all developed intellectually, are amongst the chief principles of the followers of Saidi Nursi—to whom saintly and miraculous qualities are frequently attributed. A strength of the movement is that Sunnite, Shi'ite or mystic can all subscribe to its principles.

However effective this movement may prove to be, its intellectual weakness is apparent; its writings do not really reach as far as a repetition of the ideas of Young Ottomans, like Namık Kemal (1840—88), Ziya Pasha (1825—80), and Ali Suavi (1838—78), or, more important, those of the best known Turkish thinker of the Young Turk and Atatürk periods, Ziya Gökalp (1875—1924).[25] It is still fundamentalist ideas which lie behind the revivalist movement for the most part, but the work of the modernist thinkers we have mentioned requires some examination—superficial though this must be in an introductory work of this sort—for their influence over more educated minds.

It will be recalled that the Young Ottomans of the mid-nineteenth century opposed the uncritical westernizing reforms of the Grand Vezirs, Ali and Fuad Pasha's. They opposed uncritical acceptance of western-style reforms for two related reasons. Firstly, they thought that it was enough to adopt western techniques, not western philosophy, or western systems of law. Secondly, they were of the opinion that Islam, properly interpreted, lay at the root of those western ideas which seemed to them to represent an improvement on those currently dominating the Ottoman world.

Namık Kemal was at pains to show that Islam, properly interpreted, contained the essential principles of modern liberal-democratic government. The first and great stumbling block, which Kemal never properly surmounted, however, is that in Islam it is immensely difficult to establish the principle of popular sovereignty. By virtue of the original submission of men to God sovereignty is His and Kemal's arguments for the secular origin of government to allow the development of a theory of popular sovereignty are not admissible. The rights of man, as allowed under Islam, cannot depend on a law of nature behind and beyond the Koran. In fact, for Muslims there is no natural law existing in any sense independent of God; He is immanent in all nature. Since Namık Kemal does, often inadvertently, introduce into his thinking the non-Islamic concepts lying behind the thought of European political thinkers like Locke, Rousseau, and Montesquieu (whom he much admired), his attempt at a fundamental alignment of classical Islam and modern liberal thought failed. However, in providing interpretations within the restricted Islamic framework he had more apparent success. For instance, the Koranic injunction to Mohammed to consult with his followers is developed as a justification for the adoption of constitutional government. Again, the oath of obedience the community swears to a newly-elected Caliph is represented as a form of contract between people and ruler which is in force only insofar as the Caliph governs by Holy Law. So grounds can be found for a general right to determine who, under God at least, shall enjoy sovereignty and under what conditions. In this regard Namık Kemal sidestepped the contradictory ruling that the Caliph holds his power in trust from God, not from the community.

At a fundamental level, the only level at which to satisfy the most searching intellects, Namık Kemal's attempted synthesis of classical Islam and liberalism was too confused and even self-contradictory to be a success. Ali Suavi's reformulation of classical Islamic values, on the other hand, was simplistic, much less ambitious and, within its limited and sharper focus, more effective and convincing. For instance he eventually took the view that the separation of powers Namık Kemal tried to justify was only necessary if there was no strict moral code, like that which he saw to exist in Islam, by which to judge political acts. He was also clear that whilst man was sovereign over himself in those areas left free to him, the notion of popular sovereignty was meaningless in Islam, as it must imply that *vox populi* is greater than *vox die*. Only Holy Law could transfer sovereignty to a lower plane. Secular rulers only executed the Holy Law, or its interpretation by the *ulema*. All this was purist and not very helpful, but it set the tone of Islamic thinking on politics and it is a line of thinking behind some of the popular literature. Nevertheless the achievement of the Young Ottomans was to help create a general opinion that Islam was not opposed to some modern western and liberal governmental practices. To an extent they severed religion from the Ottoman tradition, thus making it easier for the latter to be attacked without this being seen as an attack on true religion.

This narrower, but still accommodative, Islamic view was in essentials propagated by a group of Islamic writers during Young Turk times. They did not, however, dominate the scene for they had to encounter the opposition of two other doctrines. One was that the Ottoman Empire should go more or less without reservation for a complete policy of westernization. Ahmet Riza, for example, the most persistent Young Turk critic of the Hamidian regime from his self-appointed place of exile in Paris, was captivated by Comte's positivism. Whilst not anti-Islamic, Ahmet Riza favoured an elite leadership for Turkey by those able to understand what the social sciences when applied to Turkey actually required by way of policies. Abdullah Cevdet (1869–1932), another noted thinker, who published a journal in Geneva, was a thorough-going advocate of westernization who wanted to raise the people's general standard, and indeed to alter their mentality, but who also stressed the need for elite leadership.[26] Rigorous westernization, secularization and elitist tutelary policies were later the hallmark of Atatürkism.

The most interesting attempt to reconcile modernity with Islam was undoubtedly made by Ziya Gökalp, who was very influential among Young Turk intellectualist circles. Ziya Gökalp regarded Islam, like any religion, as a "historical phenomenon subject to change and dependent on the social circumstances in which it developed . . . But for the anti-Islamic attitude of Atatürk, Gökalp might have become the initiator of a fruitful scientific investigation of Islam in Turkey and perhaps even the father of an interesting reform movement."[27] In his approach Ziya Gökalp was revolutionary, so revolutionary in fact as to attempt to separate religion from the state, a seemingly hopeless task in Islam, which seeks to establish on earth a divinely ordained system of social and political rights and duties. Whilst Namık Kemal, like many Islamic modernists, sought to demonstrate that the system was inherently liberal and democratic, Gökalp tried to show that the Holy Law, which incorporated the system of social right and duties, had become ossified and should rightly be subject to constant revision in the light of evolving changes in social structure. This was much more promising than inflating scant and debatable texts to show that they contained the seeds of this or that particularly favoured foreign doctrine. Yet, like the apologists, Gökalp had also to start with a text, in this case the opinion of a celebrated jurist (Abu Yusuf) to justify his own radical interpretation. Abu Yusuf had said that customary law (*örf*) was to be preferred to Koranic command or prohibition if the latter is in fact derived from customary law—a remarkable judgement. Inspired by this view, Gökalp begins by asserting a fundamental difference between two sources of the Holy Law— (i) the Koran and the sayings and deeds of Mohammed (who according to the Koran possessed the wisdom to apply ultimate principles to problems of everyday life) and (ii) the customary law (*örf*) which Gökalp defined as the collective conscience of the Muslim community.[28] He then moved on to claim that this conscience of the Islamic community expressed in customary ways of living was in nature divine. For this social conscience was the product of the natural law of social evolution, and all law must emanate from God, (since Islam does not recognize natural law in which God is not immanent). It therefore became possible to claim that the social element in Islam could have even greater validity with regard to social and temporal matters than the direct injunctions of the Koran and Tradition.[29] The acceptability of this argument depends *inter alia,* and principally, on the truth of the claim that there are evolutionary laws which hold good of societies, a matter of some dispute.

Once the conscience of the community was considered at least on a par with the Koran and the Tradition the way was wide open to separating religion and society, the development of the latter being free from religious direction. So too it logically followed that the administration of law should be free from religious control, that legislation could be left to temporal authorities, that the state could be separate from the church. Some pious Muslims were no doubt grateful for this solution when Kemal Atatürk completed the separation of church and state. At least it was a straw at which to grasp.

Nationalism and Atatürkism

It will be appreciated that Gökalp was not in the everyday sense secularist—he did not advocate a non-religious basis for life, but rather sought, if inadvertently, to create a basis for religious tension between the claims of the law and those of the community.[30] The question then arises whether Gökalp's position on Islam could be reconciled with his views on nationalism, which he promoted above all else.

The principal difficulty of reconciling his re-interpretation of Islam (let alone much less daring interpretations) was that Gökalp was a Turkist. For a time he seemed to dally with a broader version of Turkism which looks to the amalgamation of all Turkic and related peoples in a mythical Turan, but eventually he directed his thoughts and feelings to Anatolian Turks and their near cousins in Central Asia. This Turkism was grounded on shared religion and culture; in this definition of culture language was necessary, though hardly sufficient. For Gökalp culture lay in the latent values of society which were to be found among the ordinary folk and which could be brought to the surface and activated through dedicated effort since these values are hidden forces. So a nationalist is a person who is sensitive to the ideal inner nature of his society, which then awakens in him love, enthusiasm and even worship. "The nation is a group composed of men and women who have undergone the same education, who have received the same acquisitions in language, religion, morality and aesthetics."[3][1] There is no racialism in this, nor any sympathy for nationalism as deriving simply from an intention to continue a life in common. For Gökalp Switzerland could not constitute a nation, nor could the Ottoman Empire. Consequently for him Ottomanism became theoretically as well as practically impossible. Nor in his nationalism was there much scope for individual self-determination; like his principal mentor, Durkheim, he regarded society as more important, but this collectivist vision no doubt also had some roots in Islamic fraternity and equality as well as in his mystical bent, which all but turned the spiritual God of the Koran into society itself.

The snag in Gökalp's thinking at this stage was, however, that he equated society with nation, and insisted on language as a necessary route to the national soul. This created a dislocation between religion and nation, at least between Islam, with its waning Arab connections, and Turkism. Gökalp appeared to believe that he had limited religion to a spiritual dimension, but in fact he found its vitality in a notion of society he could not square with his conception of a nation. To this day Islam fits uneasily and unsatisfactorily into the Turkish nationalist context, if at all. Gökalp stressed the primacy of a culture which, he knew very well, was only in part Turkish. The 1931 programme of the People's Party dropped religion. "The nation is a political and social body composed of citizens who are bound together by unity of language, culture and ideal."

Not only was national culture supremely important for Gökalp, he also developed a partly original theory, not withstanding his debt to Ferdinand Tönnies, to the effect that national cultures are to be distinguished from multi-national civilizations. The national culture is unselfconsciously composed of ideals and feelings stemming from the national cultural heritage—its folklore, popular literature, language, ethics, religion, aesthetics and so on, all nationally welded together. Civilization derives by contrast from an artificial, purposive, rational creation of knowledge and an understanding of history, art, economics, science, philosophy and even language, built around common intellectual attitudes. So there is a European civilization distinct from the many European national cultures which exist alongside rather than *within* it. Any individual consequently operates at two levels or in two different spheres, the one emotional and the other rational. Convincing or not, this approach allowed Turks to dissociate themselves from Ottoman civilization without losing a sense of identity and to attach themselves to European civilization for the purposes it could serve. *Islamic* "civilization" was a stumbling block, but once it was shown that Islam should rightly be a spiritual, not a temporal or social religion, it could neither properly constitute a civilization nor hinder any Islamic nation from joining whatever civilization it wished. The Atatürkist passion for Turkey to be regarded as civilized in a western sense is not to be seen as merely imitative, or as emanating from lack of confidence, or levantinism. Gökalp here articulated and legitimated a number of Turkish thoughts and feelings in a very sensitive field and greatly helped rescue national dignity. Whether he overestimated the power of Turkish culture to withstand European civilization is a moot point.

Other aspects of Gökalp's thought also influenced numerous Turkish intellectuals, including those who were to play a large part in formulating the basic policies of the Atatürkist regime. For example, Gökalp advanced a belief in populism but thought it necessary for government to be in the hands of an elite, an elite which brings civilization to the ordinary people but has to absorb Turkish culture from them. He was also in favour of a national leader to develop a national consciousness and to teach the people democracy. But there was not much of the romantic conception of a leader as the incarnation of the folk spirit. Atatürk was exactly the sort of leader Gökalp thought necessary. Gökalp was also opposed to class struggle and recommended a system in which private capital was allowed to function, provided it operated to the benefit of the state. Not surprisingly Gökalp was in favour of a corporate state in which the professional organizations and guilds would cut across incipient socio-economic class divisions. He did not see the dangers. Fascism had yet to appear; and trade unions in Europe partook more of a class than of a corporate identity. Gökalp also advocated a form of state capitalism on the grounds of the weakness of private enterprise in Turkey—a policy of statism which formed one of the six principles of Atatürkism or Kemalism, but which was not officially adopted until as late at 1937. Gökalp's thinking was mirrored in Atatürkism, but not in every respect.[32] Despite his radical interpretation of Islam his concern for religion was rather too great for the many westernists found in the Atatürkist regime. They did not wish to find a place either for the Caliphate or for the education in religious ideals which Gökalp advocated, and they were prepared to go to the West for more than just the civilization Gökalp found there. In fact Atatürkism reflected the ideas of many Turkish intellectuals, not just those of Gökalp, but his formulations of ideas current at the time are the most comprehensive.

Atatürkist offical ideology proclaimed Turkey to be republican, nationalist, secularist, statist, populist and reformist. Its nationalism abandoned the Pan-Turk, or Turanian, ideals which strongly coloured Gökalp's nationalism for a long period of time, and also became more secular. In content, this Atatürkist nationalism was restricted to the geographical area of post-war Turkey and developed a fascination with pre-Islamic Turkish culture. Self-regarding, suspicious of foreign aid, insistent on the privacy of the nation-state, nationalism reached an intensity in Atatürkist times which has since moderated. One reason for its diminution in strength has been the post-second world war re-assertion among some Turkish intellectuals of the significance of the Ottoman and Islamic past which the secular nationalists blamed for most of Turkey's misfortunes. The need to strengthen moral defences against Russian communism was one reason for this development, but there was generally a recognition that the Turk could not slough off his immediate past and had no real need to do so. This feeling was most evident not perhaps among the Turkish elite as such, but among the new elements rising to prominence

from small town and village backgrounds where the new secular
nationalism had not time to catch hold. The development of anti-
secular, anti-Atatürkist nationalism had earlier appeared in the
writings of a former confidant turned enemy of Atatürk, a
Dr. Riza Nur, who contrived to combine in a projected programme
for a new political party republicanism, the restoration of the
Caliphate, and the political union of all Turks under those of
Anatolia. He was also opposed to industrialization, fearing it
would break up traditional society.[33] This was an appealing
amalgam for those with no eye for the bizarre, and it has consequently been popular and influential at a certain level where
inconsistencies and illogicalities count for rather less than
emotional appeal. Many groups have come to promote nationalism
based in varying degrees on racist and Muslim principles, with the
preservation of the *status quo* against attacks from the left as
perhaps their prime raison d'être. Nevertheless secularist
nationalist organizations have also appeared. The most purely
Pan-Turkist current also reached greatest prominence during the
second world war when it emerged as a "mixture of racialism,
a romantic passion for the past (antedating the Ottoman history),
an irrational belief in, and exaltation of, personal valor and of war,
purity of blood, and discrimination of all groups considered non-
Turkish."[34] This can hardly return in all its force now, but
elements of it exist on the Turkish right.

We have seen earlier in this chapter how, despite the religious
activity, or perhaps religiosity, now prevalent in Turkey, there is
little fundamental and realistic thinking about any new Islamic
state. Together with republicanism, secularism and nationalism
the principles of revolutionism (or reformism), statism and populism were written into the Constitution in 1937, having previously
been the basic tenets of the Republican People's Party.

In the Atatürkist period *İnkilâpçılık*, reformism (or revolutionism) was officially interpreted as thoroughgoing reform of state
and society along western lines, a policy which became more,
not less, vigorous after Atatürk's death. The striking point about
this reformism, or revolutionism, was that the Turkish people were
largely held to be responsible for their own backwardness by
Atatürk himself; the blame was not just heaped onto imperialism.

"If they want to be treated with justice and wish to occupy a place with dignity among the nations of the modern world, they must keep a constant vigilance over any tendency to lapse back into slumber, and the bondage of arrogant self-glorification."[3] [5] "Few nations, Professor Berkes concludes, "have faced such devastating self-criticism from their leader after a hazardous and dubious struggle to survive." Reformism remains as a plank in nearly all political party platforms, as we still see; it may be interpreted as the liquidation of backwardness in the forceful Atatürkist fashion, but there is much more emphasis now by parties left and right of centre on reformism as modernization, the modern concept, and the basis of Turkish national structure and values. However, *İnkilâpçılık*, interpreted as revolutionism has been powerfully revived by leftist groups, as might be expected. One important journal edited by Doğan Avcıoğlu was called *Devrim* (Revolution); it existed between 1969 and 1971, when it was closed down, and constantly called for revolution as representing the real Atatürk spirit.

Statism (*devletçilik*) has also been widely interpreted, and indeed from its emergence first in Young Turk times has caused serious dispute between state interventionists and the supporters of private enterprise. As it was formulated it was not in Atatürkist times directed against individual economic enterprise. The state was to promote economic development to make up for the deficiencies of capital or business skills. Atatürkists regarded themselves as neither capitalist nor socialist. The right of the state to take private enterprises into public ownership is now guarded in the Constitution, however. Whilst complete state direction—if not ownership of the means of production—is a socialist aim, some statist policies encouraged private enterprise to develop—for example, by turning semi-finished products of national enterprises, like leather into finished articles (shoes).

This brings us to the last of the six principles, populism (*halkçılık*). As formulated this closely reflected Gökalp's views. Populism was defined to exclude recognition of any special privileges to any individual, family, class or community; it saw society as composed of various professional groups arising from division of labour, but working in harmony. The aim was to secure order and solidarity in place of class conflict. The distribution of benefits in society was not to be strictly egalitarian, but based on the contribution made. An Ottoman Turk would have agreed wholeheartedly with the conception of a society composed of interlocking, mutually supportive socio-economic groups. Since those days populism has declined as a concern of the major political parties, the inevitability of socio-economic class divisions being urged more and more. So the originator of the doctrine, the People's Party, now has a new socialist orientation. The moderate right wing parties do not mention it, but the right wing National Action Party makes something out of the concept, as we shall seee, if only by seeking to prevent the class conflict promoted by Marxism. Many of the former chief supporters of populism, the intelligentsia, seem to have moved now to one or the other varieties of socialism, a process which came to fruition in the years immediately after the 1960 revolution.

Modern Trends

Socialism has found powerful intellectual advocates in Turkey since the floodgates were opened in 1960, particularly between that date and the military intervention in 1971. How important each strand of thought was, or will be, in helping fashion Turkish political values can only be measured by the extent to which socialism, of whichever sorts, has been incorporated by political parties in their programmes and policies, and by the electoral support they have received. Whether this is a correct gauge of the extent of the adoption of socialist principles must be open to doubt, but to this we shall return later. For the moment we need to know what sorts of socialism have been advocated and how widely socialist doctrines have been disseminated.

Socialism is too varied and complex a doctrine to be easily defined, but it may be said to be composed of four main tendencies, all represented to some degree in every socialist movement which appears.[36] First there is *egalitarianism*, the principle which comes down from classical times, a principle which in its purest expression leads inevitably to the emphasis on a community of persons whose energies can find nothing but *social* expression, a community where selfishness, self-centredness or emulation can find no place. Egalitarian revolutionaries are relentlessly dedicated to the fight of the poor against the rich. Babeuf is a pure model, Marx more equivocally so. Some distance behind in dedication to a vision of a new socialist society come the *rationalists*—those who deplore the unscientific wastefulness of capitalism. Often with the Marxist creed to hand, they believe in a Marxist science of politics and ethics, and are sometimes determined to hasten along the inevitable through elitist political and administrative control in the interests of a socialism as yet but dimly perceived by the masses. The third tendency is that towards *moralism*, a much milder tendency stemming mostly, if not completely, in Europe from a religious tradition which deplores the inhuman, "exploitative" aspects of capitalism, its onslaught on human dignity, its advocacy of competition, rivalry and even hatred of man against man, its baneful influence on the emergence of a brotherhood of men holding fast to the sanctity of human life and the need sometimes to prepare for the life hereafter. Social democracy, or democratic socialism, as it has now become, leans heavily on this approach, though it is not actually the special monopoly of socialists. Politically this tendency in socialism stops somewhere short of complete public ownership and detailed management of the economy whilst usually occupying the commanding heights, and it believes in socialism through persuasion and liberal-democratic electoral devices. Finally, there are the *libertarians*, the "new left" of the western industrialized societies, who stress the repressiveness of the capitalist system, the ways in which it damns individual expression of the natural man, a creature who only through the liberation of his passion and emotion reaches real happiness. This strand, less prominent outside the developed world, obviously clashes with egalitarianism, which suffocates the individual in some senses, and most certainly with rationalism. There is a certain dislocation, too, between the moralism of the social democrats not impressed by Rousseau and the restrictions imposed on human beings by egalitarianism in particular, but also by rationalism. In the third world generally it is the egalitarian strand in socialist theory which has predominated, most notably in China and Cuba, but with large additions of the rationalism necessary for rapid economic and social development along scientific socialist lines. In Turkey, however, as in some other states, the moralistic element has some strength. Not that there has been a long socialist tradition—even moderate socialist doctrines did not get into the air until the 1950's; and not until after the 1960 revolution were the more searching aspects of socialist doctrines given currency. In fact, many Turkish intellectuals and men of affairs on the left have for long been, and still are, under the influence of the liberal and democratic ideas which, originally stemming from Europe, have been reinforced by the social egalitarianism of the American example, and not least by the greater efficiency apparent in capitalist or part-capitalist modes of development. "The period between 1957 and 1960," it has been said, "might be rightly considered the sentimentalist, universalist phrase of Turkish socialism."[37] It was markedly represented in the fortnightly publication, *Forum,* and later—after the 1960 Revolution—in the early issues of the weekly *Yön* (Direction)[38], and in People's Party circles. It led eventually to the left-of-centre stance of that party, and the loss of its more liberal members. It was then freer to develop a more *rationalist,* statist, emphasis not uncongenial to the elitist spirit of the original Atatürkist party.

The *moralist* element could be strengthened in the People's Party if it were not so secularist in tradition. This is because there is another *moralist* socialist current running in Turkey—among those of Muslim conviction who do not find a natural haven in the former party of Atatürk. Islamic socialism came to be discussed in the 1960's, reflecting thinking on Islamic socialism in Arab countries. The subject is complex and cannot effectively be entered into here. A few indications of the directions of this thought must suffice.

In the first place Muslims have no difficulty in recognizing that the doctrine which asserts "There is no God and Marx is his Prophet" cannot be reconciled with Islam. However, when Muslims look back into the Koran and into the Traditions they find, as Namık Kemal found for liberalism, certain pointers to the divine nature of socialism. For it may be asserted that the Koran and the Traditions contain many injunctions as to sharing, and censures those who become rich without sharing. Moreover, even when the Arabs brought home much booty, the early Caliphs did not succumb to the lures of riches, but continued to live sober lives. Again, Islam recognizes, it is claimed, the principle of social security through requiring levies for charity, and, there is the ideal of Muslim brotherhood implicit in an Islamic community. In addition, Islam stresses personal morality, and finally, although Islam clearly recognizes the need for private property and the individual's right to dispose of it, this right is circumscribed in the general interest.

Some of the texts on which Islamic socialism is based are not altogether unambiguous, but the general way of life of the Muslim—the emphasis on community, a stress on some aspects of egalitarianism, the allowance of a moderate degree of property held in trust to God— all argue for the appositeness of a moralistic type of socialism to the bulk of the Turkish population, which is still religiously inclined. It could be argued that this moralistic socialism is more formal than that of the Christian or European world, that a Muslim or post-Muslim man agonizes less than Christian or post-Christian man about moral problems (since there has been more explicit guidance), but there is clearly in the Muslim tradition much that would support a moderate socialism. The temporary coalition of the People's and National Salvation parties in 1974 was not so bizarre as at first appears.

One feature of *moralistic* socialism is often the belief that socialism can be introduced through the procedures of liberal-democracy. This is essentially the view of the People's Party insofar as it is socialist, and was also that of the Worker's Party of Turkey from 1961 to 1969 when it was under the leadership of Mehmet Ali Aybar. That socialism could come about peacefully was challenged by Doğan Avcioğlu, a very influential member of the Party, impressed, like many, by the possibilities of the popularity of right wing parties among a traditionalist electorate. He argued for an alliance between the military and the intelligentsia, for the imposition of socialism, and for economic development, thus harking back to the Kadro movement of the late 1930's. In this formulation national liberation from neo-imperialism was stressed over class conflicts, and the role of the intelligentsia over that of the workers, held to be too weak in Turkey to initiate action. The western capitalist world is of course the main enemy, but local capitalists and large landowners were rigorously attacked by Avcioğlu or contributors to the journals he edited. Socialism was not fundamentally very different from the socialism of many writers in his journal, *Yön;* their ideas were modelled on ideas of Western socialist groups, chiefly those of the British labour party. The difference lay in the mode to be employed to reach the objective. In his second journal, *Devrim*, Avcioğlu openly preached revolution.

This moral socialism, by whichever road it was to be reached, allowed for Turkish conditions and was supported in the 1960's, and probably still is, by many of the official and professional elite; it forms most of the basis of the policies now of the People's Party. In the 1960's it was not rigorous enough for some groups however. There were those who preferred a much more scientific or *rational* socialism; they emphasized planning and production. Others preferred an organizational and educational onslaught on the people through the formation of revolutionary cadres, and deplored parliamentary methods, which led to vote seeking and the dilution of socialism; they despised any concessions to Turkish conditions. In fact, deference to Turkish conditions in some writing indicated a slide in the direction of Maoism, in suggesting a broad class alliance against the evils of western imperialism, excluding only the *compromador,* high bourgeoisie. But perhaps of all these varied leftist approaches the most interesting was that which directly attacked the idea of a military-intellectual alliance for the revolutionary introduction of socialism on the grounds that the bureaucracy, which the intelligentsia would man, was the prime cause of Turkey's underdevelopment. On this view it is the bureaucracy which has been chiefly responsible for intro-ducing western imperialism, from which it has sat back and profited. The view that Turkey would have developed quite satis-factorily but for the western imperialist stranglehold is rejected. It was the bureaucracy which had held back the masses in a con-dition of traditional deference and would continue to do so. The bureaucracy would exploit the masses under the guise of socialism. This Trotskyist attack on bureaucracy can of course be used by both socialists and non-socialists. It is a common complaint about third-world socialism that it does little more than restore a traditional bureaucratic control. But the idea that the bureaucracy is able to control private enterprise is not generally accepted, certainly not by those on the left. It is widely assumed that the bureaucracy will simply become the tool of the bourgeoisie if any significant private enterprise is permitted. The leftists generally claim that despite his many virtues, Ecevit will be unable to end western neo-imperialism.

To conclude, the main socialist strand in Turkish leftism is moral, rather than rational or egalitarian, and there is not much libertarianism. This moral socialism owes something to Islam, is respectful of Turkish conditions, and does not seek to promote class conflict. It profits greatly by the stress on neo-imperialism, since this makes socialism appear a matter of national self-assertion in a country where nationalism is not a spent emotion.

CHAPTER V

THE NORMATIVE FRAMEWORK
THE CONSTITUTION

A constitution might be defined simply as the set of rules or procedures by which governmental organizations are related to one another, but constitutions are usually more than a statement of fact. For constitutions are normally expected also to lay down the rules that *ought* to be followed—they are normative in two senses. First, they may state how political power should be controlled—for example what rights, if any, individuals should possess, or how the legislature should be related to the executive. The role of constitutions in modern history in limiting and controlling arbitrary power derives from this understanding of the purpose of a constitution; the hallmark of a real constitution has often, therefore, been seen to be its *garantiste* quality in this regard.[1] Yet constitutions are not just liberal; they are used as normative instruments in another sense. They are often programmatic; they incorporate what are thought to be the political aims of their societies. So the Soviet Union, and many other states, have equipped themselves with programmatic constitutions in which liberalism can find no or little place.[2] Other constitutions tend to mix these sorts of substantive, or programmatic, norms with those of more liberal provenance. The present Turkish constitution is of this latter-day mixed type.

To speculate on the role of constitutions in politics is to raise a number of important, intriguing and often quite baffling questions. These cannot be entered into here, but the important, if obvious, point must at least be made that to establish a constitution is a major political act. Any constitution must be the creation of a politically powerful person, or group, or must emerge from bargaining between, or among, politically powerful persons or groups. The constitution may represent the norms of the society to which it relates—the more likely the more numerous and socially significant the persons or groups who bargain for it. Or it may be forced on society as a disciplinary or educative instrument, in an attempt either to change political and social norms, or to express the "real" norms of society which are thought to be suppressed in partisan political struggles. At this point it might be supposed that the longer a constitution lasts, the longer it can be expected to last—it will come to mirror social norms. A moment's reflection reminds us that this is not necessarily the case, however; much depends on the capacity of the constitution to change with changing norms in society. Moreover, what may easily happen is that a major political group arises which, under the cloak of normative language, actually changes a constitution to suit its own interests, in which case the constitution is not, in the sense used here, a constitution, but merely a set of rules organizing power to the convenience of those who hold it. It is with considerations of this sort in mind that we need to examine constitutional development in Turkey.

We have already seen that the provisions of the 1876 Constitution could hardly affect the autocratic functioning of the Sultan's government.[3] Nevertheless the Constitution was an important expression of political norms to which a large section of the educated elite may be assumed to have subscribed. In addition, it was a clear statement of political principles ready-made for adoption by all those in Hamidian times who were disaffected by the regime. The 1876 Constitution was hallowed by its rejection. Its principles were the prime revolutionary principles of modern Turkey; for this reason the 1876 Constitution was a crucial instrument in the formation of Turkish political values. It was a profoundly educative document; it was also a very popular document, for the cry for the Constitution was on everyone's lips in 1908.

The Young Turks lost little time implementing the principles expressed, but then suppressed, in the 1876 Constitution. They began to transfer political power from the Sultan and his ministers to parliament. Consequently both houses of parliament (who now elected their own presidents) were allowed equally with the Sultan's government to initiate legislation and the Sultan's consent to a proposed bill could, if necessary, be dispensed with by a two-thirds majority in both houses. In addition, the Council of Ministers was made responsible to the lower house of parliament, the Chamber of Deputies. To prevent evasion of this control

parliament was also empowered to meet each year without the
Sultan's permission. Moreover, whilst the Council of Ministers
was made jointly responsible to the Chamber of Deputies for
general governmental policy, the ministers were individually
responsible for affairs under their own jurisdiction. This largely
nullified the power of the Sultan to appoint the Grand Vezir and
to approve his nomination of the other ministers. Finally, the
Sultan's power to dissolve parliament in the event of an unresolved
dispute between the Council of Ministers and the Chamber of
Deputies was greatly restricted. In fact, in the case of disagreement
the Council of Ministers had to resign, or give in. If a new Council
of Ministers were formed which still was in dispute with the lower
house, then the Sultan had to dissolve parliament and order new
elections. So parliament was made supreme.

These last provisions occasioned the most important constitutional dispute of the Young Turk era. In 1911 the Committee
of Union and Progress, influential in government, but now faced
with a hostile lower house, sought to restore executive power by
introducing a constitutional amendment making it much easier
than it then was for the government to dissolve parliament in the
event of a dispute between them. The Committee managed to have
parliament dissolved, but only under the arrangements introduced
in 1909 which protected the position of the lower house and led
to long and acrimonious debates. A new Union and Progress
dominated lower house passed the amendment, but ironically,
at this point, the military wing of the liberals suddenly became
dominant in government. In 1912 they pressed to completion
through a sympathetic upper house their opponents' amendment
to strengthen the government over parliament. The Committee
of Union and Progress was hoist with its own petard. The Constitution was said to be in ruins;   what had certainly happened was
that the balance had finally been tipped in favour of the executive.[4]
The next attempt to create assembly supremacy over the executive
had to wait until after the war of liberation. The revolutionary
single-chamber Grand National Assembly which emerged out of
the war of independence, while triumphantly asserting the
principle of national sovereignty, as we have seen, firmly declared
that it was the body to govern Turkey and took care that its

president was also *ex-officio* President of the Council of Ministers.

This democratic and revolutionary surge had somehow to be adjusted however, as in Young Turk times, to the practical needs of government—long recognized in the Turkish tradition. The Turkish war of independence did not throw up a Robespierre. Yet it had a dynamic and forceful revolutionary leader in Mustafa Kemal Pasha, even though he was an established and much respected member of the modernizing, indeed, westernizing, wing of the Ottoman intelligentsia. It accorded neither with his experience, nor with his temperament, to be held in control by an assembly. Before long the strain became apparent.

In October, 1923, when, partly thanks to Mustafa Kemal, assembly government found itself in some disarray, he cajoled the Grand National Assembly into declaring Turkey a republic, with himself as President.[5] With this office Mustafa Kemal could command wider allegiance in society than as President of the Assembly; there is little doubt that for many Turks he was regarded as a substitute, or even a new, sultan. Constitutionally the political system now appeared more "parliamentary" in character than the revolutionary "convention" regime it bade fair to replace, but unfortunately for this development, not all the deputies approved the change, however much it might have satisfied a popular desire for a personage at the top.

Very significantly, when the amendment in question was passed it was only by 150 out of the 287 members of the Assembly, the remainder abstaining. Assembly debates shortly afterwards on the draft of the 1924 Constitution became very heated on the question of the separation of powers. Many deputies were adamant that the concentration of legislative and executive powers in the Assembly was an indispensable principle of modern Turkey. Apropos the suggestion that the President should be empowered to dissolve the Assembly, one deputy declared, "We . . . . the real representatives of the nation . . . . are absolutely determined that the Sultanate will never return!"[6] The opposition was sufficient to restrict the powers of the President very severely. The President was left with the power to choose the Prime Minister and to approve his choice of ministers, but the government had to be submitted to the Assembly for approval.

Moreover, the President could neither veto legislation nor dissolve the Grand National Assembly.

Despite the concession to the idea of a separate executive, the principle norm established in the 1924 Consitution was the concentration of all powers in the Assembly. This guaranteed the representation of the national will, but did not do a great deal for individual rights, which significantly, perhaps, were stated in the last section of the Constitution in formulations none too precise and depending much on future regulation by law. The Constitution was not originally programmatic however. It was only in 1937 that the People's Party's six principles of republicanism, nationalism, populism, etatism, secularism and reformism were incorporated.

The partial constitutional victory for assembly power proved hollow and turned out to be more dangerous, possibly, to the development of liberal-democratic institutions than a more realistic recognition of a greater separation of executive power might have been. For it became necessary for Mustafa Kemal, if he was to succeed in his social revolution, not just to keep the Assembly quiet but also to capture it for the revolution, since the Assembly represented popular sovereignty. He was first able to control the Assembly by the opportunites for authoritarian rule offered by the emergencies of 1925, 1926 and 1931. He also created the People's Party, which soon dominated the Assembly, and he had sufficient prestige to gain support from the military for his strong but modernizing policies, whilst excluding them from politics.[7] After Mustafa Kemal Atatürk the political habits generated by the 1924 Constitution made it possible for the Democrat Party to dominate the Assembly during their decade of office (1950–1960), though by leaning on a massive popular vote for legitimacy instead of on a single party.

It was against this background of the dangers inherent in concentrated representation of sovereignty in an assembly, and the dangers to which it actually gave rise, that the present, 1961, Constitution was drafted. It was felt, in the first place, that the representation of sovereignty should be dispersed. Consequently Article 4 of the Constitution lays down rather clumsily, that "the nation exercises its sovereignty through authorized organs in accordance with principles laid down in the Constitution." The Constitution then proceeds to attempt to deny the exercise of arbitrary power by the now bi-cameral Grand National Assembly. There was little pressure to separate powers to the extent of seeking to augment the powers of the President by having him directly elected, for instance, after the American or French fashion. However, he was now permitted to dissolve the important lower house of the Grand National Assembly on the request of the Prime Minister in the event of repeated votes of no confidence in the government.[8] By contrast the judiciary was made much more independent and secure, a development prompted by the measures taken by the Democrat Party government to influence the judiciary in its favour. Their government had made changes in the civil service law to allow the premature retirement of judges and the dismissal of university teachers in addition to curtailing press freedom, the right of public assembly, and even the formation of electoral coalitions. Most important, the Democrat Party government had also set up a parliamentary commission to investigate the activities of the Opposition whom they suspected of connivance with the military. Not surprisingly then, the framers of the new Constitution, from whom any members of the Democrat Party were naturally excluded, sought to disperse power and to regulate it. Power was dispersed for instance, by allowing autonomy to the television and radio authority and to the universities, by emphasizing the freedom to form associations without prior permission, by granting a large measure of freedom to the press, and by guaranteeing the right to strike. The exercise of power was regulated in a number of ways. As we have seen, a constitutional court and a second chamber were established and the duties of the Council of State were prescribed in the Constitution. Provisions were also included in the Constitution requiring political parties to manage their affairs democratically, and arranging for elections to be conducted under the supervision of the judiciary. Yet the Constitution did not go so far as to incorporate recommendations of the first constitutional commission[9] which had proposed, *inter alia,* a constitutional warrant for proportional representation and a form of corporate representation for the Senate as a check on democracy. In the end result the Constitution blended purely constitutional control with a wide increase in individual and group freedoms intended, it seems, to foster broader experience in self-management as a means to the development of a more pluralist society.

The Constitution not only deals with freedoms and checks on arbitrary power; however; it also lays down a series of social and economic rights and obligations—like the right to social security and medical care, the right to leisure time and to just remuneration for work. More concretely, the state is obliged to provide land for landless peasants and to assist with the provision of agricultural implements. The state is also authorized to expropriate the whole, if necessary, of any immovable private property and to nationalize private enterprises under specified conditions of compensation. In a crucial article (Article 4) the general philosophy is stated to be the regulation of economic and social life in accordance with justice and the principle of full employment, a policy which is deemed to include investments which promote social welfare and which envisages development planning.

Articles of this import were subject to much debate, with the less welfare minded members of the Constituent Assembly hostile to the new "social" state, even when it was explained that "social" did not mean socialist; they insisted that there should be some recognition of the value of private enterprise. As a result, some changes were made in this direction. The new Constitution cannot be called socialist, but it does positively enjoin the establishment, as economic means permit, of a welfare state. This is why most of those engaged in constitution-making did not want to hobble the government with all sorts of restrictions designed to protect democracy, but likely to stultify action. The programmatic and *garantiste* norms were in some degree in conflict, though a compromise assigning about equal weight to each was finally agreed and ratified by referendum (6.35 milion for, 3.95 million against, with 2.4 million abstentions).

In its blend of liberal-democracy and social welfare can the Constitution be said to be truly Atatürkist? Reference is often made after all to the Atatürkist principles of the Constitution.

If we view the new Constitution in the light of the principles enshrined in the ideology of the Atatürkist state it is easy to show that the Constitution is not *populist* in the sense of seeking to create a united society, despite its concern for social welfare. To accentuate freedoms, like that of the autonomy of the media, or to guarantee the right to strike were hardly ways to induce social harmony. Nor did the Constitution trust the people to express their voice directly through a national assembly untrammelled by the delays and questionings of constitutional checks and balances. The people, it was asserted, had been duped by the Democrat Party, and could be so duped again. So the new Constitution became less democratic (and a shade less *republican*) whilst becoming more liberal. It is hard to say whether it is more, or less, *nationalist*, but in seeking to restrict the alleged religious exploitation of popular religion it certainly showed a continuing concern to be *secularist*. By insisting on economic planning it was more *statist* than the previous regime had been. As to whether the Constitution is *revolutionary* (or *reformist*), that is a very difficult question. *Revolutionism* (or *reformism*) ostensibly indicates a disposition to movement or change, a somewhat unsettled state of mind which rejects immobility. Yet for many Turks for revolutionism to have meaning there must be clear objective. On this view the Constitution is a conservative compromise.

Of the achievements of the Constitution the gains in freedom were, as ever, to prove the most precarious. For it was the growing abuse of the new freedoms which seems, in the main, to have led the military to declare on the 12th March, 1971, that they would intervene unless a government was formed to remedy the anarchic condition of the country and to apply in an Atatürkist spirit the reforms the Constitution required. Changes were subsequently introduced to limit liberty and promote order.

The chief changes were as follows. First, in 1971, the article in the Constitution regarding freedom of the press was changed; henceforth it was possible for newspapers and journals to be closed down without waiting for a judicial decision, lest there be danger in delay, though the court has to support the closure within three days. A change to Article 26 restricted the free use of radio and other means of communication granted in 1961, by asserting the claim to protect national unity, the republic, national

security and general morals—the broad justification for many of
the changes made. Another restriction of liberty was the freedom
now given to the authorities (Article 30) to imprison persons for
seven days before showing cause. A precaution against administrative anarchy was the removal of the right of non-manual public
servants to set up trade unions (Article 46). Not surprisingly, the
autonomy of the universities and the radio and television
authority was severely curtailed (Article 120 and 121). Moreover,
the government was now authorized to step in and control a
university in danger of not performing its functions of teaching
and research, with presumably, the power to dismiss university
teachers. In addition university teachers were no longer permitted
to join political parties, a matter of some dispute in 1961.

Whilst these freedoms were curtailed, the influence of the
military was enhanced in a number of amendments. For instance,
conditions for the imposition of martial law were eased in its
favour, the National Security Council was now given the right to
"advise" the Council of Ministers, not just to offer information,
and offences by civilians against the military were brought under
the jurisdiction of military courts. By contrast, serious amendments were not made to the role of the civil judiciary. Nor were
there any substantial changes affecting the programmatic content
of the Constitution, save that, to the satisfaction of those more to
the left, Article 38 doubled to twenty years the period of payment
of compensation for lands expropriated for distribution, afforestation or settlement.

Of the changes made by the 1961 Constitution perhaps the
most important has been the rejection of the supremacy of the
elected national assembly as representing the will of the nation.
Nevertheless, despite some leanings in the first draft of the Constitution in a corporatist direction, representation of groups of
persons in different sorts of occupation has not emerged to replace
individual representation. The emphasis on judicial review does,
however, represent an intention to limit parliamentary sovereignty
and the power of government. That there has been some bite in
this development is indicated by the hostility shown by the Justice
Party, among others, to the whole idea of judicial power.
Mr. Demirel has frequently proclaimed his party's opposition, on

democratic grounds, to the limitations imposed by judicial institutions on the will of the people as expressed through their elected representatives in parliament. It was, consequently, in the Justice Party's interest when Article 114 of the Constitution was amended after the military intervention of 1971.[10] This article originally stated, simply, that no act or procedure of the government should be free from judicial review. The amendment clouded the picture by adding a paragraph—aimed chiefly at the jurisdiction of the Council of State—to the effect that judicial power should not be used to prevent fulfilment of the executive function of government in accordance with forms and principles prescribed in legislation. It also added that judicial decisions were not administrative acts. The Council of State has decided not to change its policy— ostensibly on the technical grounds that its decisions being judicial, cannot *ipso facto*, be administrative! More fundamentally there is the realization that any dispute about the jurisdiction of the Council of State would be subject to debate and decision by the Constitutional Court, a body which has asserted it independence in a number of instances. In 1971 the Constitutional Court was also under attack. An amendment to Article 147 of the Constitution made it clear that the Court could not test the constitutional validity of constitutional amendments which are made by the Grand National Assembly, whilst allowing that procedural aspects of such amendments could be contested on constitutional grounds. This important amendment did make it clear that only parliament was to decide the content of the Constitution. Obviously conditions could arise, as during the era of Democrat Party government, when this might be abused, but the alternative could be a very rigid constitution. The healthiest situation is probably one in which friction arises, but leads to reconciliation through compromise. There has been friction in the Turkish case accompanied by an unwillingness, or lack of strength, to push matters too far. For instance the Constitutional Court has responded to the limitations placed upon it in two ways. First, it interprets widely its procedural powers regarding the constitutionality of constitutional amendments, Secondly, it has in one case, in 1975, simply declared a constitutional amendment as unconstitutional. It did this in regard to an amendment removing the requirement that in war-time the majority of judges in military courts have to be qualified as judges. Such an amendment, it was asserted, was contrary to the fundamental rights and principles of law contained in the Constitution. This was not, relatively speaking, a crucial matter, and won some general approval for being directed against the military, but it was a sign of very spirited independence. The decisions of the Council of State may be to some extent over-ridden by a hostile government simply not acting, or acting tardily, on its recommendations, as has occurred in Turkey, but the Constitutional Court cannot be ignored quite so easily on account of its more vital function. Moreover, both these courts have benefited from being relatively permanent and predictable bodies, since their membership changes slowly, in what has been since 1961 a fairly fluid political situation. Faced with the opposition of a well-entrenched party government with powerful electoral support their position could be less secure.

From these constitutional struggles it is at least clear that the Turkish Constitution is not a very tight fit with the social and political norms of Turkish society. There are strong feelings, even among those on the right of centre, that the Constitution is too much directed towards the social welfare society, and that through judicial control it both inhibits strong government and is un-responsive to public opinion expressed through the political parties. At the same time it is regarded by these same groups as too free, certainly much too free before 1971, in many respects other than that of economic freedom. By significant minorities on the far left and the far right, including the Muslim right, the Constitution is regarded even less favourably, whilst for some of those in the centre left it simply is not socialist enough. The Constitution is therefore a compromise, or rather a *modus vivendi*, which a good number of moderates do positively support, but on strictly rational grounds as the best, and perhaps the only, way to resolve discords in a society where discord readily produces strife. Few, of whatever political inclination, seem greatly enamoured of, let alone emotionally attached to, the Constitution. This is shown by the fact that in the major political institutions for which the Constitution provides, conventions do not readily spring into being as they tend to do when basic values are shared. Behaviour is formal and conditioned by what is written. The Constitution is, in other words, as yet at least, primarily an educative instrument, a blueprint for an orderly, but not unfree form of government. The balance which the Constitution enjoins is precarious; it is therefore very sensitive to political violence, which has a marked destablilizing effect. This is where the military is important. The military did not in any serious way design the present Constitution, but does seem willing to defend it insofar as it does not lead to a break-down of order in society.

CHAPTER VI

POLITICAL PARTIES AND VOTING

Before the Young Turk revolution there were two major revolutionary societies in existence outside the Ottoman Empire. These were the Ottoman Society for Union and Progress led by Ahmed Riza and the liberal Society for Individual Enterprise and Decentralization under Prince Sabaheddin, a relative of the Sultan. When, in 1906, the former group allied itself with a revolutionary group of officials and officers in Salonica, and when at the same time relations improved between Ahmed Riza and Prince Sabaheddin, the prospects for a successful revolution were markedly increased. These societies were not political parties, however, and it was only in 1913 that the Society for Union and Progress decided to become a party, following the example of a crop of others, but notably that of the Liberal Union, a coalition of its opponents.

The common feature of these political parties was that their forbears had been nationalist, conspiratorial and revolutionary. They had railed against the Sultan's despotism, but they despised it because it was ineffectual more than they hated it because it was oppressive. When the Unionists came to power they emulated the Sultan's government in coercing their opponents—and more harshly—but they did not seek to destroy them. They did not set out to overthrow the bureaucratic elite which had managed the state for the Sultan because they were themselves junior members of that elite. The Young Turks were nothing like the Bolsheviks; they had no hatreds to work off against a domineering aristocracy, no theory of a necessary inter-class hostility. They were variously liberal, positivist, religious or secular in outlook, but their enmities were personal or based on group loyalties. The political parties which came into existence were internally formed from within the elite groups in the system. No groups external to the system were pushing for recognition.

This early history of Turkish political parties is not un-important. The incipient party system no doubt cloaked for a time the confrontation between the religious and secularist elements in society that was to come to the fore later with Kemal Atatürk. Yet even the religious parties of Young Turk times could claim with some justice to be part of the system.

With the Atatürk regime and the attack on religion, insofar as it was integrated with the state, the values of the political system came to be more narrowly defined. A specifically religious party came to be regarded as outside the system. Attempts in the 1950's to set up such parties were denied expression. A tradition was also established during the Atatürk regime of denying legitimacy to political parties formed on a class basis. Consequently when the Turkish political system became multi-party in 1946 it required conformity to a rather limited set of liberal and democratic values.

The restrictions articulated by the Atatürk regime went further than excluding Marxism and Islam. Liberalism itself was greatly curtailed, but the authoritarian single-party regime which was established was not totalitarian. No extravagant ideology of race, culture, or state was developed to embrace all civilization and deny all religion. Party membership was not restricted to an elite; there were no purges, no uniformed party militia and there was no rigidly disciplined party cell organization of the sort met with in totalitarian parties. Nor was the People's Party a substitute church; all classes of society were still too close to Islam for that. In any event the "spiritual" was not, despite Gökalp, released from the "material" in Islam; it was not floating free and available for mobilization by pseudo-religious political movements. The Party was nevertheless centralized and authoritarian in its selection of policies and leaders. It tried to carry the message of the revolution to the country at large through its People's Houses, though it organized neither mass meetings nor demonstrations in the totalitarian style. Moreover, party membership was never restricted to a dedicated minority chosen for the sacred task of leading the revolution and re-fashioning society in the image it might be loftily assumed that the Turks really desired. Turkish nationalism was perhaps intense enough to serve as a basis for an all-embracing movement, but it was checked by Atatürk, who rejected extravagances like Pan-Turanist dreams. As for the internal justifications of the creation of a right-wing totalitarianism, there was neither a strong native communism to combat, nor any at all significant industrial or commercial middle classes to feel threatened.

Within the People's Party an attempt made in 1930 by Atatürk to set up an opposition party, the Free Party, failed after a short and bitter experience. Yet this was only due in part to those ultra-authoritarian elements within the People's Party who did not appreciate that political opposition was necessary for governmental efficiency as well as being more "civilized". The failure of the experiment also reflected the fact that the general populace and their influential traditional leaders greatly preferred a certain past to an uncertain and innovatory future led by a tutelary bureaucracy.[1] Yet after the 1930 debacle the People's Party made genuine efforts to sensitize itself to the wishes and feelings of the populace and to decentralize its selection of leaders, whilst advancing the process of political socialization through the People's Houses. In addition, Atatürk promoted the election of Independent deputies for the sake of subjecting governmental policies to scrutiny. It is true that in 1936 Party and State were merged at the highest levels in what could be regarded as a typical subjugation of the state by the party, but it seems that the reverse was the case. It was the government which took over the Party, not *vice-versa*, in order to check the personal ambition and authoritarian bent of Recep Peker, the vigorous Secretary-General of the Party. In 1939 party and state were quietly disentangled.[2]

When in 1946 a multi-party system was inaugurated it was not altogether out of tune, therefore, with the aspirations of a number of members of the previous single-party regime. The danger was, nevertheless, that the new multi-party system would do no more than produce a dominant party regime—that the recent tradition of authoritarian rule, combined with a list system of voting in which winner took all, would soon snuff out the democratic and liberal spirit. It certainly looked like that when after 1954 the Democrat Party began seriously to restrict the freedoms of the opposition, but since 1961 a closely balanced two-party system has operated, with the smaller parties usually playing an important role in coalition-making, but also showing a marked tendency to wither away.

Of the two major parties the now left-of-centre People's Party has been in office twice since 1961 and assumed office again in January, 1978. The first time, just after the revolution, was a shot-gun alliance with the other major party, the right-of-centre Justice Party, the gun being pointed by the military. In 1974 the People's Party entered into office with the National Salvation Party, but this lasted less than twelve months. Otherwise the Justice Party has been in power, with absolute majorities in the 1965 and 1969 elections and as chief partner in rightist coalitions from 1974 to January, 1978. Justice Party members also figured prominently in the non-party governments set up following the military ultimatum in 1971 to the formation of the People's and National Salvation parties' coalition in 1974 to which reference has just been made. An examination of the election results in the table at Appendix I shows how, despite the use of proportional representation since 1961, a dual system has operated for the most part. There are clearly rightist strands represented by the National Salvation and National Action parties which draw sustenance from national sentiment and from fear and hatred of Russia in particular and of the West as well. This right-ism derives, too, from the small traders' and the small business-men's distress at the economic effects of big business, from their fear of the incipient power of the unions, their dislike for arrogant and unhelpful bureaucracy, and from their close attachment to Islam. The Islamic wing of this rightism has been represented by a succession of parties since the creation of the multi-party system. At first it was the National Party (dissolved in 1954 but reacti-vated in 1962), the National Order Party (closed down in 1972) and now it is represented by the National Salvation Party. The popularity of these parties has waxed and waned at different times. In 1977 the National Salvation Party lost half its seats in the National Assembly, as was noted earlier, but its vote did not decline all that much. Its decline was, however, matched by a rise in votes for the National Action Party. This came into being after its leader, Türkeş, took over the Republican People's Nation Party in 1965, the name being changed in 1969. We shall see shortly the nature of this party's activities and appeal. Finally, another right-wing party, the Democratic Party, came into being in 1970 after the defection from the Justice Party of some forty deputies whose loss greatly eroded Demirel's strength in the previous year. This group is said to have represented landowners and other provincial notables who reacted against the Justice Party's policies for modest agrarian reform and taxation of agricultural wealth.[3] Against continuing pressures the Democratic Party has not survived.

Whilst defections from the Justice Party have been towards the right, defections from the People's Party have not correspondingly been towards the left. The chief defection was that of Turhan Feyzioğlu, who, in 1967, deplored the People's Party's new left-of-centre position and the creation of the distinction between bourgeois and proletarian that was implied. The Reliance Party set up by Feyzioğlu with some thirty deputies was joined by a further nine members from the People's Party in 1973. As they had set themselves up as the Republican Party in the previous year, out of deference to them "Republican" was pre-fixed to the title of the Reliance Party. Nevertheless its fortunes have declined.

Potentially perhaps the most significant party, the Worker's Party, has not done as well as its prophets foretold. Founded in 1961 by trade union leaders, its fortunes were greatly affected by the adherence of leftist intellectuals—a veritable kiss of death. The party's chief architect was its first chairman Ali Aybar, but he was pushed further and further to the left despite his own social-democratic convictions. Under its subsequent chairman, Behice Boran, the party went further left—though not far enough for some—with the result that it was closed down in 1971 and several of its leaders arrested, tried and imprisoned. The party was re-constituted in 1975, after an unsuccessful attempt by the Turkish Unity Party, adversely affected by its connections with the Shiite (*Alevi*) minority to take its place.

Party Programmes

It has become fashionable in political science not to devote much time to analysing political party programmes. We know now that voters do not pay much attention to them. Social class, parental preferences, political images, skilfully projected political personalities—all these and other irrational factors are generally accepted as more important than reasoned statements of beliefs that may well have to be compromised anyway when it comes to the difficult task of actually governing. Yet political parties do continue to hammer out programmes and struggle to get their points of view across to the electorate. If they did not do so there would no doubt be more blurred images and less definite personalities to impress the voters. In other words, it is not quite as simple as it may first apppear to separate party policies and ideologies from other more measurable factors in the appeal of political parties to the voter. And very recent voting studies suggest that too much emphasis is placed on voters' irrationality.

The immediate appeal of party programmes must nevertheless be to the educated minority. In Turkey the educated minority is much smaller than in western democracies, but the intensity of their interest in politics is much greater. The survey of student attitudes discussed earlier showed that among students from a variety of faculties, over two-thirds interested themselves to some degree in politics, with one-fifth very interested. A good deal of this interest arose from reading and from their instruction in social and political subjects. How far this elite acts as opinion leaders cannot really be judged, but the newspapers are replete with political information—and articles on political subjects, written often by academics. Some of the political commentary is as grossly partisan and personal in tone as can be found anywhere, but a great deal of it is genuinely informative and does not burke policy and ideology in favour of more sensational matters. Newspapers are also in great demand and are handed around a great deal in small communities. In continuing, as they do, to place considerable emphasis in their speeches, to literate and illiterate alike, on their political programmes political leaders in Turkey are not likely to be altogether misguided.

The party news which catches the headlines in Turkey is usually that which relates to the activities of potentially anti-systemic, and inherently exciting parties, like the Worker's, National Salvation, and National Action parties. Yet the two centre parties are much more important electorally and to their less thrilling, but more substantial, views we first turn.

The People's Party was soon embarrassed by its left-of-centre declaration, especially as its fortunes did not revive in the 1965 elections. There were many in the party who did not really approve, including important personages like Nihat Erim and Kemal Satır. The leader of the left-of-centre movement, Bülent Ecevit, was supported by the veteran chairman of the party, the late İsmet İnönü until 1971, though with some wavering before the 1969 elections. When İnönü announced in March, 1971, after the military's ultimatum, that he supported a government to be formed under Nihat Erim, Ecevit resigned his post as Secretary-General to the party. One particular bone of contention with İnönü was that by supporting Erim's government he re-created in the popular mind the all too familiar spectacle of a People's Party/ Military alliance. Many in the party had come to believe that this supposed party identification with the military (and the bureaucracy) had been the prime cause of relatively weak support for the party at the polls since 1960. Another matter of dispute was the fact that under İnönü the party had agreed that there was a need for constitutional amendments. One argument advanced by those opposed to the party's policy in this matter was that the Constitution had special force through having been approved by a referendum in 1961—a view that would have made any constitutional change a major task. More realistically, it was also urged that the situation in the country, whilst serious, could have been rectified by firmer government under the existing provisions of the Constitution. In 1972, with the support of the provincial party congresses, Bülent Ecevit fought out with İnönü, now supported by the new Secretary-General Kemal Satır, a battle for control of the party and its policy. In May, 1972, İnönü resigned rather than go along with the Ecevit faction, despite their entreaties, and Ecevit was elected Party Chairman. It was an inglorious and almost quixotic exit from politics for a statesman to whom Turkey owed so much. It also meant an inglorious exit for Kemal Satır, who later joined the Reliance Party.

For such upsets there was obviously much at stake, but whether these struggles represented ideological or personal conflicts is a moot point. Certainly Bülent Ecevit and the radicals attacked what they regarded as two ossified features of Atatürkism, namely the emphasis on national solidarity and westernization at the expense of fundamental social reform, and the unrevolutionary support for the 1960 revolution provided by the wealthier classes. These charges of superficiality, complacency and even hypocrisy were not relished by staunch and proud defenders of the Atatürkist tradition.

Yet when the party's programmes are examined there is little enough difference between those of the 1960's and the 1970's and certainly little between the "left-of-centre" programmes of the late 1960's and the "democratic left" programmes of the 1970's.[4] A survey of the principles of the 1970's shows that the party now lays great stress on the participation of the villages in their own development, of workers in their factories and civil servants in their offices. The initiative from the people is now all important; it self-consciously replaces the tutelary and paternalistic posture of the 1950's, which still lingered on well beyond that decade in some quarters. Something positive now is made of religion; it is not studiously ignored as it has been in the past. In this and in other respects the Party has learned that its chief rival's ability to mobilize the electorate derives not just from the "exploitation" of ignorance but often from a genuine helpfulness based on a closer understanding of the predicaments in which ordinary people often find themselves. The substantive points of its programmes are more clearly made than hitherto, and there is no doubt that they are meant for understanding by the less, as well as by the more, educated. There is frank recognition of the existence in society of economically based social classes, but the party is not Marxist by any means: it sees itself as the broker of class interests, not as an agent for the destruction of the bourgeoisie. The party declares, probably in good faith, that it is not opposed to the development of even large concerns in the private sector, provided that they do not offend against social justice (not defined), that profits are not excessive, that monopolies do not emerge, public resources are not used for private gain, and that large amounts of capital and advanced technological skills are not devoted to luxury or inessential industries. Nor does the party adopt Marxist views on land holding. The party means by land reform that a working farmer should own enough land to make a living for himself and his family. On another vital economic matter, foreign capital for investment, the party is strict, but not

forbidding. Noting that foreign firms have begun to take out of
Turkey more than they put in—a rather simplistic analysis of a
highly complex issue—the party will restrict the export of profit to
a reasonable degree in accordance with world standards, and will
insist on a less than a half share for foreign companies in joint
enterprises, whilst the exploitation of mineral wealth must rest
very definitely in the hands of the Turkish government. Not
surprisingly, the party also believes firmly in development through
planning, though always with regard for social justice again. The
individual is not to be ground down by the bureaucracy, however,
for the sake of society. The individual and group freedoms
restricted by the amendments to the Constitution in 1971 are to
be restored. It will be interesting to see if they are. The party is
particularly concerned that there should be no attempt to prevent
the involvement of trade unions in politics and state officials are
to be allowed to form unions again. In all this, democracy and
social justice are the key concepts. Democracy entails the participation of the unions (but not the employers' associations it
appears—by neglect perhaps) in politics; it also involves participation by workers and employees in the organization of their
work and their conditions of employment. Social justice does not
seem to envisage absolute equality, but in the absence of definition it is wide open to interpretation. Perhaps most important is
that the party openly rejects elitism on whatever grounds, but
whether this would easily be abandoned in practice in the socialistic society envisaged, in which the intelligentsia would obviously
have an important role, is open to question.

The Justice Party also claims above all not to be elitist,
certainly not, at any rate, to be led by an intellectualist elite.
Like its predecessor, the Democrat Party, the party makes
something of a fetish of its capacity to go direct to the people. So
now does the People's Party, as we have seen, but there is some
truth in the claim that the People's Party, in trying actively to
involve the people in its own achievement of democratic socialism,
is still acting in a tutelary way. By contrast, the Justice Party
claims that it simply discovers natural interests, senses feeling, and
responds to a natural desire on the part of the people for the
government to look after their interests as they traditionally

expect Papa State to do. It strives neither to reform the people, nor to get them to reform themselves. It is not a party of school-masters.

"The appeal of the Justice Party, like its predecessor, the Democrat Party, is not ideological," it has been said, It may well be true, the same observer continues, that, "the party's greatest support comes from the small-holder peasants" who "are allied with expanding, but still small, commercial, industrial, urban labour groups and newly wealthy farmers."[5] The Justice Party must indeed obtain support from these groups to some extent and the party's programmes embody many of the aspirations of these groups. For entrepreneurs there is a marked emphasis on the value of private enterprise, with the job of economic planners, for instance, seen to be to advise and assist the private sector. It is envisaged that the state shall undertake economic activities where the private sector cannot—to provide a lead, for example, in large risk-bearing operations. Whilst the People's Party does not in fact proclaim the need for total public ownership and supports private enterprise to some extent, it does not evince any enthusiasm for private economic enterprise. The contrast here with the Justice Party's very positive attitudes is most marked.

Does the Justice Party stand then for a *laissez-faire* system? Not according to its leader, who always stresses that the party is not wedded to nineteenth century liberalism, or to capitalism or indeed to any other "ism", but is most definitely opposed to com munism. The ideal is Turkish *national* development towards the goal of a prosperous Turkey. This goal of a "prosperous ease" (*refah*) is constantly stressed: and it is regarded as the key to a vision of social harmony which in its fulfilment will make socio-economic class divisions nugatory. For the Justice Party the operation of the market economy is a necessary good; for the People's Party a necessary evil. The Justice Party consequently tends not to see, or to minimize, the dislocations that can be produced by rapid economic development—like the plight of small businessmen and traders put out of business by larger concerns, or the creation of socially unsettling disparities of wealth. Of late the main section of the Justice Party has tended to look rather more closely at the generally unwelcome effects on society and politics of some of its policies. It too has come to accept the ideal of social justice. Who dare not pay lip service to it? But it makes it clear that this does not mean equality of income. The real emphasis is on a liberal equality of opportunity, combined with a need to provide social security to overcome the difficulties caused by the processes of economic development. On the very contentious question of foreign capital the Justice Party professes caution. "If foreign capital is well used it is valuable; if not, it starts a fire . . . . the advantage does not all accrue to us. The nation's profit is a matter of calculation. There is no relationship when the other side has no gain."[6]

The general approach of the Justice Party is accompanied by a rejection of religious influence over the state, the assertion of individual rights, the need for private economic development to protect democracy from bureaucratic hegemony, and an emphasis on a strong and stable state so clearly necessary to create the conditions for prosperous economic enterprise. This seems to be a liberal and democratic ideology, but it is not liberal in the sense of having hidden within it the ideal of the hard-working, self-made, individualistic, upright man prepared spontaneously to do his bit for the good of society. Certainly the Justice Party does not appear like this to its opponents. To them its greater economic freedoms seem to lead only to the tawdry corruption and exploitation of later Ottomanism. The Justice Party image does perhaps have a touch of the levantine about it. It is not so much that the two major parties differ in the actual content of their programmes, it is rather their styles which separate them and the personalities of their leaders. To their opponents Justice Party conservatism spells the venality of the past. To the Justice Party the socialistic zeal of their principal opponents still bespeaks heavy-handed Ottoman reforming bureaucracy. But the Justice Party's economic liberalism is anathemia to its opponents on the left even if they misconceive its nature due to their own doctrinaire upbringing. The Justice Party responds always to their attacks with frankness and vigour; the arguments are similar to those found in every serious journal in the West. The problem is whether Turkey has now really moved into a situation not essentially different from that of Western Europe, as the purveyors of this argumentation insist, or whether the debate is not in some way imitative and less relevant to reality than these political disputants suppose.

Two rightist parties claim to be closer to the Turkish reality than their big rivals. One of these is the National Salvation Party, even although its representation dropped dramatically in parliament in 1977.[7] The party particularly seeks to represent the religious interest, which others think is on the wane generally in Turkey. Indeed both liberals and socialists assume from their different views of progress that it will eventually wither away as development of whichever sort proceeds. The National Salvation Party rejects this mindless sort of determinism and asserts that economic development, at least, and Islam are perfectly compatible. To be Islamic is not to be materially backward, as the old People's Party used to suggest—mediaeval Islamic civilization was much more advanced than that of Europe in material as well as in other ways. Islam is not the "dead hand" on progress the Atatürkist philosophy implied. So, not surprisingly on this view, the prime factor in development is technology, not a more thorough understanding of western culture or civilization. Its leader, Erbakan, is a technologist and so are many of his immediate circle. True to a rather puritanical Muslim ethic the party stresses that this technology must be used without wastefulness; it should be utilized in the construction of factories, not luxury hotels. The party is critical of the misapplication of capital, especially if, as has been the case, it continues to destroy small producers, artisans and merchants. That the party is supported by these classes is generally accepted.[8] Unfortunately for the consistency of the party's philosophy its emphasis on technology runs counter to the interests of the small men in business and industry in the long run and there is not much suggestion as to how the development of technology might be controlled. The party seems to assume that Islamic moralism will be enough. This is of course dependent in the longer term on the firm adherence of the population in general to Islamic values. This in turn entails the inculcation of these moral standards through schooling combined, no doubt, with very firm authoritarian leadership in government. Both these are consistent with the Islamic tradition.

Not surprisingly, therefore, the party requires the state to attend assiduously to the moral education of all its citizens. On the governmental side the party firmly supports the freedoms accorded by the Constitution, particularly freedom of thought and belief, but proposes a return to Assembly government, the amalgamation of the offices of President and Prime Minister and the President's election by direct vote. The use of the referendum is also favoured. This faith in democracy derives from a perhaps shrewd belief that the Turkish people would still prefer authoritarian, but Islamic, government if properly allowed to express their inner convictions.

The most heavily authoritarian strain in the Turkish right is represented by the National Action Party. Whilst it is now of more importance electorally than it was, it is also noted, and feared, for its support by strong-arm groups of commandos (Grey Wolves). The fact that at party congresses many of those attending wear uniforms is also not reassuring. The other political parties fear this party as a great potential danger to democracy. Supporters of the People's Party, in particular, have resented the inclusion of the party in national front governments, when its influence can be readily expanded. Influence of this sort was used by the National Salvation Party when in coalition with the People's Party in 1974. It is said that at that time almost 5,000 religious functionaries were appointed and many officials in various ministries were either dismissed or retired.[9]

The policies of the National Action Party appear to be those mainly of its leader, Alparslan Türkeş, though there is also some more intellectual support.[10] Türkeş has a history of involvement in pan-Turkist and anti-communist political activities from 1944 and was one of the fourteen expelled from the military junta in 1960. The Grey Wolf groups which support the party gained notoriety in 1968 and 1969 for their vicious attacks on left-wing organizations, notably in the universities, and have been active ever since. It is not known how large these youth organizations are, but they appear to have had military training in special camps where the curriculum consists mainly of physical training, lectures on nationalism and, more recently, of religious devotions.[11] They are fired by nationalism and anti-communism; most important, as always in politics, they are dedicated and well organized.

These groups and the six and a half million voters who at present support the party presumably agree with at least some of the party's aims. These have been expressed by Türkeş in the form of "nine lights".[12] These nine lights are neither unusual nor remarkable, but together they point to a direction. The "lights" are nationalism, idealism, moral improvement, a rational and informed approach to the solution of problems, social concern, village development, freedom and respect for the individual, development and populism, industrialization and technical proficiency. Türkeş is at pains to point out that "the nine lights reject national socialism, just as they reject capitalism and marxism."[13] In fact he considers national socialism and fascism as "a degenerate deviation from capitalism,"[14] though not as Marxists would have it, as the final phase of capitalism. This accords with his view that there should be a properly regulated system of private ownership. National socialist and fascist regimes are "reactionary dictatorships which do not believe in human rights and freedoms." The party is said to be devoted to Türkeş, the Turkish nation and to Turkism. This Turkish nationalism includes a concern for the well-being of Turkish society, a concern which rises over and above a concern for individuals. Yet a belief in the democratic road to power and in the maintenance of democracy after power is attained is constantly reiterated. International ideologies, whether liberalism or marxism, are rejected on the grounds that they are both imperialist. The weakness of Turkish intellectuals, it is asserted, is that they tend simply to copy what seems better abroad. Instead they should rely on Turkish traditions. Whilst the party does not consider itself fascist, it certainly accepts that is is conservative, but how far this conservatism embraces the Ottoman as well as the pre-Ottoman tradition is a difficult point. For largely tactical reasons the party has turned more and more to Islam of late, but it is clearly the earlier Turkish tradition shining through the Ottoman layer which is important. Within this nationalism language, not race, is stressed, but its real roots are said to lie in a long history of an independent Turkish identity too ancient and profound for the Turks to have any need of either the national socialism or the fascism of new nations like

Germany or Italy.

Whilst moral encouragement is available to outside Turks, the real enemy of Turkish nationalism is the communism which the party considers a threat to Turkey. Class conflict and the dictatorship of the proletariat are both absolutely rejected. It is maintained that a civilized division of labour along professional lines and the formation of groups and classes which social life necessitates does not give cause for the emergence of an exploitative and arbitrary hierarchy. Moreover, the party believes that leadership should lie in the hands of a nationalist educated elite, and certainly rejects as completely unjust the dictatorship of the working class. Instead, Türkeş proposes, for socio-economic purposes, to form six vertical groupings (not horizontal classes) composed of workers, peasants, artisans, officials, employers and professional persons. These groups are largely to be left to manage their own internal affairs; from their representatives will be formed the membership of a truly national National Assembly, which will function without a Senate. This is in fact a version of the corporate state which fascist Italy tried to operate, but which resulted in control by the party. The idea of a corporate state, which long antedated fascism, is undoubtedly attractive to all those who deplore the frustrating results of socio-economic class conflict and the disrupting effects of the action of some individuals and groups in liberal-democratic states who use freedom without responsibility. The problem is whether in the state envisaged by Türkeş the nationalist zeal will not in fact lead to the subjugation of the individual and the exploitation of workers, and even managers, in the interests of those who man the state apparatus. The role of the individual is insisted upon, but significantly the device of referendum is preferred to election of representatives on the grounds that representative democracy is bourgeois directed.

Much must depend, however, on the temper of the party which would be in power. How it would develop if it were to obtain power must be open to question, but its record in power as a member of Demirel's coalition has not been reassuring and the violence of the commando groups against leftist elements is deeply disturbing. Yet it must be said that the party's philosophy, even if not developed to any intellectual depth, does not show some typically fascist or national socialist attitudes. The party's doctrine is not urged as a substitute for religion; it is neither avowedly anti-intellectual, nor anti-individual, nor anti-democratic. It does not base itself on racial purity or encourage racial hatreds; nor does it extravagantly exhort Turks to a national wilfulness or reliance on force. Instead the party makes much of the more respectable aspects of fascist doctrine like the rejection of determinism, the need for more socially orientated individual behaviour and for greater respect for traditional canons of morality and their activation. If to a marked degree fascist in its thought, feeling and action, the party is not ostensibly totalitarian; there is not the insistence on the individual's total immersion in the state that characterized national socialist and fascist regimes.

The National Action Party's chief enemy is the left, which has not been effectively organized as a contender for political power since the closure of the Worker's Party in 1971. That such a party will emerge is always a distinct possibility, though much depends on how far left the People's Party leans and, of course, how far the electorate can be convinced that a revival of the far left in politics in desirable. Nor should it be forgotten that since 1971 less leftist propaganda has been permitted.

The Turkish Worker's Party started off as a leftist social demo-cratic party which moved further leftwards in much of its internal thinking and in its chief personnel during its existence, but did not reflect so great a change in its programmes as this might suggest. Started by trade unionists, greatly influenced by intellectuals, it was not long before deep rifts, personal and ideological began to appear. The moderates and the party programmes were at one with those of more rigorous views in proclaiming the existence of the economic and social exploitation of the workers, whether in field, factory, workshop or even in minor civil service posts. They all called for the abolition of the landlords (ağa's), who are accused of dominating the lives of their peasants. They agreed, too, on the nationalization of foreign trade, banking and the major economic insitutions, and on the rejection of neo-imperialism and its agents, the compromador bourgeoisie. Thereafter significant differences appear. While the moderates would leave the peasants

with land large enough to provide a living for the family, others
dub this as bourgeois. Private enterprise would have a very restricted role for some, none for others. The party generally came
to the view under its more left inclined leadership that the capture
of power by democratic means was impossible, or that power
could only be corrupting if won with the help of small businessmen and traders when the masses still lacked true social consciousness. On this view trained cadres of dedicated propagandists
(operating among the workers) not vote-getters, were vital.

Political Party Organization

Whether the centre and rightist parties can educate the public
to their points of view against the influence of leftist activity must
depend to a large extent on the size and effectiveness of their
party organizations. Every political party is obliged to establish
a general congress and a central governing council but the law
allows other central organs to be established as well. The general
Congress is composed of members elected by the Provincial
Party Congress with senators and deputies as *ex officio* members
and with the important proviso that the latter are not to form less
than half of the total membership. Elections by the Congress
to membership of the Central Governing Body and of the Party
Chairman are by secret ballot. This imposed framework is not so
democratic, however, in practice as to bring about revolutionary
change in the long established habits of centralized power. In the
People's Party, for instance, the Central Executive Committee of
fourteen members, and in the Justice Party the General Administrative Committee, are the foci of power, as small top bodies tend
to become, whether elected or not.[15] These executive committees
prepare the agenda for the General Congresses where elections to
positions of party leadership are also greatly influenced by the
party executives in office. These latter are in close liason with
local factions dominant in provincial congresses, which choose
delegates for the General Congress.[15] Yet in 1964 the acting
leader of the Justice Party, Saadettin Bilgiç, was not elected leader
despite his control over the provincial party organization. On the
other hand it has not subsequently been possible to unseat
Demirel despite efforts within the party to do so. In the People's

Party İsmet İnönü's leadership was for many years unchallenge-able, if admitteldy as much for his historic personality as for his dominance of the party central organization. Yet in 1971 and 1972, as we have seen, Bülent Ecevit began a successful challenge to his leadership. At first supported only by the Izmir provincial organization and the youth groups, he gradually extended his influence, winning support at provincial party congresses despite communiqués sent to them by İnönü.[16] Finally, in May, 1972, an Extra-ordinary Congress called by İnönü resulted only in his own defeat and departure. Both this and the Justice Party experience show that when critical issues arise, the control of the central party organization is not the crucial factor. The issue in 1964 was whether the Justice Party should be far right, or just right of centre; in 1972 the issue was whether the People's Party should be elitist and reliant on the military and important sections of the landed and industrial worlds, or whether it should continue to adopt a left-of-centre stand and trust its fortunes to the will of the people, freely expressed, for a near socialist programme.

That the provincial and sub-provincial party organization is not normally dominant, however, in the decision of major issues must owe something to the fact that their organizations are of the cadre rather than of the mass type. In the large towns the parties tend to have large numbers of active members engaged in political party activities year in year out, and functioning through well articulated units. In the smaller towns, however, local party organizations tend to operate effectively with regard to propa-ganda and recruitment of supporters only at election times. At other times only certain parts of the organization function un-interruptedly. In particular, the sub-provincial executive com-mittees have a permanent importance because they receive from constituents requests for governmental action in particular cases, which they decide whether to promote or not. The powers of provincial party leaders are also significant. They are said "to have increased substantially over the years due to their influence on decisions concerning eligibility to vote in election primaries and their ability to build up networks of personal supporters through patronage distribution."[17] In this connection the whole system of party primary elections has never been completely applied and is in considerable disarray. A change in the legislation regulating primary elections was made in 1973 which gave formal recognition to a wide variety of practice—which can come to mean extensive central nomination of candidates to stand in elections beyond the five per cent provided for in the Political Parties' Law.[18]

Clientilism and Patronage

The strengthening of central and local political party cadres in this way may well represent something of a reaction against the widespread conviction that political parties in Turkey in general, and in the less developed areas in particular, are not primarily organizations which can be said to aggregate national opinions on major national issues; they are said to be instruments, rather, through which local benefits are sought from the central government. Frequently, it is true, local party organizations are dominated by influential local groups, or by notables in the countryside; and if independent local party organizations do not hold promise of gaining influence in Ankara, they will be by-passed and largely ignored. The party loyalties of many Turks in the less developed regions of the country are weaker than their loyalties to powerful local individuals.

This latter situation is almost certainly the case in Eastern Anatolia where two basic sets of social relationships seem to exist. The first type of relationship is that between a landowner (*ağa*) and his quite numerous sharecroppers. They not only work for him, they also vote for him or his nominees out of deference, or even out of fear. In return for this support they are generally protected, assisted in times of economic need, and helped in other ways, as in the provision of medical care, for instance, in a part of Turkey where such services tend to be at their most rudimentary. Of course, it is often asserted that the peasant clients of such *ağa*'s are exploited. However that may be, the relationship between the *ağa* and the peasant is not just economic in nature. Nor is it strictly limited to the immediate realm of patron and client. For both have at their disposal another network of social relationships derived from developed forms of an institution of ritual co-parenthood known as *kirvelik*. This institution is created when a person, normally a relative, and of higher status, is asked to be a co-parent, usually on the occasion of ceremonies initiating a boy into manhood. A reciprocal relationship is thereby formed. *Kirvelik* thus " secures a social contract among relative strangers from different ethnic, religious and kindred groups and occupational categories who can hardly otherwise be expected to trust each other. It affords the advantages of extended ties of agnatic kinship and affinity, but avoids the disputes over property and leadership that are concomitant with these other relations.'' [19] Clearly, if such an institution is extensive, and this is not altogether clear, it is a factor of some political importance. In the absence of trade unions and associational groups in Eastern Turkey, "*kirvelik* provides useful means for generating informal interest groups and voting manpower in Eastern Turkey."[20] This clearly extends the normal patron-client relationship in a highly significant fashion. As a result, a man of substance may be able to mobilize many more than just his own clients behind him.

This present situtation in Eastern Turkey must resemble that which existed more generally in Turkey in 1950 at the outset of multi-partyism. In fact, it is often held that the Democrat Party was able to develop its support in the countryside with the speed it did because it brought patrons to it side who quickly and effectively mobilized the peasant voter. Yet this may need refinement. For it has been persuasively argued that the significant divide in Turkey at that time was still the rift between the centre, represented by bureaucracy, and the periphery, composed of local notables and their clients; the role of the Democrat Party was to organize the periphery against the centre. This it was able to do as a result of economic development and developments in communications in the 1940's which allowed towns and villages to be linked laterally in new ways and to a greater extent than hitherto. The Democrat Party, it has been said "was not so much a party of notables as it was a party that speculated with a political ideology which it thought would be strongly supported by the rural masses and by their patrons."[21]

Another important and different interpretation relies on the fairly well substantiated claim that factionalism has always existed in Turkish rural society, deriving from hostilities between lineages and inter-group conflicts. "These factional oppositions were transformed into political competition at the local level with the advent of electoral politics."[22] If this is generally true, then the maintenance of a two-party system in large measure in Turkey, even since the adoption of proportional representation, may be in part explained. One patron's adherence to one party encouraged his rival's adherence to its principal opponent. These patrons would not necessarily be landlords only, but also rich merchants, sheikhs, or tribal leaders. This was a perfect example of the operation of political clientilism, which is significant not just for mobilizing support, but also for mobilizing it across socio-economic lines.

With economic development the situation has now changed. As state resources have become more abundant it has paid local magnates in most parts of Turkey to pay attention to, and dominate, local political party organizations. They then have more to offer by way of patronage. This they need because their clients are also now more demanding than they used to be as a result of better education, less deference and wider prospects for their own individual advancement in life. Political clientilism is in fact giving way to political patronage funnelled through political party machines. A greater element of bargaining is also beginning to appear as peasants become increasingly aware that their vote has a price in material benefits.

This bargaining element in political relationships suggests that the political parties are not just the tools of the notables or the bourgeoisie in any direct material sense. Certainly the highest positions in the two major political parties are not the preserve of notables or bourgeoisie: they are mostly filled by persons of professional and official background. A study of the membership of the principal central organs of the two major political parties between 1961 and 1970 showed, moreover, no real differences as to occupational background between the leadership of the two parties, nor much difference as to educational qualifications either. In the Justice Party 81%, and in the People's Party 72%, of these leading party figures came from offical and professional occupational backgrounds in about equal proportions from each. Lawyers were predominant in the People's Party with teachers next. In the Justice Party lawyers still constituted the largest group, but commerce and agriculture were rather better represented than in the opposing party. In both parties all these leaders were highly educated and also provided quite stable leadership over the period, the average re-election rates being for the Justice Party 56% and for the People's Party some 67%.[23] The central party organizations were obviously able to survive pressures from any new social groups to dominate them.

An important test of the significance of clientilist politics over patronage and bargaining would be the extent to which local political organizations were in the hands of landlords, sheikhs (in tribal areas) industrialists, businessmen and merchants. Recent substantial research is not available, but a study in 1964 revealed that "provincial political party organizations were staffed by relatively young educated local professionals and businessmen" and that "farmers, landowners and public servants were not well represented."[24] This suggests that a very limited role is being played by local notables at least, but it was noted that "the least developed provinces tend to have the lowest proportion of professionals . . . . and the highest proportion of agriculturalists,"[25] and that the Justice Party was more generously staffed "by merchants and traders."[26] Nevertheless the evidence for overall substantial domination in party leadership, whether feudal or bourgeois, is not overwhelming. The political elites of the parties have apparently converged in terms of occupational background, the professional element being most notable; it should be remembered, however, that in the less developed parts of the country, notably in Eastern Turkey, clientilism is still rife. It is in these areas that independent candidates and small parties tend to prosper. It is not uncommon for a local magnate to transfer his allegiance, and his following, from one party to another, or simply to have himself elected as an independent.

Voting

It might appear a legitimate conclusion from our discussion so far, including our discussion of political culture, that Turkish voters are only interested in the local benefits to be expected from a political party once it is in power. Certainly this has been a

strong factor in the support given to the Justice Party, of whose
supporters, when asked in 1969, "a good majority mentioned the
government's performance as the major factor in their choice."[2][7]
The second main reason for their support was the recognition that
the Justice Party was the real heir to the very popular Democrat
Party. Religion came a long way behind these considerations as
a reason for the voters' support for the Justice Party. As for the
People's Party, its supporters were chiefly impressed, not by the
left-of-centre policy, which few outside the middle classes had
heard of in 1969—the situation may be different now—but by its
being the party of Atatürk and İnönü.

Such surveys as these will no doubt be refined, though they
will for a long time have to contend with a simple lack of understanding of the questions asked, especially in the less developed
areas, as well as with a traditional inclination to give circumspect
rather than true replies. A more scientific, if rather less alluring,
mode of enquiry is to examine voting behaviour by reference to
indices of economic and social development. Such studies are
prompted by hypotheses regarding the relationship between
political participation and modernization which derive from that
body of theory which has come to be known as "development
theory."[28] This seems particularly apposite for Turkey since some
parts of the country, notably the eastern provinces, are markedly
less developed than provinces in the western part of the country.

One study of voting in relation to levels of economic and
social development first establishes a reasonable overlap of low
urbanization, illiteracy, poor communications, unequal land distribution and minority language speaking (chiefly Kurdish) in the
Eastern and South-Eastern regions of Turkey.[29] The opposite
qualities distinguish the western provinces, though it should be
said that large land holding is also a feature of the Mediterranean
region and of some Black Sea prcvinces. Also in the Eastern and
South-Eastern regions of Anatolia, where Kurdish is spoken, the
majority speak Turkish—at 70 per cent and 57 per cent respectively.

When indices of economic and social development are considered alongside voting figures it is found that the more
developed regions tend to vote for the larger parties, save in

central Anatolia, where it seems *Alevi* (Shi'ite) Turks prefer communal solidarity represented by adherence to a small party. Otherwise the small parties do well in the less developed regions. These
parties tend also to be very local. But then all parties in less
developed regions show support concentrated in localities rather
than diffused. In Hakkari province in eastern Anatolia nearly 40%
of the ballot boxed returned 90% or more of votes for a single
party.[30] This evidence of strong communal solidarity is found
much less in other regions.

In a very substantial analysis at provincial and regional level,
Dr. E. Özbudun concerns himself with the relationship between
levels of socio-economic development on the one hand and voting
turn-out on the other. Changes in both turn-out and voting
preferences are studied from 1950 to 1969.[31]

To take voting by region first, Özbudun identifies nine regions,
as shown in Appendix II.[32] On the combined basis of indices of
development employed in various studies he ranks the regions in
order of development as follows: Marmara, Aegean, Mediterranean,
North Cental, South Central, Black Sea, East Central, North-
eastern and South-eastern. From his examination of party voting
in regions Özbudun finds that in the 1950's the major parties had
different regional strongholds—The Democrat Party in the western
and more developed provinces and the People's Party in the east.

Some concrete evidence for the greater "working class" appeal
of the People's Party appears when comparisons are made between
urban and rural voting figures. In this regard, in 1969 the Justice
Party's loss of strength was most marked in the towns, whilst the
People's Party showed gains in urban areas. Again in 1973, from
the limited evidence available, it seems the People's Party collected
more urban votes, especially in the large towns of Istanbul, Ankara,
Izmir and Adana.[33] Moreover, there is evidence to suggest that the
"lower class" shanty town dwellers who started to defect from the
Justice Party in 1965 and 1969 moved to support the People's
Party in 1973.[34] Whether urban support for the Justice Party in
towns of between 25,000 and 100,000 inhabitants has also maintained the decline noted in them in 1969 is not yet clear. These
middle sized towns are where the Democrat and Justice parties
have found ready persons to mobilize.

When the analysis of voters' party preferences is pushed down to provincial level the pattern at regional level reappears, but with more clarity. Before 1969 Justice Party success, like that of the Democrat Party earlier, correlated positively with higher levels of provincial socio-economic development. In particular, the Justice Party did well in provinces characterized by high scores on literacy, more primary school education, greater numbers employed in manufacturing industries, and where Turkish was predominant. In 1969 the extent of primary education was the single most important factor in a positive correlation for voting for the Justice Party.[35] As for the People's Party only in 1969 did significant correlations emerge in these respects. The only minor party to register success in more developed provinces was the Turkish Worker's Party, but in 1965 it was found, in conditions of an equivalent degree of provincial urbanization, that "the partial correlation between the TLP (Worker's Party) vote and the percentage of males in manufacturing industry became strongly negative."[36] The conclusion is suggested, and accords with the impressions of observers, that the main strength of the Worker's Party lay in the urban middle classes.

In 1973 the People's Party voting correlated even more strongly with provincial socio-economic development (owing a lot to its new popularity in the large cities) but it is also true that the Justice Party draws an above average share of its votes from the more highly developed provinces. Is there any difference in the nature of this voting? When socio-economic analysis which distinguishes between urban and rural development is used it is found, for 1973, that the Justice Party does best in provinces with high *rural* development, whether the level of urban development is high or low. By contrast the People's Party does well in provinces of high *urban* development whatever the levels of rural development. The two major parties combined obtained 70 per cent of the votes in the provinces of high urban and rural development, and only 52.7 per cent in those least developed on both counts. It is of interest that the National Salvation Party was almost equally strong in all provinces.

We have noted earlier, drawing from Dr. W.M. Hale's analysis of the situation in 1969, that in the less developed regions there is a strong tendency for a party to obtain almost all the votes in villages or groups of villages. Özbudun's analysis for 1969 shows that the poorer a village, the more votes it gives to one party. In 22 per cent of the poorest villages more than 80 per cent of the votes were given to one party, with another 56 per cent of the villages giving between 50 and 80 per cent.[37] This tendency is on the decline, it seems, however, and the typical Turkish village "seems to be one with a clear majority for one party but also with considerable support for other parties."[38] The Justice Party seems to do better in the more modernized villages, to judge from 1965, but may be declining since, to judge from the 1969 and 1973 figures, the People's Party is gaining some ground in such villages. Most remarkably, perhaps, at village level is the popularity of the major parties. The claim, discussed earlier, that Turkish villages are often divided into two opposing factions is often advanced to explain this adherence to bi-party'ism. It is also the case that village bi-party'ism correlates positively with village socio-economic development, though this could be because villages with two opposing factions are just those most likely to manipulate the political system to obtain material improvements. This warns us against attributing too much causal significance to socio-economic factors. Indeed, it might be suggested that the two party system effectively in operation until the advent of proportional representation in 1961 was itself a factor in forcing village factions into two groups where more than two existed.

Assuming a high degree of faction-based competition these villages should then show high voting turn-out rates. Yet it so happens that the more developed villages which, as we have seen, favour bi-party'ism, actually vote less than do the less developed. It is not too surprising then to discover, further, that rural turn-out is greater than urban, and that the voters in the more developed provinces are proportionately less numerous than in the less developed. This characteristic of Turkish voting is actually by no means easy to explain, and flies in the face of most political development theory, which assumes that political participation, including voting, increases with socio-economic development. It may well be, of course, that more "developed" Turks do not vote as much because they have increased their political participation in other ways. Only further research would tell. It certainly seems to be generally accepted, at any rate, that the larger vote in the less developed areas is due to its being mobilized by local leaders relying on a traditional loyalty or fear of retribution, or is due, simply, to greater communal unity.

Finally, it is possible as a consequence of diligent research by Turkish scholars, to examine a little more closely patterns of voting in the major cities of Ankara, Istanbul and Izmir.[39] Information for Istanbul is not as full as for Ankara, and especially as for Izmir, and these latter two cities have each been divided for analytical purposes into four "classes", namely upper middle, middle, lower middle, and shanty town (*gecekondu*) dwellers. When the voting of these different groups is analyzed it is principally found that the *gecekondu* dwellers support the Justice Party strongly, though this support weakened in 1969. There is also evidence to show that in some parts of Istanbul this support for the Justice Party weakened considerably in 1973, with a resultant increase in the People's Party's vote.[40] Nevertheless it would be sanguine to believe that the Justice Party is being squeezed out of the *gecekondu*'s where it has enjoyed much popularity for its capacity to help ordinary people with their problems. The People's Party's main urban vote, it will be recalled, comes from the middle and upper middle classes. The Worker's Party began to make some headway among the lower as well as the higher urban groups in 1965 and 1969, but their proportion of the total vote was very low.

As far as they go, these analyses suggest that any socialist party has a long way to go if it is to have an electoral impact, but their are some signs that the left-of-centre People's Party is just beginning to bite. The question here, as elsewhere, is whether the People's Party is more popular now on account of its new programmes of social welfare or on account of its enhanced capacity these days to provide practical help and advice to would-be voters. Dr. Özbudun is of the opinion that with further modernization "the urban poor become more responsive to sectoral inducements and more inclined to engage in class-based political participation."[41] In his view, with modernization deferential loyalties weaken and are replaced by attachment to political party machines (like that of the Justice Party) which provide concrete benefits in return for votes. This is then superseded by another stage when voting reflects class cleavages. The recent increase in the People's Party's popularity among urban and developed areas is on this theory attributed to the party's class appeal. There is certainly some evidence to suggest that the party's leftist policies are becoming more attractive to some voters. Karpat found that in Istanbul *gecekondu*'s in 1973 the People's Party's leftist ideological stand "attracted many of the young as well as those who sided with the Marxist Labor Party."[42] but an investigation among *gecekondu* dwellers also showed that their principal reasons for choosing a political party were its contribution to national welfare, its utility for the *gecekondu*, its capacity to provide for the poor and its affinity with *gecekondu* citizens. The urban middle classes are no doubt much attracted to the planned socialist state, especially those not engaged in private enterprise, but the urban poor mostly appear to want practical social welfare more than the promises of total change forecast by new ideologies. In the past, in Turkey as elsewhere, parties of the right as well as of the left have been able to supply this need.

CHAPTER VII

SUSTAINING FORCES
THE MILITARY AND THE BUREAUCRACY

The Military

The Ottoman Empire rose by the sword and fell by the sword. Both its chronic ailment from the late seventeenth century onward and its mortal crisis of 1918 were brought on by military defeat. Both, at the most obvious level, were military problems. Hence the army became Ottoman Society's natural instrument for effecting a regeneration. The remedy, it turned out, was the creation of the Turkish Republic.[1]

This alerts us to the nature of the role of the military might be expected to play in Turkish politics, but it is first necessary to examine the part actually played by the military in Turkish political life since 1908.

As we have seen, in that year Sultan Abdul Hamid II was persuaded by the Committee of Union and Progress to restore the Constitution. Most of the Committee's members were in the army, but they did not take over government; instead they sent a Committee of Seven to the capital to influence government. Why the Committee did not take over a quite demoralized government is not altogether clear, but they perhaps did not see in themselves the capacity to rule.[2] This underconfidence has been ascribed to administrative inexperience, youth and lowly class origins—they represented the lower bureaucracy and lacked on that account, it is said, the self-confidence of their Young Ottoman forbears. Certainly one experienced Ottoman statesman, the Grand Vezir, Kâmil Pasha, "had never thought the Committee capable of seizing absolute power."[3] In fact the Committee was put to the test by the part liberal, part reactionary counter-revolution of 1909; it managed to bring in the army to restore order and depose Abdul Hamid in favour of his brother, but the army command was now supreme over the junior officers of the Committee. The chief of staff to the General, Mahmud Şevket Pasha, whose army destroyed the counter revolution, was none other than Mustafa Kemal, who was not among the Committee's members. Yet the army command did not take over government. Moreover, Mahmud

Şevket Pasha tried to stop young officers from joining the Committee and thus participating in politics. To some extent this was successful; the Committee set itself up as a political party, and developed a supporting organization. Yet when the Committee attempted to strengthen its hold by manipulating parliament and elections in its favour, a group of Saviour Officers with liberal connections came into being intent on restoring legal government and getting the army out of politics. They were successful in greatly reducing the influence of the Committee of Union and Progress for a short while, but the Unionist military coup led by Enver Pasha in 1913 removed the liberal Grand Vezir, Kâmil Pasha, and Committee power was consolidated with the failure of a Liberal Union inspired coup a short while later. In a very confused national and international situation the military had obviously become increasingly politicized, despite the efforts of the high command.

These disturbing events have been described in some detail because they acted as a warning to later generations of the dangers of politicization of the military, and not least to Mustafa Kemal. He shared neither the Pan-Turk dreams of some of the Unionists, nor the liberal and religious predilections of the Committee's opponents. Yet in his modernizing, positivistic policies, Mustafa Kemal was as good a Unionist as any Committee man. The difference was that he led his revolution from the top—from the position of military leader. For Kemal the military was to be both the agent and the guardian of the reforming ideals of his regime. Alarmed by the demand of some generals to hold military commands whilst being deputies Kemal took courage in his hands in 1923 and 1924 to force generals to decide between the army and politics. When they chose the latter he was able to defeat them with the help of the People's Party machine. He was then able to discredit them when they were accused, but dared not be convicted, of involvement in the assassination plot of 1926. For this victory over military politicians Kemal relied on that element of the military which, under Marshal Fevzi Çakmak, believed in a non-political role, but at the cost of conceding a position of importance to Çakmak, even though as Chief of the General Staff he no longer had a place in the Council of Ministers after 1924. In

the remainder of the period of single-party rule there were currents of communism and Pan-Turkism in the military, but they
remained subterranean, save that in 1944 twenty-three pan-
Turkists were brought to trial for attempting to obtain military
converts to this doctrine. Among those imprisoned for short
periods was Captain Alparslan Türkeş.[4]

When the Democrat Party was seeking to get into power after
the second world war its leaders took pains to obtain sympathy
and support from the military. In fact the party was quite successful; a number of senior officers resigned from the military to
become Democrat Party candidates, whilst Marshal Çakmak
joined in the formation of the National Party. This expression of
support did not, for Menderes, obviate the need to purge the top
military after the Democrat Party achieved power in 1950. As a
result of this action and subsequent neglect of junior officers'
pay in a period of inflation, the military reverted to its pro-
People's Party sympathies. Indeed by 1957 army groups were
conspiring to intervene in politics. In 1958 General Cemal Gürsel,
Commander of Land Forces, was recruited by the military conspirators, who could henceforth place fellow plotters in crucial
positions in the military command.[5] The occasion for the 1960
military intervention was the special parliamentary investigatory
Commission set up to enquire into charges of sedition against the
People's Party, whose connections with the military the government now feared. This created a revolutionary atmosphere which
was ignited by a spontaneous protest march made by military
cadets on the 21st May, 1960.

Not long after the formation of the military junta it became
clear that there was a split between older and more senior
moderates on the one hand and younger more radical officers of
lower rank on the other. With the expulsion by the moderate
element of the fourteen radicals, including Türkeş, the moderate
army leaders outside the junta with active commands joined
together in an Armed Forces Union to watch over the activities
of junior officers, who were much upset by the expulsion of the
"fourteen". The Armed Forces Union was also fearful of the
junta, afraid lest Gürsel establish a directorate of major junta
leaders.[6] Gürsel then tried to dismiss the Commander of the Air

Force, a member of the Armed Forces Union, but without success. That body responded by forcing the dismissal from active command of two members of the junta, and the retirement of a number of generals. The junta was disciplined, in fact, by the senior officers in active commands; the Chief of the General Staff, Cevdet Sunay, now attended meetings of the junta, whose bid for power against the established military hierarchy was at an end.

The military was not at all reassured, however—neither by the 1961 election campaigns nor by the results. Now convinced that military disengagement had occurred too soon they had previously expected that the public disgrace of the Democrat Party leaders would have persuaded a horrified and enlightened electorate to vote for the People's Party. When this did not occur the military was greatly disillusioned, so no-one was surprised when a powerful military group led by Cemal Tural, Martial Law Commander and Commander of the First Army in Istanbul, signed the "21 October Protocol" which threatened intervention in order "to entrust the revolution to the true and competent representatives of the nation, to prohibit all political parties and to annul the election results as well as abolish the NUC."[7] Called to a conference by the military commanders the parties which had emerged as heirs to the defunct Democrat Party agreed not to seek an amnesty for Democrat Party members sentenced after the revolution, not to reinstate dismissed officers, and to accept Gürsel as President with İnönü as Prime Minister. During the two ensuing coalition governments headed by İsmet İnönü there were two abortive coups, (22nd February, 1962 and 20th—21st May, 1963) both led by Talât Aydemir, a colonel in charge of relatively meagre forces in addition to the Army and Gendarmerie cadets. These coups were attempted during periods of political crisis when the neo-Democrat Party members of the rightist parties were particularly intransigent. That both attempted coups failed was due to the firmness of the high command and their trust in the political resourcefulness of İnönü. For his leadership of the second coup Aydemir and one other officer were executed, and many other severe sentences were handed down—a sign that so far as the military threat went the regime had grown in strength.

With the acquiescence of the military to the emergence of an elected Justice Party Government in 1965 under the control of the moderates, the period of the military's withdrawal after the 1960 revolution may be said to have ended. The military's concern was to prevent hostile politicians from taking revenge and to preserve the democratic framework; they also wanted to ensure that the social reforms contained in the Constitution were put into effect. In the late 1960's, by contrast, the military was primarily concerned to maintain stability against threats to the democratic regime from new forces on the left. The Justice Party governments have taken care of the military, with the result that the military have prospered in a number of ways—in particular the economic and social standing of the officer has improved considerably, whilst retired officers have found good positions. Moreover the army has a stake in the mixed economy promoted by the Justice Party government in particular. The Army Mutual Assistance Association obliges regular officers to invest ten per cent of their pay in this institution, which has invested its massive funds in numerous enterprises including Renault in Turkey. From these investments many socio-economic benefits accrue to members of the armed forces. Consequently since 1961 the military has developed a large stake in political stability. During the late 1960's the military came to see Turkey's two major internal enemies as communism and public disorder, though not always appreciating that its denunciation of the far left encouraged the far right, whose attacks on their adversaries helped create the disorder the military detested. The Chief of the General Staff, General Tural, ordered that a book entitled *Means of Combating Communism*, should be read throughout the military.[8] Like the government the military feared the far left; in 1967 General Tural warned the army to be ready to take action against subversive elements. The military, it has been said "was totally committed to the existing regime and no longer pretended to stand outside or above politics."[9] The President. Cevdet Sunay, went so far as to assert that the Constitution was closed to socialism, though the Constitutional Court decided it was open to "limited" socialism, whatever that meant. Despite these attempts by the authorities to delimit politics, radicalism dominated the universities and socialism influenced some of the workers at least. Interesting at this juncture was the military's hostility to legislation—supported by Inönü no less—to restore civil rights to former Democrats; the military was not afraid of the Democrats as such, but was fearful of any undermining of Demirel's relatively moderate regime by the rehabilitation of those they had deposed.

After 1969 Demirel's government was anyway grossly weakened by defections, with the result that law and order suffered and the military became alarmed. It seems that the military attributed the situation to non-implementation of Atatürkist reforms, but this appeared second in the famous 12th March, 1971, military memorandum after parliament's and the government's alleged responsibility for permitting anarchy to develop. The military commanders threatened to take over power unless a strong and viable government was formed to remedy the anarchic situation and implement the reformist laws required by the Constitution. This military intervention, it is said, was prompted by restlessness among younger officers, including Muhsin Batur, the Air Force Commander, who had presented two memoranda calling for reforms.[10] Moreover, in January, 1973, eleven colonels, a major and two retired members of the National Unity Committee were charged with conspiring to change the Constitution and overthrow the Grand National Assembly. So there is some, if not very substantial, evidence for the view that the high military command forestalled more radical action by junior officers. Certainly, too, the first government set up under Nihat Erim after the military intervention was avowedly reformist (and technocratic) and included eleven non-parliamentary members. With openly expressed military approval the government announced its programme of reforms, including the nationalization of natural resources, land reform, a tax on agricultural wealth, and renewed industrialization. Yet these reforms did not get under way. The reason was that the political opposition from right wing and right centre circles was too strong, and under Ecevit's influence the People's Party was careful, as we have seen, not to revive its old image of the party of the military/bureaucratic establishment. At this juncture the military did not intervene further—felt it dared not intervene, more likely, given the complex issues at stake. By contrast it pushed hard for constitutional amendments to limit freedoms and in this had ample support from the rightist parties in parliament. What the military did pursue with energy, under a regime of martial law, was the rooting out and trial of persons whose actions were allegedly subversive of the constitutional regime. Heavy-handed and unsubtle—as military organizations often are in politics—the military arrested and had tried and convicted by military tribunal a large number of persons on the left, including the leaders of the Turkish Worker's Party, which was alleged to have strayed too far in the Marxist/Leninist direction, but was closed down by the the Constitutional Court for its divisive activities in encouraging Kurdish autonomy. The military showed much less enthusiasm for reform than it had in 1960, when they tackled rent profiteering, obtained agreement on the principle of taxation of agricultural income, established an abortive Declarations of Wealth scheme, raised land and building taxes and exiled to western Anatolia fifty-five *ağa*'s from eastern Anatolia, even confiscating their land—at least for a time. But they did not achieve much by way of lasting reform. It was the brief alliance of sword and pen that was important in 1960. With the setting up of the Constitutional Commission "the professors transformed the *coup* into a revolution."[11]

The military's disinclination to rule directly is mainly due to its awareness of its incapacity to manage a complex society. Nevertheless the military has always been respected and feared—at least until 1973, which year may prove to be a turning point in civil-military relations. When in that year the President ended his term of office the military suggested a candidate— expecting, as in 1966, that the political parties would not demur. On this occasion, however, the military was not able to impose its choice on parliament, even although the officer candidate in question, General Gürler, had resigned as Chief of the General Staff in order to take a place in Senate as a presidential appointee. In remarkable unison the political parties opposed the election, of a candidate who "had been one of the main forces behind the March 12 Memorandum and as such was identified by many politicians with military interventionism."[12] In unison still, they voted for their agreed candidate. He was a retired admiral, seventy years of age, Fahri Korutürk. He was fortunately acceptable to the military since he had not been involved in politics and had a military background. Had a more politically involved candidate been put forward the military might well have argued that there was a threat to the Constitution; in this case they could do nothing which would in the general view look at all legitimate. Neither side was the outright victor, but the developing convention of appointment of the Chief of the General Staff to the presidency received a setback.

Turkish civil-military relations are much less complex than those of, say, Syria or the Lebanon, where ethnic and religious heterogeneity, and hostility, is reflected in military organizations that are often deeply and bitterly divided. The Turkish military is overwhelmingly Turkish, Sunni Muslim in outward faith and Turkish speaking. It is on this account straightforwardly nationalist in sentiment; there are not debilitating conflicts of loyalty between social or ethnic groups and the nation. Nor does the Turkish officer ally himself with any social class, feudal or bourgeois, as is often the case in Latin America. Only now, with military involvement in the market economy, is he developing contacts with the bourgeoisie, but this is a limited contact, mainly economic, whose consequences should not be mindlessly exaggerated. The Turkish officer is not bourgeois and cannot be assumed, without evidence produced, to possess what are commonly, but often gratuitously, assumed to be bourgeois attitudes. In fact, the Turkish officer has been part of, or close to, the official class since Ottoman times. This means that when the military intervenes in politics it does not arrive like a thunderbolt out of the blue. Its journey into politics is a short one; it is always standing in the wings.

Yet it should not be assumed from this that the military is up to its neck in politics, or indeed that it wishes to be so. As we have seen, even in the Young Turk era when there was every temptation to intervene, the internal and external political situations being so chaotic, there was a profound desire on the part of the army command to keep the army officers out of politics; even the action taken by the Saviour Officers had the ostensible purpose, at least, of excluding the military from politics. The great urge of the time was to develop new instruments of rule that were purely political in nature. Not sur-

prisingly this was Mustafa Kemal's policy too. With great skill
and with much difficulty, for he was dealing with generals, not
with majors and colonels, he eased the military out into the wings,
not pampering them in the process, but not seeking to diminish
their prestige either. This last the Democrat Party government
under Menderes managed to achieve, but not consciously, or out
of fear; rather it was out of carelessness allied to euphoria arising
from the overwhelming sense of legitimacy imparted by electoral
success. Yet in 1960 the military did not intervene just because
they were neglected. They were perturbed by the worsening
economic situation, the partiality shown by the government
to the entrepreneur and by what they regarded as "the complete
debasement of the political coinage," [13] the responsibility for
which they laid on the Democrat government. The attempted
repression of its opponents by the government led to inflam-
matory reaction by the Opposition under İnönü, a reaction which
simply reinforced the Democrats' intention to stay in power at
whatever cost. Each of the two major political protagonists began
then, very dangerously, to proclaim that the military was on its
side. This made the military think very positively and urgently
which side it really was on. So it is not surprising that before long
the military did intervene, deciding to put an end to a dictatorship
whose onset, according to the Republican Opposition, was well-
nigh imminent. This action also had the effect of stifling the
growth of political divisions in the military, where politicization
was advancing fast. And, as ever with the military, they are powerfully moved to intervention when, as in Turkey in 1960, civil
disorder is rife. These immediate pressures to intervene were
crucial in 1960. They should not be overlooked by over-
emphasizing factors like the socialist inclinations of some of the
radicals in the military junta, or the military's fears for the future
of the Atatürkist principles under continued Democrat Party
government, or even the reduced economic and social status of
the military. These may have been necessary, but they were not
sufficient, conditions. There is often a tendency in the social
sciences to look for economic and social reasons at the expense
of the plainly political.

In 1971 the military again intervened to restore order and to preserve the system, though this time from elements outside, rather than within, the political system. By comparison the 1960 intervention was much more subtle; it involved a re-structuring of elements contained in the system to ensure a harmony of working parts. In 1971 the system was defended from outside attack, a relatively straightforward operation when, as in this case, the dissident elements did not have substantial support and protection from society. There is so far no ideological attack evident from the military on the system itself. There are no doubt strong socialist as well as strong nationalist currents among the officer corps, but they have not dominated military actions yet. Any such currents probably exist among younger members of the officer corps, but in 1960 the high command asserted its authority over the junta, as we have seen, and even if in 1971 the high command was prodded into action by those of lower rank, thus forestalling a coup, the military hierarchy was kept intact. This is an immensely stabilizing factor. As we know from military inter-vention elsewhere, coups affected by junior officers are all too prone to generate further coups.

The Bureaucracy

If the military stands for democracy with development can the same be said of the bureaucracy, its erstshile twin? We saw when discussing political elites that the Atatürkist *crème de la crème* of the Turkish bureaucracy were the graduates of the Political Sciences School (now Faculty) in Ankara. They filled posts in the prestigious ministries (Finance, Interior and Foreign Affairs) but more recently they have not hesitated to make their careers in the newer administrative departments that have arisen, or expanded, as a result of social and economic development. From a recent penetrative study of this group by L.L. and N.P. Roos there is much to the learned which may well have wider implications.[14]

In the first place a series of studies based on various criteria (e.g. job evaluation, job satisfaction, an individual's social status and educational achievement) show that the newer administrative departments in the Turkish administrative system enjoy the highest status.[15] These include ministries like Reconstruction and Resettlement, Highways, Industry, and Tourism and Information.

The ministries of the Interior and Finance, the traditional areas of employment for elite entrants, by comparison, have declined in status, though the Ministry of Foreign Affairs and some other older departments have not done so. The conclusion here is that those areas of the administration concerned with development have come to the fore, which is not necessarily the case in all societies said to be dedicated to development. Not surprisingly those Political Science Faculty graduates who work in these higher status organizations are those most satisfied with their jobs.

Job satisfaction does not stem only, however, from the high status of the organization in question. The Political Science School graduates of 1965 were overall more satisfied than dissatisfied with their jobs, and with no particular factor causing either satisfaction of dissatisfaction. Salary level, political factors, the chance to increase knowledge, the interest of the work, authority, responsibility, security, promotion prestige and geographical location were all mentioned in varying, if not very significant, degrees.[16] It is interesting in this regard, too, that political interference, which featured as a prominent cause of dissatisfaction in the 1950's, was nothing like as important in the 1960's; the most likely conclusion is that higher civil servants have become used to it over the years. The Ministry most affected by this phenomenon of democratic politics is not unnaturally the Ministry of the Interior, whose provincial governors and assistant governors are most open to influence wielded at the centre by local politicians. Again, not surprisingly, provincial governors "were identified as especially prone to leave the Ministry of the Interior."[17]

The relations of bureaucrats to politicians—and to the new business groups of modern Turkey is of the first importance. It is often asserted that Turkish bureaucracy has been bourgeoisified and has lost not just its official role, but also its impartiality, its capacity to hold economic pressures in balance with other important national concerns. For instance, a bureaucracy which cannot prevent tax evasion by small businesses—a serious problem in Turkey now—can easily be represented as having sold out to the entrepreneurial classes.

On the other hand, and from the other side, the criticism is often heard that the administrative elite is hostile towards successful industrialists and businessmen to the extent that economic growth is harassed and hindered by bureaucratic controls. Obviously there is a fundamental question of political philosophy at stake, but leaving that aside, it is the case that the Political Science School graduates are not generally hostile towards businessmen, or towards politicians.[18] Yet when we look at it in more detail the situtation is more complex. There seems to be a substantial minority who have negative feelings towards interest groups and most pronounced, rather unexpectedly in the newer administrative organizations. Politicians are thought by a good minority of graduates in these new organizations to hinder national development, though this includes persons who "might have sought employment in the new ministries and state economic enterprises to try to avoid dealing with politicians who would annoy them."[19]

Between one quarter and one third of provincial governors stress the significance of political factors in their work—much less than might be expected. It seems that their own prime concerns in the countryside are with the need for more education of peasants and relief of their poverty. These anxieties are not those of the peasants, however, who wanted (in the 1960's) water and new roads as first priorities. From the evidence available this is what the peasants actually got for the most part, especially from those provincial governors who "perceived themselves under heavy political pressure from their constituents."[20] Politicians, followed at a good distance by local magnates, were the principal intermediaries between government and the villages.

Three principal conclusions may be drawn from these studies. First, the mobility of the most prestigious recruits to the higher bureaucracy to areas of new development activity shows that new areas of importance are not deprived of talent. Secondly, this mobility must have been a way of allaying frustration for this elite group in achieving satisfactory careers. Thirdly, this elite has been brought into direct contact with the entrepreneurial elements in Turkish society, a contact which has not, it seems, been altogether without some friction. But it may, at least, have led to some softening on both sides—and may also have helped political stability. It seems unwarranted to assume that these

prime products of the Atatürkist system are going to become
lackeys of the bourgeoisie without a struggle.

Yet the importance of these graduates must not be over-
stressed. Their influence is diluted.[21] This may be offset by the
fact that the other higher officials among whom they work are
also highly educated, but this is often in scientific and technological subjects,[22] the shortage of technically qualified
personnel being in the lower grades.[23] Whilst such an education is
in some ways invaluable for administrators, it is also limiting, even
although such officials do tend to regard themselves as generalists.
In addition, many higher civil servants are inhibited from developing a very broad governmental outlook by the fact that they
spend most of their careers in one ministry. These circumstances
may account for the frequently made observation that their
individual initiative is not much developed. If this is the case, it is
certainly not due to fatalistic attitudes derived from a religious
background, nor, say, to an excess of legal training (many are not
so trained). But apart from structural reasons, it may derive from
the respect for those in positions of power which is embedded in
Turkish political culture.[24]

Unless the situation has changed radically over the past
decade, minute legal prescription of some areas of administration
is matched by excessively wide discretion in others.[25] The result
is either to stifle initiative or to encourage excessive anxiety and
insecurity where broad guidelines are absent. The response to the
latter   situation is to refer problems for decision to the top—a
practice long the bugbear of Turkish administration. Add to
anxiety and insecurity the presence of numerous ministerial
inspectorates, which are regarded by ordinary officials as a sort of
police force, and the result is to discourage initiative for fear of
being found out in error.[26] The problem is that to free civil servants from control in order to encourage initiative may only be
to free them to give expression to traditional forms of behaviour.
For instance, there is something to be said for allowing a certain
amount of disorder in the salary system. The rigidities of the
normal structure have long been overcome, in fact, by developing
dubious devices, like payment on a daily basis, which allow
needed personnel to be paid sufficiently attractive salaries. It is

argued that this could be taken further. "This side door recruit-ment—if opened to administrators as well as to technicians—might attract more potential innovators, and loosen up the present rigid salary schedule."[27] Similarly, it has often been argued by western administrative experts on the basis of their own systems that even greater latitude should be allowed to individual ministries and other governmental organizations in, say, recruitment and promotion, in order to provide greater flexibility to meet particular pressures. This is to some extent justifiable, since each administrative organization is controlled by quite rigid central legal procedures. Yet to relax this central control is to encourage the re-emergence of those traditional attitudes, whether popular in origin or deriving from Ottoman administrative practice, which are offensive and disturbing to those in the Atatürkist tradition. They are quite rightly afraid of corruption setting in as outside interests impinge more and more upon the bureaucracy. That Ottomanism lies not far beneath the surface is suggested by one experienced and perceptive observer:

> The Turkish bureaucracy to this day retains much of the flavor of this late Ottoman period with its conscious adaptation of French patterns. A citizen's errand to a government office typically begins with a written request. A series of initials and signatures must be scribbled on the left and lower margins as the document is passed up the hierarchical ladder. An offical evaluation, disposition, or reply is prepared at each step and fastened to the growing bundle with an ordinary steel pin. Each successive paper col-lects its quota of initials and signatures, of stamped seals, and of tax stamps. If a fee is payable, an invoice must be prepared by an accountant and initialed by an auditor, and a receipt prepared by the cashier, and several more tax stamps must be duly licked, affixed, and cancelled. The experienced petitioner has bought an ample supply of such stamps in all conceivable denominations at a cigarette store before venturing into the labyrinth of offices—for to stoop to trafficking in these magic bits of gummed and per-forated paper with lowly subjects would be far beneath the dignity of august state authority. Its stamps and signatures in place, each document now is carefully numbered according to two different indexing systems. Each signature is duly dated, each incoming and outgoing document carefully inventoried in a folio register. The language of requests, dispositions and other official correspondence reverberates with the reverential circumlocu-tion of the Ottoman Imperial chancery. Each incoming paper, and a carbon copy of each one going out are duly placed in pronged cardboard files. In the perennial twilight of asthmatic offices dossiers upon dossiers slant in

glass-doored cupboards or teeter on high piles on the creaky floor. The harried clerk now can tug contentedly at the green visor on his forehead and smooth out the black sleeve protectors on his forearms. His task is well done. When a document is needed a month later only the most assiduous and extensive search is likely to extract it.

These exacting procedures were once devised no doubt in the hope of protecting both citizen and state from arbitrary and capricious action by individual administrators. They do effectively tend to stifle the   civil servants' initiative and they even more surely dilute his responsibility. But the intricate system engenders its own antidotes and immunities. Documents are carefully drafted but hastily read. Signatures are uniformly illegible. The fees for most tax stamps barely repay the time and effort of purchasing, licking, and cancelling them. Above all, the system puts a premium on "connections." The lowly petitioner starts to wind his way upward from the Secretariat for Incoming Papers through a tedious progression of ante-chambers. Not so the well-connected citizen, who instead sips a trayful of amicable cups of coffee with his cousin or classmate or cousin's classmate who, as luck will have it, occupies the well-upholstered armchair in the director-general's office—while a bevy of lesser spirits at the mere flick of a hand scurry back and forth with the growing pile of necessary papers.[28]

The whole problem of whether the bureaucracy is basically traditional, legalistic or developmental in its basic attitudes has been the subject of a recent study.[29] The object of this study was to determine how far Turkish bureaucracy could be said to be patrimonial, legal/rational and rational-developmental. By patrimonial is meant a bureaucracy which stresses traditional authority restricted only by general moral norms reinforced by symbolism and headed by a leader of established legitimacy. Such a bureaucracy is characterized by an emphasis on persons, rather than on functions, which are left ill defined. Classes of functionaries may be defined, but on the basis of status, not of functions performed. Appointment and promotion are personal matters; indeed such a structure may be riddled with kinship networks.

By contrast the legal/rational model, as advanced by Max Weber, envisages administration as a system of abstract rules built into a legal code by reference to which the bureaucrat functions. Obedience to a superior, or authority over a junior, rests on this legal basis. Hierarchy is important, but obedience is not a personal matter. The tasks of the administration are arranged in functionally distinct spheres. Decisions are taken rationally on the basis of sound information, normally in the form of written documents.

Appointment and promotion are regulated so as to obtain the best qualified person for the functions to be performed. Favouritism and family or political pressures have no place; the bureaucrat has a settled career within the bureaucracy, not looking outside for stimulation or reward.

This rigid formulation has been criticized on various grounds. Two criticisms are first, that it is just too inhuman, and secondly, it is too rigid a formulation to allow for coping with the problems of development administration in uncertain and often unstable environments of the sort found in most societies, but in the developing world in particular. A modern third model is therefore sometimes suggested which stresses *inter alia* that hierarchy should be a flexible instrument for control, that supervisors need not be superior in knowledge to those under them, that officials should look outside the bureaucracy for their professional and social contacts, that uniformity within the organization is not desirable, that technical qualifications should be stressed over others, that politics should not be allowed to interfere with administration, that initiative should be rewarded even if the results are disappointing, that authority should be given to those who can do the job to get on with it without undue reference to superiors, and that bureaucrats should regard themselves as colleagues, not as members of a strict hierarchy. The system might be described as one of controlled flexibility for rational-developmental ends.

When studies of Turkish administration are examined in the light of these three sets of criteria the conclusion has to be accepted that the system is mixed, but that the legal/rational and traditional elements are predominant despite the increasing employment of scientifically and technologically educated personnel in recent years. As yet the pressures of outside organizations, like employees' associations and trade unions, for a more active and productive bureaucracy have not borne fruit. There is not much evidence of radical re-thinking of administrative problems inside the administration, as an Advisory Committee in Administrative Reform concluded in 1972. Lip service is paid to new planning and to other approaches along rational/developmental lines. The legal/rational structure developed in Ottoman and Republican times is still very important. Moreover, it is influenced quite powerfully by traditional attitudes, and we have seen how these appear at the operative end. In more important matters, like recruitment, many exceptional practices greatly reduce the effectiveness of legal-rational devices like competitive examinations designed to obtain the best candidates. Similarly, seniority is still accorded an excessive importance over merit in promotion. In the determination of numbers and types of posts to be established the relationship between personnel and the duties to be performed is still left in an Ottoman haze.

Consequently, if the attitudes of civil servants are examined to determine how far they are philosophically or psychologically disposed to these three sets of criteria, we might expect the rational developmental responses to be very restricted. As it turns out, however, from Dr. Heper's thoroughgoing research into these matters, this surprisingly is not the case. Traditional attitudes are the weakest, legal/rational attitudes are strong but, generally speaking, the more modern rational developmental approach is stronger still.[30] From these findings some hope for the future may be drawn: it may be that new ideas are seething underneath the surface. Or, of course, to be more pessimistic, it may well be, as the author of this enquiry is well aware, that it is simply lip service that is again being paid to modernity[31]—it is often said to be a traditionally Turkish trait to give the expected reply. More fundamentally, of course, there may be some solace in the suspicion that the ideal type approach to the study of public administration has its limitations, however valuable, heuristically. Many quite administratively effective bureaucratic organizations are very mixed in character. Efforts at reform should always be made, but if they are only partly achieved this may result in a more enduring success.

If there is a query about the development mindedness of Turkish bureaucracy is there also any doubt about their commitment to the ideals of democracy? Certainly to judge by their opinions expressed in response to an enquiry into this sensitive matter former and present higher civil servants are well-nigh unanimous that "democracy is the least evil of available political regimes", contemporary officials being in fact rather more warmly in favour.[32] Some of the respondents thought that for democracy to work, however, experience, tolerance, discipline and such-like qualities were needed. A small number among the modern group thought that democracy in Turkey was "bourgeois democracy", but this new (and unsettling) viewpoint is clearly restricted to a minority. A number of present higher civil servants think that democracy ought to operate more quickly and that "it should be reinforced with institutions."[33]

This pronounced partiality for democracy may be checked against preferences for other less democratic propositions. There is near-unanimous support among the contemporary higher civil servants for the view that "democracy is not a system which allows anyone with strange or extreme opinions to voice them"— a reaction perhaps "to the extremes of right or left and the political thinking which has developed in recent years."[34] Democratic though they may be in principle a great majority of the contemporary respondents (85%) think, like their forbears, that "one of the most important needs in Turkey today is for well educated and experienced persons to play the major part in elaborating governmental policy." In fact, 44% of another sample of higher officals see policy formulation, together with policy deliberation and decision in the choice of given policy alternatives, as their first role (22% for policy formulation). In making decisions 34% do what they think is best; otherwise they defer to precedents, the views of their supervisors, or the public or their colleagues, in that order, but never, it seems, to the views of their subordinates![35]

The earlier groups of higher officials were Atatürkist to a man, an adherence to principles which include secularism, revolution, and rationalism and which are not inherently democratic, or only imply democracy within narrow limits. The present higher officials are almost as much Atatürkist in these respects. As many as 87% of the sample disagreed with (29.3%) or were completely opposed (57.7%) to compromise over these Atatürkist principles in order "to free Turkish political life from its basic difficulties." However, the contemporary civil servants stress the importance of guarding Atatürk's reforms less than the older group and urge much more the need to find solutions to economic problems. This was then pursued further and the officials were asked which of certain

criteria they thought most important in determining policy and
development programmes. As their first choice 25% named the
adoption of scientific principles, as compared with 20% who
opted for secularism. revolutionism and the like. They seem also
to believe that politicians did not or could not give an ear and
effect to their proposals, but the older group interestingly declared
that it was the job of professional associations and other
institutions, like universities, to put forward proposals for legislation. On another tack both former and present officials believed
that the Turkish people are not sufficiently in tune with the political regime; moreover the present officals deplored the disunity
of political parties, the divisions in the intellectual elite and the
fact that basic divisions were occurring in society. Fortunately
for Turkey, however, Turkish higher civil servants still agree that
non-material outweigh material considerations in their work,
though they appear rather less dedicated to selfless service than
they were. How then should a civil servant serve the public best?
Turkish higher officials divide between "seeking to identify public
needs and reflecting them in governmental action" and "performing well their routine duties." When they were asked what their
principal task was, over three-quarters replied that "they should
serve the bureaucracy, the government or cabinet to the exclusion
of other parts of society, if necessary."[36]

From this review of the characteristics of Turkish bureaucracy
it is not too easy to reach very firm conclusions. But to take
the question of democracy first, it does seem clear that provided
extremism is avoided and that Atatürkist principles are not over-
thrown, Turkish bureaucracy will not turn against the system.
It will be mindful of its role as public servant and respectful of
democratic politics as long as its voice in the long-term public
interest is heard. It is obviously not antagonistic towards
politicians, though if with coalition government there are large
scale dismissals or transfers of senior personnel and their replace-
ment with buraucrats of more agreeable political complexion, then
attitudes could change.

As to the bureaucrats' capacities for inspiring developmental
administration, these seem rather doubtful. They regard themselves rather more as generalists than specialists,[37] which accounts

perhaps for their being "mixed" when defined by ideal type. Whether specialization greater than at present exists is necessary for the functioning of a fully modern administrative organization is open to doubt, however. Coordination of disparate efforts seems so essential. Perhaps the liberation of the more rational-developmental urges which lie under the surface will spur Turkey on to more developmental effort. Or perhaps it is a question of the will to improve and understanding and acceptance of the ends in view. Atatürkism in its hey day provided the targets and the will to achieve them. Specialization in an expertise may provide firmness with regards to individual ends, even if the overall purpose is no longer clear, but whether the will to move mountains is present is doubtful. Given the large range of its autonomy the bureaucracy must somehow be made enthusiastic about the liberal and democratic system if it is to develop real energy in the public weal. Positivist and reformist in outlook, Turkish higher officials do not easily take the view that they might also serve simply by helping society to live and mould itself as it wishes. At present they regard the political system as the least evil, but this may not be enough either for economic and social development or for liberal-democracy.

CHAPTER VIII

PRESSURES ON POLITICS
WORKERS, EMPLOYERS AND STUDENTS

Trade Unions

There can hardly be any doubt now about the significance of trade unions for politics in the developed and liberal-democratic states of the western world. In a country like Britain it does not need a union even, but just a breakaway section, to hold the country to ransom. Miners can simply refuse to mine coal—or others to move it to power stations—or yet others can shut down the nations's electricity supply by simply refusing to maintain equipment. Less drastic, but still important, strikes can close down assembly lines vital for export production or they can paralyse public services like refuse disposal. This sort of action by one union is rarely stopped by another—in Britain at least—despite general inconvenience, because there exists a powerful worker solidarity born, no doubt, out of the grim sufferings of the populace of the first country to industrialize. Add to this a class system—more aristocratic than bourgeois in origin, it might be argued—that perpetuates hurtful social, rather than economic distinctions, and does not ease industrial relations.

In the developed West the unions were formed as a means of combating the often terrible hardships that accompanied industrialization. With the aid of some intellectuals the workers organized themselves in order to obtain real benefits from the industrial system, or to attack it for their misfortunes. In Britain, using the political freedoms available, they came, through the Labour Party, to exert a powerful influence on the industrial society in which they worked. They forced themselves into the political system and to some extent the ideals of the labour movement were corrupted (or made more realistic) through this involvement in politics. The labour movement has been, and still is, powerful, but it has not until recent years been radical.

By contrast, in some countries which industrialized later than Britain more paternalistic care was taken of workers by the state from the outset—in Germany for example, where paternalism has been good for industrial relations and industrial development, if not, arguably, for the vitality of social and political life. In the United States conditions were altogether different. Labour unions became strong, but did not adopt ideas markedly different from those of society as a whole. The emphasis was on economic rather than on political struggle.

In the third world the position of workers' unions has been different again. Often unions in the colonial countries were in the forefront of political struggle against the colonial power. In such cases they were politicized. After independence such institutions became part of the new establishment. They were often favoured for their past and potential support by extensive social legislation on their behalf—a policy which made it unnecessary for workers to set up their own protective organizations or to develop existing ones. Moreover, to be an industrial worker in developing countries is usually to be much better off than most of those scraping a living in agriculture, or in services of a menial kind. Consequently it is unusual for industrial labour to constitute a revolutionary force. Moreover, many members of the work force are still first generation and still possess the conservatism of the peasant. Often, too, as we have seen in the case of Turkey, they maintain contacts with village society, sometimes by owning land there, and by keeping their families in the villages. And finally, even if the workers do become radical or revolutionary, in third world states they simply do not possess the disruptive capacity of some workers in highly industrialized societies. They cannot bring society to a halt, not even with a general strike in most cases. This is because, firstly, they do not collectively dominate the main springs of the economy, and secondly, they are not for the most part highly organized in a relatively small number of large industrial organizations—industrial establishments are small and scattered; Industrial disputes can generate sporadic violent confrontations; these can be quite massive demonstrations which pose real problems of control for the police and military, but they are also shortlived. Turkish trade unions possess many of the characteristics of trade unions in less developed societies, but as the country develops, they are increasingly a force to be taken into account.

A brief survey of the history of Turkish trade unions never-theless shows that they also possess some singular features.[1] In the first place Turkish workers have not featured much in the Turkish national struggle, so they do not have any special place in the nation's roll of honour beyond a fairly general conviction that they have not been dealt with very generously in the past. By contrast the military and the students are groups whose historical significance is recognized.

The first strike in Turkey occurred at the naval dockyards in Istanbul in 1871.[2] In 1908 there was a general outbreak of strikes in Istanbul, mainly directed against foreign enterprises, which spread to other towns, some of these disturbances taking on the character of local general strikes.[3] In 1909 both strikes and union activities were forbidden in public places and utilities, an act which had the incidental effect, it seems, of destroying union activity elsewhere, though for reasons which are not altogether clear. The national war of independence gave the workers a chance to earn some place in the national affection by the strikes that were effectively organized in areas occupied by the Allies, but the workers' role was overshadowed by that of the military and even by that of the peasantry. Workers' representatives were invited to participate in a national economics conference held in Izmir in 1923, but their demands for the right to form unions and to strike fell on deaf ears. It was no part of the Atatürkist philosophy to encourage social dissension of any sort. In 1925, after the Kurdish rebellion, the law forbidding the creation of professional organiza-tions effectively disposed of the matter of unions, a prohibition underlined by a law passed in 1938 which forbade any organiza-tion with a class basis. In the meantime, in 1936, a Labour Law was enacted to regulate working conditions and to provide *inter alia* for some rudimentary insurance for workers, a regular working week (48 hours) and for compulsory arbitration of disputes. Strikes and lock-outs were both banned. Inspired by German and Italian models the state adopted a paternalistic role which accorded well with Turkish social and political culture. After the second world war, in 1947, in the new liberal and democratic atmosphere the formation of unions and associations was permit-ted. Collective bargaining was also allowed with arbitration courts as a last resort, but strikes were still banned. Nor were either employers' or employees' organizations permitted "to engage in politics, or political propaganda, or to act as the instrument for the activities of any political organization." They also had to be "national organizations" which did not engage in activities "unpatriotic or against the national interest."[4] Although all political parties promised the right to strike, the Democrat Party included, nothing was in fact done. The major political parties looked for support in, and exercised some considerable influence over, the trade unions during the late 1940's and during the subsequent decade, with the result that the unions became more and more interested in politics. But it was not until 1961 that the unions were given the right to strike when, as we have seen, it was included in the Constitution. Even so, the right was not enacted in law until 1963 after some pointed demonstrations by the unions. In achieving this important freedom the unions undoubtedly owed much to the intellectuals who became prominent under the rule of the military junta. But the climate of opinion about workers had been changing with the increased contacts made after 1950 with the International Labour Office, with the general acceptance of the view that the right to strike was inherent in democracy, and as a result of some fear that concessions had to be made to the unions if they were not to lose faith in the political system. Nevertheless, some restriction was still maintained. Although allowed to strike under the terms of the 1963 legislation, the unions were not permitted to strike for political reasons.

The principal unions now inducted into the political system developed in 1952 a national organization, the Turkish Trade Unions' Confederation (*Türk İş*, as it is popularly known). This has ever since remained the principal organization representing labour. In 1967, however, a minority of unions broke away to form a rival organization, the Federation of Reformist (or Revolutionary) Workers' Trade Unions,[5] known in Turkey by its Turkish acronym, *DİSK*. *Türk İş* is supported by about two-thirds of all workers in unions. About eight per cent belong to *DİSK* whilst about one quarter of unionized workers belong to unaffiliated unions, which are numerous but small. The work force in unions is about forty per cent of the total employed, a figure which does not compare unfavourably with the position in more developed countries, especially when it is remembered that the bulk of employment in Turkey lies in agriculture, where unionism is weak, and is likely to remain so.[6]

The potential strength of Turkish unions is partly unrealized because the union structure is weak and lends itself to divisions. Since unions may be freely formed, there is a large number of local unions which are inclined to make local and sometimes suspect agreements with local employers. These unions are often not part even of the federations of local unions, which, at the national level, are confederated with the non-federal national unions in *Türk İş*. This body would naturally like to bring more of these non-affiliated unions under it wing. Consequently, in 1970, at the instigation of *Türk İş* and initially with the support of the People's Party as well as that of the Justice Party then in power, the government passed amendments to the 1963 law to require any national union or federation to have the support of at least one-third of the unionized workers of the industry concerned. The same general principle was also applied to any confederation, which had to be formed by at least one-third of the unions and federations. This ruling would adversely affect *DİSK* if it did not abandon its name (and with it the prestige) of *confederation* and become merely a *federation*. Another amendment made it procedurally more difficult for workers to change unions and sought thereby to introduce more stability in membership, especially for *Türk İş*. Although these amendments were passed by parliament, they were annulled in 1972 by the Constitutional Court before they were put into effect. This attempt to reduce the numbers of smaller unions was defeated, but it is doubtful whether unions denied national status would not have continued to exercise the right to make local agreements, the real reason for their existence. Nevertheless the whole confused issue was treated generally as an attack on small unions in general and on *DİSK* in particular. The organization of trade unions had become a matter of prime political importance.

Significant in the attempt of *Türk İş* to restrict the role of the smaller parties was the cooperation between *Türk İş* unionist deputies from both major parties in the Assembly.[7] *Türk Is,* being a loose confederation, has within it members of all parties. Not surprisingly, therefore, it has not sought any connection with any one political party. As we have seen, any formal relationship is forbidden by law, but informal support is always possible.[8] This "above politics" policy of *Türk İş* has long been a matter of contention within the Confederation. The breakaway of some unions to form *DİSK* in 1967 arose from dissatisfaction with this policy, especially as some of the leaders of the disaffected unions involved were members of the Worker's Party. The decision to secede was greatly influenced by the attitude displayed by *Türk İş* during the course of a now historic miners' strike in Zonguldak in 1965 when two workers were killed and twenty-two wounded. The action of *Türk İş* in supporting the government without proper investigation when it asserted that the strike was illegal and communist inspired led to serious criticism of the Confederation. Then in 1966 a strike in Paşabahçe glassworks in İstanbul culminated in a conflict between *Türk İş* and six unions which supported the continuation of the strike, and the appropriateness of a plant-level agreement against an all-industry agreement negotiated by *Türk İş*. The six unions were temporarily expelled from *Türk İş*. As four of them had previously set up a council to oppose the political neutrality policy of the Confederation, the development of a rival confederation was an easy step.

The policy of the breakaway confederation, *DİSK*, is frankly socialist. It seeks power for the working class, but denies that it is Marxist. It certainly does not advocate proletarian revolution, which would anyway render it liable to prosecution in the courts. Its support of the Worker's Party when it existed in turn ensured that its activities were channelled towards political involvement. It has strongly criticised *Türk İş* for siding with the government, for accepting financial aid from the American government agency *AID*, and above all for its refusal to follow a socialist policy. These accusations cannot be denied by *Türk İş*, which has had to co-operate with governments in power to get necessary social legislation through parliament. The accusation that *Türk İş* has been dominated by the Justice Party can hardly be accepted however. Nevertheless this has always been a sore point for *Türk İş*, which, in order to avoid this accusation, always seems to have made a particular point of attacking Justice Party governments for neglect of labour issues. By way of counter-attack against *DİSK* the larger confederation has always maintained, and not without justification, that it has obtained better material benefits for its workers through its concentration on economic, as against political, matters.

The extreme socialist attack led by *DİSK* has lost a lot of its impact in more recent years, but with the adoption by the People's Party of its left of centre policy, and its increasing success at the polls, there has been much pressure on *Türk İş* to abandon its above politics policy in favour of declaring itself to be social-democrat in belief. In 1970 Mr. Ecevit, addressing the eighth General Council meeting of *Türk İş* criticized the Confederation for the ineffectiveness of its neutrality policy in achieving its own declared ends.[9] Responding perhaps to pressures like these a movement appeared in *Türk İş* in 1971, led by the leaders of four unions, who declared that *Türk İş* needed a socialist political ideology. Being themselves members of the People's Party they not surprisingly proposed an approach to that party, despite the fact that it had finally joined the opposition to the amendments to laws governing trade unions which *Türk İş* wanted. This move was followed later in 1971 by a call from twelve *Türk İş* unions for the adoption of social democracy as its creed. This was a more significant development as the twelve had among them eight members of the twenty nine member executive committee of *Türk İş*. Their programme envisaged a tripartite economy comprising a state sector, a private sector and a public sector relying on co-operative and union resources. They declared themselves opposed to both capitalism and Marxism. At a different level they deplored the fact that *Türk İş* was exposed to the influence of different political currents and to a process of bargaining which prevented the emergence of shared views among the workers. In addition to moderately socialist demands they also wanted to see the end of an antiquated Ottoman sour-faced response by government officials to all initiatives from the workers.

An alliance with the People's Party cannot legally be explicitly advocated, but this is how the demands of the "twelve" were interpreted. The official response of *Türk İş* is simply to re-iterate the above party policy. The Secretary General (now Chairman), Halil Tunç pointed to the difficulties inherent in a situation in which the government might be of a different complexion from *Türk İş*, when the temptation for government to intervene in union affairs could be very great. In the event of a match between government and the Confederation the latter could not easily enter into dispute with the government. That *Türk İş* is not ideologically adverse from social democracy as a set of principles almost goes without saying. As Halil Tunç said, "Socialism exists in the philosophy of trade unionism. A trade unionist is not normally to be found on the right, but conditions are different in Turkey. There are both workers and trade union leaders on the right. The initiative of the four is premature."[10]

In one sense it might be argued that time is on the side of those who believe that Turkish unions will become more socialist as they come, through education and experience, to realize their true place in the socio-economic structure. On this argument they will gradually lose their deference for paternalistic owners and managers, and the reinforcement of deference deriving from the peasant experience of workers will weaken as they become more completely townsmen. But there is nothing axiomatic about this and much will depend not only on the attitudes of employers, but also on the way in which workers are educated to make sense of the new world in which they work. Certainly, as yet, the workers are not all socialist by any means. A survey of a sample of workers in Istanbul, published in 1975, revealed the existence of still very conservative attitudes.[11] Nearly three quarters of those interviewed in the survey believed that it would be appropriate for unions to make contributions to mosques should such be needed. Almost sixty per cent thought that unions could defend workers' rights without getting involved in politics at all, and the great majority read rightist newspapers. Moreover, a higher degree of education did not positively correlate with less conservative attitudes, and workers mostly believed that the unions' most important functions were to establish good relations with employers as well as to increase union strength. This latter was stressed as the most desired long-term union objective, but was closely followed by the need to protect and develop Turkish national and religious values. The workers did express concern over wages and working conditions, but not markedly. When they were asked the crucial question how they were treated by employers and management nearly a quarter replied "well", half replied "normally" whilst about one-sixth claimed they were treated badly. It could be argued that dedicated socialist intellectuals will easily lead the workers into a commitment to politics, but the workers do not show much of a preference for that kind of leadership. Moreover, their own leaders, grown from the ranks, do not need now as much as they did the aid of the intellectuals. They were valued in the early stage of organization, but they are not so much revered now.

More recent developments in the history of the relations between trade unions and politics do not then suggest a development of classs consciousness among the workers strong enough to push their unions along the road to closer union with socialist parties. Indicative of its neutralist approach, in April 1977, just before the 1977 general elections, Türk İş offered both the Justice and People's parties its full support in the elections provided that the parties allocated one-fifth of their parliamentary seats to the Confederation. This was an unrealistic demand given the pressure for the very few placed at the direct disposal of the parties, as the Confederation must have been aware.[12] Although the Justice Party made a mildly favourable response, Türk İş could do no more in the finish than allow its affiliated bodies to vote as they wished. The negative response from the People's Party owed much to the fact that it has of recent years established close connections with DİSK, whose numbers have also increased. Despite its former close connections with the defunct Worker's Party DİSK did not choose to create a liaison with the revived Worker's Party set up in 1975, and in the 1977 elections DİSK advised its members to vote for the People's Party.

One of the principal requirements for the growth of DİSK has been the capture from Türk İş of the Union of Public Service Workers (Genel İş), a respected and wealthy union which has not expended funds in strike action and in other ways. Together with this union has also come its head, a former stalwart in Türk İş

Abdullah Baştürk, who has often spoken out against the dangers of the extreme left. He has transferred to DİSK not just as president of his union, however; he is now president of DİSK itself, where it seems he has outshone the socialists with his socialism.[13] In fact strike action was taken by DİSK in March, 1978, in protest against a bomb attack by rightists (presumably) which killed five Istanbul University students. This action was not to the liking of Ecevit and the People's Party and caused at least a temporary rift.

Just after the 1977 elections Türk İş urged deputies to support an Ecevit government. A stable centre government is still the best for Türk İş, but the difficulty of centre-right governments is that they have of late had to share power with the National Salvation and National Action parties. Both these parties now have attached to them small confederations of unions. There is always the fear that in conditions of multi-party government such parties will try to politicize important sections of society, including the unions. Whether an "above politics" policy is enough to ward off this threat remains to be seen.

Commerce and Industry

As we have seen, in 1947 the People's Party government allowed associations to be formed, whether by employees or by employers. The employees lost little time in organizing themselves, but the employers took much longer. For this delay there were three principal reasons. In the first place, workers' demands had not built up the momentum they were later to develop so a counter organization was not imperative; at that time the market also operated to the advantage of the employers and the right to strike had not yet been granted. Secondly, it was only in 1950 that an important measure of freedom from state supervision was accorded to chambers of commerce; the Union of Chambers of Commerce and Industry was now permitted to advise, when requested, parliamentary commissions and ministers. On this basis the Union was able to develop its organization in order to represent industrial and business interests. Thirdly, in the settlement of industrial disputes the Union was given no important functions to perform.[14]

Nevertheless the Union has been very active in commercial matters. It had the task in the 1950's and 1960's of allocating on behalf of the government import quotas to member chambers (which meant part control of valuable foreign currency reserves) and the registration and control of the prices of imported goods. Such important functions brought with them a great deal of influence over important governmental decisions. This continued until 1968 by which time, it appears, the Union of Chambers of Commerce and Industry was so intricately interwoven with the Justice Party that there was simply no need to continue with the regular meetings with the government which had begun after the revolution in 1962.[15] The government formed after the military intervention of 1971 withdrew authority from the Union to allocate import quotas, so contact is now much reduced, the government approaching individual chambers as necessary for the transaction of this business. Nevertheless more formal contact in the provision of statistics and other information is maintained. Obviously the power of the Chambers of Commerce depends on the political complexion of the government in office. The Union was influential over economic planning in the mid-1960's when the Justice Party was in power. Its pressures on the government to aid the private sector in some rather special ways resulted in governmental action, but the measures were quashed by the Constitutional Court in 1969.[16] Between 1962 and 1968 the union had some twenty-six quite major items accepted by the government, but was unsuccessful with some twenty others—from modernizing the ports to having certain types of tobacco planted in the Marmara region.[17] Since the 1971 military intervention the Union has not found much favour with government, not even with the Salvation Party when it was in coalition with the People's Party since it has come to be regarded as a pro-Justice Party organization.

In 1969 a separate Union of Chambers of Industry was set up to express industry's interests better than the existing Union could with its heavy weighting towards commerce. But more important has been the development since the 1960 revolution of the Confederation of Employers established in 1962, its Turkish acronym being *TISK*. In addition to having representation on a number of governmental advisory bodies the Confederation has acted as a powerful pressure group, sometimes in conjunction with the Union of the Chambers of Commerce and Industry. The Confederation strongly supported *Türk İş* in its desire to reduce the number of trade unions. Not surprisingly the Confederation has shown its approval of the 1971 military intervention, appreciating the greater measure of law and order that ensued. Yet this did not stop the Ankara Military Law Commander warning the Confederation in 1972 (along with the trade unions) that lock-outs and strikes would be forbidden, if they did not come to their senses. Of the workers confederations *TISK* has tried and partly succeeded in establishing a dialogue with *Türk İş*, with which it claims to share a belief in "a powerful and healthy union movement in a free and democratic regime."[18] At about this time, however, *TISK* began to develop more critical attitudes towards trade unions and indeed directed itself towards "weakening labour unionism."[19] One of its objectives is to involve state enterprises in the employers' union. This would certainly leave private sector employers less exposed in the struggle with the socialist unions, but whether any government would wish to embroil itself in industrial dispute more deeply than at present is doubtful. The proposal embarrasses any government but particularly a socialistic one which has the interests of the workers at heart.

Students and Politics

Of all unions those most difficult for a government to deal with in a less developed country are student unions. They do not control many resources save their own numbers, but of all they are the most politically active—certainly this is the case in Turkey.

Many reasons have been advanced to explain student activism, but there is no science of the subject. There are many valuable studies of particular situations, but they are all so extensively different that they ask to be contrasted rather than compared. Where the variables are restricted in number, when, for example, student activism is studied in one society and within very similar institutions, the conclusions then suffer through lack of universal validity. This does not mean that comparative method has no value, but in the social sciences there are too many and varied

factors to be taken into account for comparative method to be
used to create a science. What comparison may do is to give
greater order to description and, more important, to suggest
hypotheses for the study of particular situations which may turn
out fruitful and which we may otherwise ignore. Having set this
warning bell ringing to remind us of the shortcomings of
comparison a few general reasons for student activism might now
be hazarded—constituting a distillation of the main features of a
variety of situations—which might be considered of some significance in a relatively under-developed country like Turkey, and
which might at least be borne in mind when examining the
Turkish situation.[20]

In the first place students in developing countries are often
deeply conscious of the fact that they are the prospective political
elite. So they feel responsible for the welfare of their society to
a marked degree. Moreover, where they are accustomed to such a
situation they are likely to feel very aggrieved when, as society
develops, they are no longer the only prospective elite, or when
they discover that they do not have a ready entry into lucrative
new positions created by socio-economic development. Secondly,
students now feel, perhaps more than they did, that their societies
are being oppressed by the economic imperialism of the western
world. This makes them all the more concerned with their nation's
political leadership, especially as national feeling runs high
amongst them. Nothing seems to excite active resentment as much
as the belief that oneself or one's nation is being exploited.
Thirdly, the universities to which students belong are institutions
in societies where, outside immediate family and declining kinship
groups, there is usually a shortage of institutions. Consequently
the universities and their student groups have an important voice—
and an articulate one. University teachers are themselves often
engaged in serious debate on public issues. They are not
necessarily political in the narrow sense of the word, but as we
have noted, they consider themselves to have a serious public
mission, and that their students sometimes draw inspiration from
this is not surprising. To these basic considerations must be added
the facts that students often exist in universities in very large
numbers where they are often insufficiently taught, where they

suffer from quite inadequate facilities and simply have too much spare time. In such a situation they easily constitute a readily mobilized force which may exert a pronounced physical influence on politics, especially if the university is located in the capital city in close proximity to government. Moreover, it is in the tradition of many societies to be rather lenient towards youth and for adult citizens to be very disturbed if students get injured in clashes with authority. Ironically this lenience towards youth in Turkey is not so much matched now by the traditional respect of the young for the middle aged and the elderly. The generation gap is the more unbridgeable in Turkey because it is often still a cultural gap between young people and their parents. In this regard it is surprising how quickly the latest movements in the developed world, fads or fashions, create an echo in the third world, especially among its youth, no matter how inappropriate to the local environment these novelties are.

Of students in Turkey what first do we know of their background and their attitudes? Of Ankara University students questioned in 1965 (we refer below to a later, 1969/70 survey) it was found that most of them read the leftist press (though by no means all) and that politics dominated their newspaper reading, as well as their everyday conversation, though not with their teachers.[21] This last point is of some interest since it conflicts with the general impression that university students are often inspired by the example of their teachers.[22] The students in 1965 revealed that, like their forbears, they believed in the multi-party system and that the government should be *by* and not just *for* the people. Over half were not too dissatisfied with the politicians (quite remarkable at that time of coalition troubles) and a good majority definitely did not want a dictatorship. Despite their interest in politics, they showed the usual, and no longer surprising, lack of basic knowledge of the basic modes of operation of the Turkish political system. More significant was the confused nature of their political beliefs. They mostly wanted to follow a middle road in politics, but the combination of a fundamental belief in socialism with a pronounced sense of the value of private enterprise was not uncommon among them! How they would reconcile these contradictory opinions if pressed can only be conjectured. But it is of interest to note that they believed that the military, the landlords and religious leaders were more influential than they had a right to be, and that peasants, workers and officials (an interesting addition) much less so.[23] This information suggests that students in Turkey are in fact less political than at first appears, or than might be assumed from comparative studies. In fact over half the students in 1965 thought that students should concern themselves with politics, but the large majority admitted that they interested themselves very little. Nevertheless a good number were of the opinion that student interest would increase.

The political sympathies of over half the students lay with the People's Party, with the Justice Party coming second, though by a long way (12%). These moderate predilections did not stop them from participating in various meetings and processions (59%)— which confirms the suspicion that many students just like the excitement of demonstrations—but very few actually engaged in party activities (3%). The tendency of the world outside to assume that all students who participate in meetings, demonstrations and the like are either activist or extremist is mistaken and can be dangerous. It can lead to attacks on students, or to the condoning of attacks on them by extremist groups, which has resulted in Turkey in wanton and senseless bloodshed. Such attacks have been and are still occurring on Turkish university campuses on an alarming scale. Activists easily involve others in political acts especially if there is an undercurrent of resentment occasioned by poor facilities of various sorts. The 1965 study predictably shows how very much more politically interested, more authoritarian and more to the left are the officials of student societies than are the students themselves.

The 1969/70 sample of students from the Hacettepe (Ankara) and Atatürk (Erzurum) universities showed a lower proportion of students whose fathers were officials, officers, teachers (altogether 44%) than the 1965 sample (58%). There were also many more fathers who were peasants or workers (18.5% and 9%) in the later survey than in the earlier (11% and 1%). This is probably not an indication of dramatic change in recruitment patterns, the differences relating more to the nature of the samples and particularly the inclusion in the later sample of provincial university students from wider social backgrounds, who are now clearly being recruited into the higher educational institutions, at least in the provinces.

From this second survey we learn that 31% of the students support the People's Party and 10% the Worker's Party, as compared with 48% and 6% of the 1965 sample, respectively.[24] Those who share their fathers' political preferences constitute over one-third in the later sample, (37%) but seems higher in the earlier sample, though direct comparison is not possible since the questions asked were rather different. What does emerge clearly is that students who support the People's Party closely follow their fathers' political preferences. Other points of interest are that a large majority of the students, particularly those from poorer and village backgrounds thought that the Soviet Union constituted the greatest threat to Turkey, whilst a third of those inclined towards socialism believed that socialism had its foundations in Islam. The girls particularly thought this to be so and those generally who came from villages both large and small. Some 40% of the students thought that relations with the United States completely undermined Turkey's neutrality.

The later survey also takes us into fields other than the political. For instance, only about one-fifth of the students thought they would find employment after graduation and nearly a third thought they would not find employment easily. The responses may not suggest a state of deep anxiety, but only an optimist could be reassured. In addition, a very large majority of the students expressed themselves as dissatisfied with the social system in which they lived, but it is interesting that the most dissatisfied (dentistry students) were those who mainly believed they would easily find employment! About two-thirds of the sample thought that influence played an important part in finding a good job easily. As to their work in their universities, they were not much satisfied with their modes of teaching, though the actual content of their courses was not much criticized. Asked whether they were generally satisfied with their classes 57% at the Hacettepe Universtiy replied that they were, but less than half as many were as happy in Erzurum. Girls are always, in Turkey it seems, at least, more satisfied than boys however, and there were more girls in the Hacettepe sample.

Obviously surveys of this sort can be no more than a guide to attitudes among students, especially as conditions differ greatly as between universities and even between faculties. Nevertheless it would not seem very far wide of the mark to suggest that dissatisfaction with teaching, employment problems, over-crowding and other contingent factors allied with a marked social-democratic or socialist trend among students does provide an opportunity for dedicated activists to influence for their immediate purposes a large proportion of the student population. There is, moreover, quite a tradition of student involvement in politics which goes back to late Ottoman times. After the establishment of the Republic by Mustafa Kemal, students were generally quiescent. Atatürk provided the dynamic leadership students favour, he needed a modern administrative elite for government and for industrial expansion and he made a particular point of declaring that it was the destiny of Turkish youth to defend and preserve the Turkish national heritage. Yet it was not all harmony. Towards the end of the 1920's there was marked student unrest expressed through a preference for Gökalp's solutions to those of Atatürk, particularly for the former's synthesis of religion with modernization. A more virulent and more Türkist nationalism than that espoused by the Atatürkist regime also declared its presence in disruptive anti-foreign demonstrations in 1933 led by the National Federation of Turkish Students.[25] This Turkish nationalism clashed with the markedly authoritarian socialism of the *Kadro* movement, which for the time being proved more influential, with the result that the students' organization was closed down, though many of its leaders subsequently filled important positions in government and politics.[26]

In the multi-party period from 1946 to 1960 the National Federation of Turkish Students revived, only to be challenged very shortly by a new student organization, the Turkish National Student Federation, which devoted itself in its early years under able leadership to student rather than to political affairs. Gradually, however, it was sucked into national politics like its rival organization, especially by the policies of the Democrat Party government when it sought to restrict some political freedoms. What followed was an inglorious period during which both major political parties vied for the support of student organizations. Only in 1957 when the Democrat Party government dismissed a popular professor[27] did student opinion generally veer towards the People's Party and later threats against democratic procedures clinched the case. In 1960 students demonstrated against the regime; this did not actually bring about military intervention, but it prepared public opinion and helped produce riotous incidents, which the military can never look upon idly. The military supported students against the police and some of their teachers provided encouragement;

More than anything their role in 1960 increased the students' sense of their own importance—their sense of their mission as idealistic youth to save the nation from the dangers of religious reaction and capitalist (and therefore foreign) exploitation. This second theme was much developed after the revolution in the context of a concern for social justice, a concern much advanced by the efforts of the Worker's Party in the universities. The main object of student ire was the Justice Party government, often represented as an American lackey. That party responded by making efforts to influence the course of student politics. With this sort of move by the Justice Party, and by others, it was not surprising that student organizations fell under the control of students with pronounced political ambitions in national politics, with the result that the major divisions in multi-party national politics were reflected in university student organizations. Again not surprisingly, but after a lapse of time, these organizations began to lose the respect of the more moderate students and of the public. In fact, the public does not now have the regard for students that it did once possess. This is sad in some ways, but it does lessen their potential influence. This has not reduced student activism, however. In fact, with expansion and its consequent increased teaching and accommodation problems, the students have devoted marked attention to university affairs too. In 1968 matters began to get out of hand when there was a widespread student boycott of classes in a number of universities. Students wanted a reform of the system of higher education and more attention to the question of future employment. This non-political action soon became political; needless to say activists will seize every opportunity to exercise leadership whatever the questions in dispute. In January, 1969, the American Ambassador's car was overturned by students in Ankara, an action said to have given "a powerful thrust to the leftist student movements."[28] Another source of encouragement for the leftist students—the groups active at this time—were the stirring actions of French radical students. In addition, the very unfavourable reception accorded by the National Assembly to Worker's Party members, coupled with the failure of that party in the 1969 elections, persuaded the left that the development to socialism through parliamentary methods was simply not possible. On the 16th February, 1969, two people were killed and many injured in an affray known as Bloody Sunday when there was a massive demonstration, in which students were involved, against the visit of the American fleet to Istanbul.[29] The remainder of 1969 saw numerous incidents in the universities which Demirel's government could not, or would not, prevent.[30] Particularly ominous was the rise of groups of rightist students and others whose capacity for violent action more than equalled that of their opponents.

In 1969, leftist students organized a Federation of the Revolutionary Youth of Turkey, an organization which soon became known as *Dev Genç* (Revolutionary Youth). It was an umbrella organization under which many leftist groups operated, often in that bitter hostility to one another which characterizes the relations of left-wing groups. These groups were all anti-imperialist, and increasingly advocated violent assault on the regime, and in some cases indiscriminate terror. This characterized one notoriously extreme group, the Turkish People's Liberation Army, some of whose members were trained by Arab Palestinian guerrilla fighters. This violence met with extreme counter violence from the Grey Wolf commando groups, as they became known, for whose organization Türkeş assumed responsibility.[31]

Since 1971 clashes between leftist and rightist students have declined in scale, but have by no means disappeared. In some universities the rightist groups have intimidated, if not terrorized, leftist students, and there have been hundreds of political assassinations. Indeed the decision to hold premature elections in

June, 1977, instead of October was due to increasing political violence chiefly among students. During governments led by Demirel both before and after this election it was often asserted that the discovery and prosecution of rightist assailants was not vigorously pursued. Whether that is true or not, under Ecevit's government there has been greater public confidence in the government's capacity to restore a larger measure of public order and some very severe measures are under active consideration (November, 1978). Yet as we have seen, in March, 1978, six students were killed in a particularly vicious bomb attack on allegedly leftist students in Istanbul University, while other smaller, but often fatal, incidents are regularly reported—and, increasingly, not just in universities.

The prevalence of violence in universities and the suspect attitude of the government and police led in 1970 to a great burgeoning in the number of public statements made by student organizations.[32] Many of these statements were directed against imperialism and the United States, but the dangers of religious reaction were not forgotten. In earlier years students had protested against private schools, the general educational system, the shortage of university places and the like. Much earlier, after the second world war, they had denounced communism. How that has all changed! By 1970 they had absorbed neo-Marxist doctrines.[33]

In the extensive study of students and politics in Turkey by Professor Szyliowicz it is suggested that the political variables of repression by the government and the legitimacy of regime and government in student eyes particularly affect student politics. In addition, the relative deprivation felt by students with regard to their own or their country's prospects is also seen as important. By relative deprivation is meant the negative feeling engendered by contemplating the sad differences between reality and potential, whether one's own, or one's country's. It is difficult to "operationalize" these concepts, but it is certainly the case that Atatürk's period was one of legitimacy plus repression, and that the post-war period of multi-party politics has not been very repressive of student activities and has been accompanied by negative feelings among students. During the decade 1950–60 many students did no doubt feel that the *government* was not legitimate, and a minority among the students since 1960 believe that the *political system* is not legitimate. To link these concepts with "relative deprivation" is not too easy, but we may note and agree "that in the twenties and thirties regime and government legitimacy remained high even though there were many indications that students were subject to feelings of relative deprivation."[34] This quotation seems to refer to personal deprivation. Where societal deprivation is felt then "both the government and the rules of the game are both viewed as illegitimate."[35]

Interesting though these formulations are, it is perhaps going too far to make much of a distinction between students' personal dissatisfactions and their dissatisfaction at the way their society is ordered, since they invariably link their own dissatisfactions with the inadequacies of the system. Furthermore, a distinction between the government and the political system should not be pushed too far either. Too rigorous an attack on one's opponents within the system frequently discredits the liberal-democratic system itself. We do not know whether this present generation of students is deeply disaffected with the system. If they are—and the signs are certainly that more are than was the case in 1965— it may not only be because they now discern, thanks to their absorption of Marxist doctrines, the contradictions and social injustices in the system. It may equally be that they are responding simply to the incapacity of the governments of the day to satisfy their own expectations and to manage society in accordance with generally accepted standards of what is appropriate. In other words, if the present system can be made to run more normally some of the anti-systemic student opposition may disappear. This would also make it easier for social science teachers in the universities to propose to young ideologues that some of their accepted truths may well turn out to be very debatable hypotheses. Apart from the need for effective police action a concerted effort by those political parties which believe in the existing system is needed if political violence in the universities is to be stopped. One self-denying ordinance they could immediately adopt, if they were so minded, would be to refrain from attempts to influence student politics in their own particular directions. The students need to be less, not more politicized, so that political education can reassert itself. The only real attack on extremes that is valuable for the preservation of the centre is an intellectual offensive from the centre, persuasive and persistent. Vicious attacks from the right on the left play into the hands of those on the left by drawing students of moderate disposition into their ranks.

CHAPTER IX

CONCLUSION
DEMOCRACY AND DEVELOPMENT

Is Turkey a democracy? And what are the factors which go to make Turkish democracy what it is? These are intriguing questions to pose, but by no means easy to answer.

The obvious way to begin is to state what constitutes democracy and then to see how far Turkey matches up to the definition. This approach may well be sound, but it is not an easy exercise because there turn out to be on examination different forms, or models, of democracy, even if in practice the models are not mirrored in any one democracy. The only way to proceed is to postulate the major forms of political organization which attract the epithet democratic, and then to judge where Turkish democracy fits.[1]

The first model to be mentioned, if nowhere extant, is that of the direct democracy of classical times, which entailed the continuous participation of all the people, who initiated all proposals resulting in decisions or legislation and controlled their implementation. Direct democracy in small units was insisted upon by Rousseau, reviving the classical tradition, and according no legitimate place to representation. It is a model in which all have the opportunity to participate equally and directly.

This classical strand is woven into a second model which may be labelled Radical Democracy.[2] This model embodies theories from other sources as well, particularly from those which stress the natural rights of man (e.g. Paine and Jefferson) and from utilitarianism. The basic principle in this model is that government exists to help the individual realize his own rights and satisfy his own interests. Consequently the people should be able individually, and in co-operation if they so wish, to initiate and declare what is to be done directly, without the use of representatives acting as intermediaries. Since government is in this fashion directly of the people it cannot theoretically speaking, be oppressive, though in practice it has often proved to be. Another important feature of Radical Democracy is that it is also seen as conducive to development of the individual's potential through his active participation in politics. For the individual the group is sometimes substituted, especially in recent American political theory, but it is the group or the individual who knows where its, or his, interests lie. The government is a mere servant to give effect to the majority of wills. That a tyranny of the majority can arise is a problem. Consequently the theory has to embody basic political freedoms to allow the minority to battle for its interests. There is nothing in this theory to allow for a general interest over and above the sum of individual or group interests whose satisfaction is said to constitute the greatest happiness of the greatest number.

In an attempt to remove the emphasis on self-interest inherent in this model another theory of democracy, which owes much to Rousseau and the Jacobins, has arisen which lies at the heart of the model of the People's Democracy. This theory asserts that every individual has a real or ideal will which when aggregated across the community in question constitutes a general will. This general will is commmunity, not individual, or group orientated. The principal practical difficulty is that this ideal will has to be declared by some person or body who knows how to recognize it. In theory which was developed at the time of the French Revolution this general will was said to be declared by a popularly elected assembly which, by rejecting sectional or personal interests, can come to divine the real will of the people. In people's democracies in the contemporary world this will is represented by the Party, which in Marxist forms equates the people's will with their "objective class interest"— with whose manifestation no individual or group interests are allowed to interfere. In declaring this general will the Party, informed by its scientific understanding and freed thereby from any arbitrary judgements, is acting as a vanguard of the people, not as its representative. These principles are reflected in the structure of "socialist democracies" in the modern world.

Liberal-democracy, as it emerged in the nineteenth century, embodied much of the individualism of Radical Democracy, but acknowledged that government was separate from, if ultimately controlled by, the people. Recognizing that government can be oppressive this model seeks to hedge government around with restrictions which embody, *inter alia,* rights of free speech and assembly for individuals and groups, a separation of legislative, executive and judicial powers and the rule of law. With these guarantees established the people are able to grant a good measure of freedom to their representatives, who need not be mandated delegates. Moreover, being trusted, and/or controlled, these representatives are allowed, and indeed expected, to concern themselves with the general interest, as well as with the individual or group interests of those they represent. In such a system, whilst an element of trust is involved, the people (or at least the electorate) is assumed to be informed, intelligent and alert enough to exercise periodic control.

This faith in widespread rationality (strongly stressed in Radical Democracy) has been shown by voting and similar studies to be sanguine, to say the least. Moreover, the possibility of representatives turning into powerful elites who make a mockery of democracy has been urged on many sides. And where group representation has been strong, as in the United States, it is claimed that groups dominate the system at the expense of individuals and the general interest. For Marxist critics, who equate political elites or group elites with a middle class or bourgeois domination of society, liberal democracy is just a sham.

To escape from critiques of this sort modern liberal-democratic theory, rejects, in the light of the most recent research, excessive assumptions of the people's irrationality in politics and claims that where political elites are plural and the elector decides which shall hold power, liberal-democracy still exists. It exists even more fully where recruitment to these elites is open. Similarly, groups which compete with one another are said to enhance democracy, again especially where wide recruitment of membership is possible, by bringing specific and important popular demands to the heart of government. This is particularly so where groups exert influence, but do not seek power. Both political and group elites, moreover, it is claimed, provide the positive leadership without which any government will falter and which democracy needs above all.

Seen against what has to be a bald summary of a web of complex and inter-twining theories, here somewhat artificially segregated, what sort of democracy can Turkey be said to constitute?

In the first place, the Turkish revolution, which began with the attack on the despotism of the Ottoman Sultan, and ended with the near dictatorship of Kemal Atatürk, parallels in some respects the French Revolution. It lacked the enormities of the French Revolution, and was played in an altogether lower key, but it developed a national assembly during the War of Independence which sought to arrogate to itself the sovereignty of the people viewed more as a collectivity than as individuals. Atatürk stopped this, but only by developing a single party which really could speak for the nation by embodying its real interests in a coherent ideology. This was a start towards the creation of a people's democracy, but the party's ideology was neither comprehensive nor penetrative enough to become the instrument of a totalitarian regime. The party dominated the Grand National Assembly, but was never quite able   to supplant it, never able to transfer its legitimacy to itself. It could be said that the party leaders never seriously tried to do so and certainly Atatürk's experimentation with liberal-democracy enhanced the importance of the assembly over the party. It is true, as we have seen, that Atatürk restricted the assembly's role by making the Executive under the President more independent of it than was originally the case. Nevertheless this did not go so far as to undermine the theory that sovereignty was indivisible and was delegated by the people to a popularly elected assembly. We have noted that this theory helped legitimate the hegemony of the Democrat Party government between 1950 and 1960.

With the greater protection for freedoms contained in the 1960 Constitution the Turkish political system is now more liberal and democratic in form. How far it approximates to a modern model of liberal-democracy with its accommodation for political and group elitism is more open to question, though no actual system under inspection would show itself to accord precisely with the model. In the Turkish case, to begin with the electorate, it is almost certainly the case that it acts less "rationally" than electorates in better educated and more developed societies. This is to say that custom, prejudice and long established economic and social connections influence voting, and other expressions of political interest, more than in most liberal-democracies of the western world. At least this appears to be the case from the limited studies available, though from our information about electorates elsewhere the differences are probably not all that great. By rational is meant here a capacity to make political choices on the basis of which policies and persons are likely to bring not only benefits to the voter but also to the society in which he lives. The indications are that the Turkish voter, when he is not acting irrationally, tends to vote and exert influence with an eye chiefly on personal and local benefits.

As we have indicated this is less crucial for modern than for nineteenth century theories of liberal-democracy. More important is whether the political leaders elected constitute an elite which is both responsive to demands and responsible, through the possibility of rejection, to the electorate. Certainly as we have seen, the Turkish system does not produce an elite at the very top able to maintain itself in office for very long periods, though there seems to be less movement lower down. It is not altogether clear how open recruitment is to the political elites. At various levels the influence of existing party members is paramount, and the device of primary elections of candidates for adoption in general elections helps enhance the influence of party officials lower down in the hierarchy. On balance, and pending further research, it seems fair to say that determined political activists are able to enter into the political elites, at least in those areas where clientilism has weakened. If this is the case a condition of modern liberal-democracy is being partly achieved.

Do pressure groups also enhance the working of Turkish democracy? At present, despite the growing power of the trade unions, their influence is not all that great, but it appears that pressure groups are increasingly being taken into account by government in developing policy in their spheres of interest. That this has been slow to develop is due partly to the fact that in conditions of relatively low economic and social development pressure groups cannot be numerous and strong, but it also reflects a general distrust of their activities by the political and administrative elites due to the influence still exerted over them by earlier liberal, and by authoritarian, doctrines.

However much pressure groups may contribute to the democratic process, they are generally and rightly regarded as too partial to be able to contribute all that much to the responsible but positive political leadership in the general interest which every liberal-democratic political system requires. The danger from the political elites in this regard is that they have a tendency either to be corrupted by an excessive pre-occupation with interests, or to be carried away with ideological rhetoric. If the political struggle is a bitter one, as in Turkey, a great deal of effort is expended on politicizing society—particularly in trying to get groups like the trade union federations, or the students, to be firmly on one's side. This is justified on the grounds that it is good for democracy to develop a wider political awareness in society. But this is very different from what really happens, which is that political antagonisms develop to such an extent that they mar the functioning of the major institutions of the state—the bureaucracy, the military, the educational system and even the administration of the law.

What a responsible democratic leadership must do is to produce realistic but creative policies and put them firmly into effect when in office whilst paying due, but not excessive, attention to interests involved. This seems trite and simply commonsensical, but it is surprising how easily thoughtful policy-making gives way to ideological dispute or extravagant attention to group demands, not to mention the temptation of short-term party gains.

Since party political elites are to some degree necessarily in conflict, concrete policy proposals of national importance have often to emanate from other parts of society. To some extent they will emanate from groups not just looking to their own narrow interests, but in a liberal-democratic system the bureaucracy is an important source of policy initiation for the obvious reason of its familiarity with the problems of government. So it is vital to have a bureaucracy whose members actually believe in liberal and democratic norms, though the obstacles in the way of achieving such a desirable condition are enormous. In the first place the bureaucracy can, and often does, exert considerable pressure to further its own corporate interests at the expense of the public interest. Secondly, a mere administrative machine, or a military hierarchy of obedient officials, is not likely to generate much creative energy—and even a civil service which subscribes to liberal and democratic beliefs can be too passive and merely wait upon events. The perfect civil servant for a liberal and democratic political system is only going to be found in Utopia, but the great danger of a politicized bureaucracy needs to be guarded against at the price of other disadvantages. For Turkey the politicization of the bureaucracy is a real danger. In recent years, succumbing to the temptation to obtain a flexible and compliant administration, new governments in Turkey have purged the upper ranks of the ministries. This is a danger to which a state with Turkey's type of political structure is perhaps particularly prone. As we have noted, the Turkish political system resembles the British in not providing for much separation of powers between politics and public administration. The headship of the administration by the President does not carry the degree of independence provided, for instance, by the American or French systems. Nor is the Turkish bureaucracy a tightly organized, and centrally directed institution able easily to develop overall views on public policy—the important bureaucratic organization is still the ministry or separate agency, despite the partial success of central planning.

That the bureaucracy should provide a measure of leadership in a liberal-democracy, even with regard to longer-term matters of policy, is seriously open to question, of course, on theoretical grounds, and will be rejected by many. That public officials are appointed, and usually to permanent posts, seems to disqualify them for an active policy role in a liberal-democratic system. Yet if the politicians who form government are deeply preoccupied with political dispute, as in Turkey, then both major, and cumulatively important minor, tasks of government are neglected. Since the demise of the single-party regime in Turkey, whose character was as much administrative as ideological, governmental and administrative coherence has declined. Given that Turkish higher officials continue to be broadly supportive of liberal-democratic values, and provided that entry to the bureaucracy is made more open and more competitive than it is now, and yet, it has to be said, exclusive of those who do not support the system, then there are grounds for strengthening the bureaucracy. This is all the more possible now that the public is more alert to its interests than used to be the case and will use political means to influence administration. There is also another measure of control available through the Council of State which, as we have seen, has been strengthened by the terms of the 1961 Constitution.

The institution which has advanced itself most as the champion of the public interest in Turkey, if in very broad terms, has been the military, often dubbed the "guardian of Turkish democracy." Paradoxical though it may seem, there is no doubt that this authoritarian institution has fulfilled this function both in 1960 and the years immediately following, and again in 1971. That it has done so is due not so much to its inherent belief in liberal-democracy so far as we can judge, but to its sense of national mission, which is no less evident in the Turkish than in other military organizations. Certainly in 1961 it saved liberal-democracy partly because its leaders, under the influence of the academics of the time, did broadly speaking believe that a liberal-democracy was an important part of the Atatürkist heritage, even if it was not achieved by Atatürk. But they were also afraid of untrammelled, illiberal democracy, and there is no guarantee that the military will refrain from political intervention if the liberal safeguards they supported are abused to create disorder. Moreover, in Turkey's deeply disturbed political atmosphere the military intelligentsia cannot help but become politically conscious and, perhaps, deeply divided on political issues and principles. In addition, the military is now involved financially in the private sector. This involvement is bound to perturb those of its officer corps who incline towards leftist political ideas, but it will worry those on the far right too, since they also believe that the military should not be contaminated by connections with bourgeois enterprise. Clearly the proper political education of the officer class needs to be developed if it is not to become an instrument of one side or another, or be riven by internal discord. The greater complexity of society which follows from economic and social development may well make military intervention more difficult, but it is never impossible. More developed states than Turkey have been governed by the military, often with disastrous results.

During the course of this study of Turkish politics it has become apparent that Turkish democracy, despite its many achievements, has not worked smoothly. This prompts us then to ask whether this is due to the existence of conditions which inhibit the success of democracy. Such conditions may inhere in the nature of Turkey's political culture or in her political tradition. Or they may derive from recent political history, or from the stresses engendered by processes of economic and social development.

To take political culture first, we have seen that Turkish attitudes to politics eschew political conflict as valuable in itself. Turks certainly are polite, deferential and persuasive in their attempts to influence fellow Turks.[3] They may distrust one another, but they are not severe in dealing with their fellows. For instance, the pain of instant removal from high office is often softened by finding some other suitable accommodation upstairs. But when Turks fall out they fall out badly and all the cultural emphasis on qualities like courage, honour and revenge finds an outlet for expression, often quite violent in nature. When such a nation is called upon openly to disagree over major matters it is natural for difficulties to arise. To break the peace is to threaten to rend asunder the social fabric. To oppose is to lay oneself open to the charge of seeking to divide the nation. "There is an element in Turkish political culture," it has been said by a Turkish scholar, "to which the notion of opposition is deeply repugnant."[4] It is not therfore surprising that organic notions of the state envisaging a corporate form of political and social organization are quite popular, as the successes of the National Action Party might suggest. In a multi-party situation, with its emphasis on conflict, attempts at coalition government since 1961 have been anything but successful. Coalition partners have invariably attacked one another publicly when in office, or have failed to agree for what sometimes appear to be quite trivial reasons. The record of the National Front governments formed between 1975 and 1977 was particularly bad in these regards. In addition, the smaller parties which participated in these governments did not play by the rules, but sought, as we have noted, to dominate certain sections of the governmental machinery by importing their own supporters into them.

These sorts of difficulties with the operation of a democratic form of government owe something also to what must be regarded as the failure of the Atatürk revolution to prepare the way for a form of democracy, or at least, for modes of participation, suitable for Turkey.[5] For the single People's Party remained a cadre party; we have observed that it only succeeded to a minor extent in mobilizing the general populace behind its objectives. By its convenient alliance with the notables in the countryside, who had helped greatly in the war of independence, the Atatürkist party and governing elite rather ignored the peasantry despite lip service to their importance. It was after all in the political tradition of the People's Party government to rule without much direct contact with the people and to establish or interpret the rules by which society should be governed. It was equally consonant with the tradition to compose differences among economic and social groups for the sake of social solidarity. But it was not part of the tradition to persuade economic and social groups actually to participate in power. If individuals or groups were to participate in power it would have to be by reference to an approved set of rules. Yet it so happened that the rules Atatürk and some other Turkish leaders had at the backs of their minds were those pertinent to the liberal-democratic systems they so admired as the highest form of civilized government. This was an important legacy but we have seen that the practice of democratic politics has often not lived up to the ideal; traditional modes of political behaviour keep breaking through the confines of the model with the result that a new synthesis is perhaps being created whose outlines are not yet clear, but which will constitute a Turkish form of democracy. At present the ideology most closely in tune with the tradition is perhaps that of the National Action Party, with its stress on harmonious interaction among the major economic and social groups, but in practice the tradition of very firm leadership would almost certainly be exploited by the party to impose a very authoritarian, if not totalitarian, form of rule. It would be too sanguine to expect social and economic groups to co-operate spontaneously within a loose party framework on, say, the Mexican model.

It might be urged, however, that the process of economic and social development presents obstacles to the emergence of liberal-democracy. As a development from this it may also be deterministically held that conditions are being created for the eventual appearance through class conflict of the communist society. This latter view is common enough among the younger intelligentsia, some of whom are prepared to give history a push, should the opportunity arise. There can be no doubt that movements of population, the break-down of traditional ways of living, greater education and exposure to outside influences, the ownership, or use, of more material goods—all will help in the mobilization of the populace in new and unaccustomed directions. That this process initially creates and fosters demands for more individual freedoms and satisfaction of individual wants seems everywhere to be the case in the third world. But industrialization and the conditions of modern economic and social life, which depend so much on the co-ordination of diversified functions also demand discipline and unity. Traditional modes of social organization can be developed to suit these new ends, for tradition is not necessarily static but has always been subject to development to meet new needs. It so happens in Turkey that the erosion of traditional modes of thinking and behaving has occurrred in an atmosphere which has stressed freedoms of various kinds. Elsewhere, as in Japan, tradition has been utilized very efficiently in the cause of economic and social modernization under authoritarian leadership. There is no guarantee that economic and social development will produce any particular sort of political system. So whether a liberal-democratic system of some sort continues to survive in Turkey must depend on a number of factors. These must certainly include the satisfaction of material wants, according to the levels of expectations, but will also depend on the degree of positive attachment to liberal and democratic principles by political activists in general and the intelligentsia in particular. To achieve this end great emphasis on a thorough political education for young members of the intelligentsia is required. Otherwise they are left to the attractions of this or the other "ism" carelessly acquired and dangerously applied. To some extent the current emphasis on radical-democratic education through participation which the People's Party advocates may help the cause of realism, but may also invoke traditionalist or ideological responses which may be disruptive of liberal and democratic norms. At any rate, there are no solid grounds for believing that the forces of economic and social change, great though they are, will of their own volition produce this or that type of regime. As Kemal Atatürk used to insist, it is up to the Turks themselves.

The problem may, of course, be viewed the other way round. The question may be asked whether Turkey can continue to develop economically under a liberal and democratic system. It is often urged that in the third world the chief effect of liberal-democracy is to encourage not only political intransigence, but also materialist expectations that just cannot be satisfied. This occurs, it is said, because competing parties dare not reject the material demands made upon government by the electorate. A party which does not seem to respond will not be elected or re-elected. If the goods cannot be delivered there is then the problem of how to contain the dissatisfaction created by the failure to meet what will turn out to be ever-rising expectations. Attempts to meet these increased expectations not unnaturally mean that savings required for capital investment cannot be made. Atatürk was able to hold back demands and squeeze some capital for development out of taxation and the Democrat Party government was a major recipient of foreign aid. But in the event of a shortage of capital to promote the investment needed to meet demands, will a liberal and democratic system not collapse, it is asked. Would a more disciplined single, or partyless, political system not be better? A single and more separate executive would also be more effective, it is urged, in taking decisive action and in restraining, by the use of force if necessary, the popular demands so irresponsibly encouraged by competing parties.

Such views are popular and seductive. They are often heard in Turkey as elsewhere.[6] One counter-argument is that in Turkey's case, at least, multi-partyism has been accompanied by significant rates of economic and social development. They might have been higher, it could be argued, under a single-party system, but then on the other hand it may be plausibly argued that Russia, having reached take-off point by the first world war, might well have developed faster without Stalinist dictatorship. In fact the evidence against liberal-democracy in this regard is not so great as to stifle the suggestion that the freedoms permitted in such a society encourage a spirit of individual and group initiative and allow for a practical *modus vivendi*, if not an intellectual recon-ciliation, between tradition and modernity. Certainly such a society may be wasteful as well as productive, exploitative as well as liberating. Yet for a political party just to seek to meet material demands may not necessarily be bad for development. Peasants may often want ephemeral consumer goods (or more mosques), but they also frequently demand roads, bridges, water supplies, electricity, local industry and more schools. Their needs are not always that different from the desiderata of the planners. The assumption that the demands of the populace are always inimical to development needs to be viewed with some caution. Nor should the possibilities of education of the populace in the problems created by conflicting demands be underestimated. The state has an educational network at its disposal, particularly in its control of radio and television. Moreover, the religious tradition is still vibrant in many third world states, including Turkey, and this often acts so as to restrict an excessive concern with material benefits on the part of the general populace.

The advocates of authoritarian government as a necessity for development rather overstate their case. They are also prone to forget that many authoritarian regimes simply stagnate economically and become corrupt. The crux of the problem for liberal-democracy lies partly in the actual operation of the system, but also in the possibility of its disintegration through ignorance of, and disrespect for, the principles on which it is based. The military so far respects these principles in Turkey, as does the bureaucracy still. Whether the trade unions and other powerful groups that may develop as Turkey grows economically will also continue to respect and support them is perhaps the most important question.

Yet the Turks do have a few solid factors working on their

behalf which must give some hope for continuing political success. They are after all trying to work a liberal-democratic system which they have themselves freely chosen and adapted to their own needs. It is not a system of government that has in any way been foisted on them by a colonial power, as has often been the case elsewhere. For all the system may creak it is nevertheless a Turkish system of which Turks may rightly feel proud. It also operates in a society which, save for the Kurdish minority, is remarkably homogeneous in language and religion, not having to cope with the daunting complexities of, say, the Lebanon or Syria. There is also a fair amount of agreement on foreign policy—firmness towards Greece, caution towards the Soviet Union and some quite widespread suspicion of the United States. Turkey is somewhat isolated, but is not on that account subject to active threat from abroad despite her important strategic position.

The most immediate problem is the domestic one of how to contain the outbreaks of violence which occur for the most part between extremist groups. As we have suggested, this violent disruption could be dangerous to liberal-democracy by creating a desire for authoritarian government, but to some degree Turkish society, like societies elsewhere, is coming to accept a degree of violence. Since a liberal-democratic system eschews political violence save *in extremis* in its own defence, it is crucial that the Turkish political system is not infiltrated by those who do not believe in the principles for which it stands, or by those who think that a liberal-democracy does not really have any.

We might finally ask whether Turkish democracy is in any danger from those who think Turkey should be an Islamic state. Clearly a strong trend in this direction exists, but Turkey is not Iran and does not have the heritage of Shi'ite Islam. In the Ottoman Empire the state was very largely supported by the religious institution, as we have seen. And when the state no longer felt the need for the support of religion it found it could reduce its influence and finally abolish the religious institution in the Kemalist revolution. The Turkish *ulema* could not resist this, whereas their Persian counterparts have been able to challenge state power very successfully. This is partly because the Shi'ite faith locates legitimate rule only in the twelfth *Imam*

and accords to him as to his predecessors the power to comprehend an alleged occult interpretation of Islam. In the absence of
the twelfth *Imam*, who disappeared about the year 873, the
Shi'ite divines, the *mujtahid*'s, exercise a wide range of authority,
which includes challenging any temporal power, even a Shi'ite one,
which denies what they regard as Islamic principles. Turkey
inherits nothing of this dynamic tradition, save among the *Alevi*
(Shi'ite) minority. Even if Kemal Atatürk had not abolished the
ulema, no-one could have arisen with the claims and influence of
the Persian Ayatullah Khumeini. There can be no such direct
religious threat to temporal power in Turkey, but a slow re-
assertion of Islamic values, and their injection into the political
system, is not at all out of the question as a reaction either to the
materialist and libertarian aspects of western civilization, or to the
spiritual emptiness of its Marxist variety.

NOTES TO CHAPTERS

I INTRODUCTION:
HISTORY SOCIETY AND GOVERNMENT

1. See Chapter II for discussion of the nature of Ottoman society and the reasons for the Empire's decline.
2. I am indebted to Dr. W.M. Hale for the information from his researches that the Atatürk regime did not shun foreign financial investment so much as find it difficult to attract.
3. F.A. Vali, *Bridge Across the Bosphorous: the Foreign Policy of Turkey*, Baltimore and London, 1971, 383.
4. W.M. Hale, *The Republic of Turkey*, International Migration Project (International Labour Office), Department of Economics, University of Durham, 1978, 49.
5. Agriculture's large part in Turkish exports requires that it should be further developed, but the area of cultivation was extended in the 1950's and 1960's beyond what was probably the desirable maximum. Further intensification is now needed, but will require considerable further investment. See J. Dewdney, 'Agricultural problems and Regional Development in Turkey,' in *Aspects of Modern Turkey* ed. by W.M. Hale, London and New York, 1976.
6. A succinct analysis is provided by C. Karataş, 'Contemporary Economic Problems in Turkey,' *Bulletin of the British Society for Middle Eastern Studies*, 4/1 (1977). Other figures in this chapter derive from publications of the Turkish State Institute of Statistics and the OECD Economic Survey of Turkey, Paris 1976. These surveys are published periodically.
7. Between 1945 and 1962 about 1.8 hectares of cultivable and similar amount of pasture land was redistributed. In 1962 there were 25.5 million hectares of cultivated and 28.5 million hectares of pasture land. Z.Y. Hershlag, *Turkey, the Challenge of Growth*, Leiden, 1968, tables 30 and 34.
8. These figures derive from the 1970 agricultural census and are contained in tables in E. Özbudun, *Social Change and Political Participation in Turkey*, Princeton, 1976, 73—75.
9. Figures derive from *Gelir Dağılımı (Income Distribution) 1973*, Ankara, State Planning office, 1976, and are given in W.Hale, 'Turkey,' in *The Middle East Yearbook*, London, 1979 (forthcoming).
10. The results of this study undertaken by Hacettepe University (Institute of Population Studies) are given in A. Tugac, 'Indices of Modernization: Erenköy; A Case of Local Initiative,' in *Turkey, Geographic and Social Perspectives*, ed. by P. Benedict, E. Tümertekin and F. Mansur, Leiden, 1974.

11. J. Hinderink and M.B. Kıray, *Social Stratification as an Obstacle to Development*: A Study of Four Turkish Villages, New York, 1970, 130–31.
12. P. Stirling, 'Cause, Knowledge and Change: Turkish Village Revisited,' in *Aspects of Modern Turkey*, ed. by W.M. Hale, 78–79.
13. This is suggested by D. Kandyoti, 'Some Socio-psychological Dimensions of Change in a Turkish Village,' *British Journal of Sociology*, 25, I (1974), 61.
14. Hinderink and Kıray, 'Social Stratification,' 231–35.
15. *Ibid.*, 238.
16. Shacks, or literally, 'houses erected overnight.'
17. As described by K.H. Karpat, *The Gecekondu: Rural Migration and Immigration*, London, New York, Melbourne, 1976, 78–9.
18. *Ibid.* 62. This account owes much to Karpat's work and that of R. Keleş, İ. Yasa, and M. Kıray. Karpat's work relates to Istanbul.
19. Town to town emigration seems to be greater than country to town emigration, but it seems that urban migrants do not live in *gecekondu* dwellings, E. Özbudun, *Social Change and Political Participation in Turkey*, Princeton 1976, 189–90.
20. T. Akçura, 'Urbanization in Turkey and Some Examples,' in Benedict *et al.*, *Perspectives*, 301–13.
21. P.J. Magnarella, *Tradition and Change in A Turkish Town*, New York 1974, 67.
22. *Ibid.*, 159.
23. E. Özbudun, 'Constitutional Law,' in *Introduction to Turkish Law*, ed. by T. Ansay and D. Wallace Jr., 2nd ed. Ankara, 1978, 32. This is a useful introduction.
24. W.M. Hale, 'Aspects of the Turkish General Election of 1969,' *Middle Eastern Studies*, VIII, 3 (1972) 395. For information on the state of research on members of parliament I am grateful to Prof. İlter Turan.
25. For a fuller account than is provided here see my *Government and Politics in Turkey*, 130–34.
26. R. Aybay, 'Administrative Law,' in Ansay and Wallace, *Introduction to Turkish Law*, 78–9.
27. The Council of State has ignored this constitutional amendment as superfluous. (*Ibid.*, 79).
28. These courts were expected to apply more rigorously than would the ordinary courts Articles 142, 143 and 163 of the Penal Code. These articles penalize action or propaganda intended to establish the hegemony of any social class or religious organization in the formation of the state. They were primarily used against the left. See W.M. Hale, 'Turkish Democracy in Travail: the Case of the State Security Courts,' *World Today* (May 1977).

II OTTOMAN LEGACIES

1. For a persuasive account see D.Ergil and R.I. Rhodes, 'The Impact of the World Capitalist System on Ottoman Society,' *Islamic Culture*, 48, 1974, 77–91 and their partly repetitive 'Western Capitalism and the Disintegration of the Ottoman Empire,' *Economy and History*, XVIII:I, 1975, 41–60.
2. Ş. Mardin, 'Historical Determinants of Stratification: Social Class and Class Consciousness in Turkey,' *Ank. Univ. S.B.F. Dergisi*, 22, 1967, 131–32.
3. B. Lewis, *The Emergence of Modern Turkey*, 2nd. ed., London, 1967, 31.
4. *Ibid.*
5. Ş. Mardin, 'Center-Periphery Relations; a Key to Turkish Politics?' in E.D. Akarli with G. Ben-Dor, *Political Participation in Turkey*, Ist., 1975, 11.
6. H. İnalcık, 'The Ottoman Mind and Aspects of the Ottoman Economy,' in M.A. Cook, ed., *Studies in the Economic History of the Middle East from the Rise of Islam to the Present Day*, London, 1970, 217. *Hisba* is the Sultan's duty to protect the general population.
7. During this period the class of notables (*ayan*) did profit from agricultural development fostered by demand for various agricultural products. But according to C, Issawi, *The Economic History of the Middle East, 1800–1914*, Chicago, 1966, 19, 'Although the landed aristocracy, the *ayan*, managed to keep sizable estates, even after the formal abolition of the *timar* in 1831, and continued to play an important role in local and national politics down to the present, the bulk of the land seem to have passed into the hands of the peasants.'
8. It assumed these functions from the Supreme Council of Judicial Ordinances. A very clear account of the complexities of mid-century institutional developments is given in S.J. and E.K. Shaw, *The History of the Ottoman Empire and Modern Turkey*, vol. II, Cambridge, 1977, 76ff. On the growth of representation see R.H. Davison, 'The Advent of the Principle of Representation in the Government of the Ottoman Empire,' in *Beginnings of Modernization in the Middle East: the Nineteenth Century*,' ed. by W. Polk and R. Chambers, Chicago, 1968. *Int. J.M.E. Stud.*, 3, 1972. A stimulating essay by K.H. Karpat, 'The Transformation of the Ottoman State.' On the 1976 parliament see R. Devereux, *The First Ottoman Constitutional Period*, Baltimore, 1963.
9. Lewis, *Emergence*, 2nd. ed., 376.

III POLITICAL ELITES

1. See J.H. Meisel, *The Myth of the Ruling Class: Gaetano Mosca and the Elite*, Ann Arbor, 1958. A very useful introduction to political elites is G. Parry, *Political Elites*, London, 1969.
2. C. Wright-Mills, *The Power Elite*, London, 1959.
3. J. Burnham, *The Managerial Revolution*, London and New York, 1942.
4. G. Mosca, *The Ruling Class*, (ed. Livingston) New York, 1939. V. Pareto, *The Mind and Society*, New York, 1935. For a succinct treatment see S.E. Finer, ed., Vilfredo Pareto: *Sociological Writings*, London and New York, 1966.
5. The reputational method has been used to discover the top elite by F.W. Frey *The Turkish Political Elite*, Cambridge, Mass., 1965. This is a classic study of members of the Turkish Grand National Assembly.
6. This analysis owes much to an article by J.S. Szyliowicz, 'Elite Recruitment in Turkey: the Role of the Mülkiye,' *World Politics*, 23, 3, 1971.
7. *Ibid.*, 393.
8. Ankara University/New York University Graduate School of Public Administration and Social Service, *Kaza ve Vilâyet İdaresi Üzerinde Bir Araştırma*, Ankara, 1957.
9. See my *Politics and Government in Turkey*, 286—87.
10. L.L. and N.P. Roos, *Managers of Modernization. Organizations and Elites in Turkey (1950—1969)*, Cambridge, Mass., 1971, 22—23.
11. *Ibid.*, 29.
12. *Ibid.*, 162.
13 *Ibid.*, 84—85, where the authors report on earlier studies by F.W. Frey, 'Education,' in *Political Modernization in Japan and Turkey*, ed. by R.E. Ward and D.A. Rustow, 224—29, and A. Kazamias, *Education and the Quest for Modernity in Turkey*, London, 1966, 242—43.
14. Roos and Roos, 84—85. See also below, Chapter VII.
15. E. Özbudun, *The Role of the Military in Recent Turkish Politics*, Harvard, 1966, 28. This view was based on 'the consensus of Turkish and foreign observers,' but received some confirmation by a study of the socio-economic background of the members of the 1960/61 junta, of which details are given by Özbudun, but, as he observes, this can hardly be considered a representative sample.
16. K.H. Karpat, 'Social Groups and the Political System after 1960,' in *Social Change and Politics in Turkey*, by K.H. Karpat and Contributors, Leiden, 1973, 267.
17. *Ibid.*, 268.
18. But the information is not very full. See, however, F. Ahmad, *The Young Turks*, Oxford, 1969, 166—81.
19. Lewis *Emergence*, 471.
20. D.A. Rustow, 'Atatürk as Founder of a State,' in *Prof. Dr. Yavuz Abadan'a Armağan,'* Ankara, 1969, 567—68.

21. Frey, *Political Elite*, 391.
22. *Ibid.*, 197.
23. F. Tachau and Mary-Jo D. Good, 'The Anatomy of Political and Social change: Turkish Parties, Parliaments and Elections,' *Comparative Politics*, 5, 1973, 556. This continues the analysis up to 1969. For more detail regarding occupational background see my *Politics and Government in Turkey*, 206. Figures for 1973 (calculated from a publication of the Grand National Assembly, T.B.M.M. Albümü, 2nd. ed., 1976) show some slight change, with deputies who were previously in official employ reaching some 18.5%, as compared with 10% in 1965. Lawyers, at some 29% formed the largest group, with farmers at about 10% and those in commerce and private enterprise just below this figure. In addition, there is a small number of deputies with a religious background, their proportion (about 4%) being similar to that of the military element. These calculations are approximations to reality because the information available is neither full nor unambiguous. The problems of classification are also quite difficult. For instance about one-fifth of those with a history of previous service in public service were in education and had almost certainly been teachers at one time. By contrast about one-third had held jobs of a technical character within the public service and before that had sometimes worked privately. This last group is not therefore so easily distinguishable from those employed in the 'free professions' and almost certainly not very different from them in outlook. The general impression is one of educational, professional and occupational variety, but with very little representation of the lowly or uneducated. The composition of the Senate is rather different. The lawyers are again the largest element, (41%), followed by those of military background (17%) then by doctors of medicine (10%) and engineers (9%). The classification is made by the Senate Secretariat and does not strictly compare with the classification used for the lower house by Frey, Tachau and myself. The source for these figures is *Cumhuriyet Senatosu Albümü*, 1976. My figures for the National Assembly differ slightly from those of F. Tachau, 'Towards a Reconciliation of Modernity and Tradition,' (paper submitted to Conference on the Future of Turkey, arranged by Hacettepe University, Ankara with the University of Wisconsin, 1974) due, probably, to classificatory differences.
24. Frey, *Political Elite*, 196.
25. According to Tachau, in 'Towards a Reconciliation of Modernity and Tradition,' of the 1973 deputies only 43% had previous parliamentary experience.
26. The best source of information on cabinet membership in English is Keesing's Contemporary Archives, but for detailed and completely accurate work Turkish sources are necessary. My own figures derive from Keesing's and the Turkish press and could be subject to minor

errors.

27. See in particular on the attitudes of the political elite, Ş. Mardin, 'Opposition and Control in Turkey,' *Government and Opposition*, 1/3, 1966, F. Frey, 'Patterns of Elite Politics in Turkey,' in *Political Elites in the Middle East*, ed. by G. Lenczowski, Washington, 1975, and M. Tamkoç, *The Warrior Diplomats*, Salt Lake City, 1976, 106—11.

IV POLITICAL CULTURE AND POLITICAL IDEAS

1. G.A. Almond and S. Verba, The Civic Culture, Boston and Toronto, 1965, 13.
2. See D.C. McClelland, 'National Character and Economic Growth in Turkey and Iran,' in *Communications and Political Development*, ed. by L.W. Pye, Princeton, 1963, 161ff.
3. K.H. Karpat, *The Gecekondu*, 201 and 202.
4. D.A. Rustow, 'Turkey,' in *Political Culture and Political Development*, ed. by L.W. Pye and S. Verba, Princeton, 1965, 184.
5. F.W. Frey and L.L. Roos, *Social Structure and Community Development in Rural Turkey: Village and Elite Leadership Relations*, Cambridge, Mass., M.I.T. Center for International Studies, Rural Development Research Project, No. 10.
6. Karpat, *Gecekondu*, 209.
7. J.S. Szyliowicz, *Political Change in Rural Turkey: Erdemli*, Paris, 1966, 159. Erdemli is on the south-east coast between Mersin and Silifke. The population of the administrative area of Erdemli in 1955 was 3,777 and included three villages.
8. For an account of the project see F.W. Frey, 'Surveying Peasant Attitudes in Turkey,' *Public Opinion Quarterly*, 27 (1963), 335—55.
9. F.W. Frey, 'Socialization to National Identification Among Turkish Peasants,' *Journal of Politics*, 30 948. Frey's percentages are double these; his are the sum of the first and second choice percentage figures.
10. *Ibid.*, 942.
11. P. Magnarella, *Tradition and Change in a Turkish Town*, New York, 1974, 155. The town, Susurluk, is in north-western Anatolia; it had a population of 12,357 in 1970.
12. Ö. Ozankaya *Köyde Toplumsal Yapı ve Siyasal Kültür*, Ank., 1971, 191—92. This vauable study of social structure and political culture is restricted to four villages, two in N.E. Antolia, and two in central Anatolia, with a total sample of 339 persons. The percentages are for first and second preferences combined.
13. Frey, 'Socialization to National Identification,' 942.
14. *Ibid.*, 944. These were villagers between the ages of 16 and 19.

15. In the less literate villages the capacity to favour any other political personage besides Atatürk is very low. Ozankaya, 118.
16. Magnarella, *Tradition and Change*, 156–57.
17. They can be compared only where the questions asked are roughly comparable. Dr. Ozankaya's study is more detailed, but does not cover some of the important matters investigated by Professor Karpat.
18. Karpat, *Gecekondu*, 206.
19. Ozankaya, *Siyasal Kültur*, 167.
20. Karpat, *Gecekondu*, 223. This is also true, it seems, in the village of Çayırhan, near Ankara, half of whose population comes from elsewhere. See S. Kili, *Çayırhan*, Ist., 1978, (Turkish).
21. The number of their pupils rose from 4.5 to 49.3 thousands between 1960/61 and 1970/71. J.M. Landau, *Radical Politics in Modern Turkey*, Leiden, 1974, 176. See also R.B. Scott, 'Koran Courses in Turkey,' Muslim World LXI, 4 (1971). One-fifth of a total of 50,000 courses were arranged by the government.
22. U. Heyd, *Revival of Islam in Modern Turkey*, Jerusalem, 1968, 17.
23. I am much indebted for what follows to the work of J.M. Landau, *Radical Politics in Modern Turkey*.
24. Çetin Özek, *Türkiyede Gerici Akımlar ve Nurculuğun İçyüzü*, Ist., 1964, 242.
25. Important for the thought of these first three writers is Ş. Mardin's, *The Genesis of Young Ottoman Thought*, Princeton, 1962. For Ziya Gökalp, see in English (there is a library of books in Turkish), U. Heyd, *Foundations of Turkish Nationalism*, London, 1950, and E.I.J. Rosenthal, *Islam in the Modern National State*, Cambridge, 1965, 28–63.
26. Ş. Mardin, *Jön Türklerin Siyasi Fikirleri*, 1895–1908, Ank., 1964, 182. To my knowledge this valuable study of Young Turk political thinkers is not available in English.
27. Heyd, *Foundations*, 82.
28. This principle, of doubtful orthodoxy, is different from the famed third Islamic principle after Koran and Tradition, of Consensus of the Community (*ijma*). Mediated by the jurisconsults (the *ulema*) this is a conservative tradition in the formulation of the Holy Law to fill the gaps left by the Koran and the Tradition, though it is a possible way of sanctioning innovations, e.g. coffee drinking in the seventeenth century. See H.A.R. Gibb, *Modern Trends in Islam*, Chicago, 1947. It could not serve Gökalp's purpose.
29. Gökalp is, in fact, not altogether consistent on this point.
30. See N. Berkes, 'Ziya Gökalp, His Contribution to Turkish Nationalism,' *Middle East Journal*, Autumn (1954), 375–90.
31. Translated in 'What is a Nation,' in *Turkish Nationalism and Western Civilization*, ed. by N. Berkes, New York, 1959, 134–38.
32. K.H. Karpat, *Turkey's Politics*, Princeton, 1959, 50.

33. See K.H. Karpat and Contributors, *Social Change and Politics in Turkey*, Leiden, 1973, 331—32. Nur donated his writings on nationalism to the British Museum on condition they were only made available to the public in 1960.

34. Karpat, *Politics*, 266.

35. As reported in a perceptive article by N. Berkes, 'The Two Facets of the Kemalist Revolution, *Muslim World*, LXIV, (1974), 305.

36. For this analysis see that of my colleague, R.N. Berki, *Socialism*, London, 1975. My treatment of the subject follows the lines of this work.

37. Karpat, *Social Change and Politics*, 348.

38. *Yön* had a large circulation. Its first issue in December, 1961, contained a statement of socialist principles signed by over 500 persons, including 150 students, 80 writers, 63 officials and 48 schoolteachers. The declaration stressed rapid economic development in the context of democracy and social justice, a mixed economy but with a large measure of public enterprise. Landau, *Radical Politics*, 52—54.

V THE NORMATIVE FRAMEWORK: THE CONSTITUTION

1. See G. Sartori, 'Constitutionalism. A Preliminary Discussion,' *American Political Science Review*, LV, 14 (1962), 855, where he asserts that 'all over the Western area people requested, or cherished, "the constitution", because this term means to them a fundamental law, or a fundamental set of principles, and a correlative institutional arrangement, which would restrict arbitrary power and ensure a "limited government."

2. The programmatic elements of the Soviet Constitution relate, it is claimed, to what has actually been achieved in the re-fashioning of society; utopianism is firmly rejected.

3. See above, p. 44.

4. F. Ahmad, *The Young Turks*, Oxford, 1969, 110. Ahmad provides the fullest account in English, but see also S.J. and E.K. Shaw, *History of the Ottoman Empire and Modern Turkey*, Vol. II, Cambridge, 1977, 282—85 and 290—92. A fuller understanding of these complex and important constitutional struggles can only be obtained from Turkish sources. A firm and reasoned case for amendment was argued by the government; the purely partisan aspect of these constitutional struggles can be over-stressed.

5. G. Lewis, *Modern Turkey*, 4th. ed., London, 1974, 91, gives a graphic account of the event.

6. Suna Kili, *Turkish Constitutional Developments and Assembly Debates*

on the Constitutions of 1924 and 1961, Ist., 1971, 43.
7. See below, p. 135.
8. His longer term of office (seven years instead of four), his ineligiblity for re-election, and the requirement that he should be politically neutral were all intended to remove him from political conflict.
9. The Onar Commission, the name of its chairman being Prof. Dr. Sıddık Sami Onar of Istanbul University. It was set up very shortly after the 1960 coup. It produced for the military junta a complex draft constitution of 191 articles, but under the influence of an Ankara group composed of academics the National Unity Committee, as the military junta became known, agreed that a Constituent Assembly should be convened. Its Constitution Committee produced a draft which was subject to some amendments by the Assembly; its chairman was Prof. Dr. Enver Ziya Karal, a noted historian. For details see W.F. Weiker, *The Turkish Revolution, 1960–61*, Washington, D.C., 1963, 41–81, and my *Politics and Government in Turkey*, 107–15.
10. For an account of recent developments, to which I am indebted in an almost complete absence of other scholarly work on the Constitutional Court and the Council of State (save for legal treatises) see R. Aybay, 'Some Contemporary Constitutional Problems in Turkey,' *Bulletin of the British Society for Middle Eastern Studies*, 4,1 (1977), 21–27. For some decisions of the Constitutional Court in the 1960's, see my *Politics and Government in Turkey*, 124–27, and for the Council of State during the same period *ibid.*, 239–43.

VI POLITICAL PARTIES AND VOTING

1. See W. Weiker, *Political Tutelage and Democracy in Turkey*, Leiden, 1973, 149–51.
2. *Ibid.*, 211–15.
3. Feroz Ahmad, *The Turkish Experiment in Democracy, 1950–75*, London, 1977, 247, where he reports on research by İsmail Cem which appeared in the newspaper yearbook *Milliyet*, 1970, 39 and 42.
4. The party does not like being called a social-democrat party on account of the connection with Marxism it considers implicit in that title.
5. W.B. Sherwood, 'The Rise of the Justice Party in Turkey,' *World Politics*, XX, 1, (1967), 55.
6. Süleyman Demirel, *Büyük Türkiye*, Ist., 1975, 297.
7. On the Salvation Party see particularly J.M. Landau, 'The National Salvation Party in Turkey,' *Asian and African Studies*, 11, 1 (1976), 1–57.
8. See D. Ergil, 'Class Conflict and the Turkish Transformation, 1970–75,' *Studia Islamica*, 41 (1975), 137–61, for an interpretation stressing

economic factors. The party is strong in less developed regimes, including the large towns in such regions.

9. Landau, 'National Salvation Party,' 47.
10. Landau, *Radical Politics*, 237, where reference is made to the writings of Dr. Orhan Türkdoğan, a lecturer in sociology, published in the weekly *Devlet* (State) which supports the party.
11. *Ibid.*, 215.
12. *Dokuz Işık*. Landau, *Radical Politics*, 223–32, contains an informative account, where it is noted that as early as 1963 a group of officers were referring to 'nine principles' in their political thinking. The very popular *Nine Lights* was published in 1965.
13. Alparslan Türkeş, *Temel Görüşler* (Basic Views), Ist., 1975, 48.
14. *Ibid.*, 60.
15. See S. Sayarı, 'Aspects of Party Organization in Turkey,' *Middle East Journal*, 30 (Spring, 1976), 191–92. This article is a notable attempt to provide a realistic account of party organization.
16. Ahmad, *The Turkish Experiment*, 315.
17. Sayarı. 'Aspects,' 197.
18. This information has been kindly supplied to me by Dr. W.M. Hale from an important forthcoming article in the *Int. Journal of Middle East Studies*. Dr. Hale notes that in 1973 Article 29 of the Political Parties' Law was amended to provide that the party lists of candidates in elections would be dertmined 'according to principles laid down in the directions and standing orders of the political parties themselves.'
19. Ayşe Kudat, 'Patron-Client Relations: the State of the Art and Research in Eastern Turkey,' in *Political Participation in Turkey*, ed. by Akarlı and Ben-Dor, 77.
20. *Ibid.*, 78.
21. Ş. Mardin, 'Center-Periphery Relationships: a Key to Turkish Politics', in *Political Participation*, ed. by Akarlı and Ben-Dor, 25.
22. S. Sayarı, 'Political Patronage in Turkey,' in *Patrons and Clients*, ed. by E. Gellner and J. Waterbury, London, 1977, 107.
23. Compiled from figures in Sayarı, 'Aspects of Party Organization,' 192–94. This includes the background study of leading party membership to which reference is made.
24. F.Tachau, 'Turkish Provincial Party Politics,' in *Social Change and Politics in Turkey*, by K.H. Karpat et al., 286.
25. *Ibid.*, 287.
26. *Ibid.*, 292. Two studies in this article, of Adana and Aydın, support in detail the general conclusions that old landed families are no longer as important in provincial party organizations as the new professionals and businessmen.
27. W.M. Hale, 'Aspects of the Turkish General Election of 1969,' *Middle Eastern Studies*, VIII, 3 (1972), 399. This account of voters' attitudes is based largely on a survey organized by the newspaper, *Günaydın*.

28. For a brief introduction see my *Political Development*, London, 1972.
29. Of studies in English see Hale, 'Particularism and Universalism in Turkish Politics,' in *Aspects of Modern Turkey*, ed. by Hale and the very detailed study by Özbudun, *Social Change and Political Participation in Turkey*. The foundation studies in English on this subject were by P.J. Magnarella, 'Regional Voting in Turkey,' *Muslim World*, 57, July and October, 1967, 223–34 and 277–87.
30. Hale, 'Particularism and Universalism,' 54.
31. The chief features of the 1973 elections are included in *Social Change and Political Participation in Turkey*, but see the more detailed work by Özbudun and Tachau, 'Social Change and Electoral Behaviour in Turkey: Toward a Critical Realignment?' *Int. Journal of M.E. Studies*, 6 (1975), 460–80.
32. Hale identifies eight regions, so strict comparison of results is not possible.
33. In percentages from 34.9 to 49.6 in Istanbul, 39.9 to 49.5 in Ankara, 33.0 to 45.9 in Izmir, and from 39.0 to 51.0 in Adana. Özbudun and Tachau, 'Social Change and Electoral Behavior,' 472.
34. *Ibid.*, 473. The generalizations derive from a study of three Istanbul 'lower class' districts.
35. Özbudun, *Social Change*, 134–35.
36. *Ibid.*, 140.
37. *Ibid.*, 171. By contrast, 11% of the highly developed villages gave more than 80% of votes to one party, and 61% gave 50% to 80% to one party.
38. *Ibid.*, 170.
39. *Ibid.*, 199–204, where there are references to the work of R. Keleş and I. Yasa.
40. Karpat, *Gecekondu*, 223.
41. Özbudun, *Social Change*, 213.
42. Karpat, *Gecekondu*, 225.

VII SUSTAINING FORCES
THE MILITARY AND THE BUREAUCRACY

1. D.A. Rustow, 'The Army and the Founding of the Turkish Republic,' *World Politics*, XI (1959), 551.
2. Ahmad, *Young Turks*, 17.
3. *Ibid.*, 31.
4. G.S. Harris, 'The Role of the Military in Turkish Politics,' Part I Middle East Journal, XIX, 1 (1965), 62.
5. A fascinating account of the development of the military conspiracy is in G.S. Harris, 'The Role of the Military in Turkish Politics' Part II,

Middle East Journal, XIX, 2 (1965), 172–76. Interesting among Turkish sources is A. İpekçi and O.S. Coşar, *İhtilalin İçyüzü*, İst., 1965.
6. Ahmad, *The Turkish Experiment with Democracy*, 168–69.
7. *Ibid.*, 178.
8. *Ibid.*, 195.
9. *Ibid.*, 198.
10. *Ibid.*, 203.
11. *Ibid.*, 162.
12. R.P. Nye, 'Civil-Military Confrontation in Turkey: the 1973 Presidential Election,' *Int. J. Middle East Studies*, 8 (1977), 213.
13. In my view one of the most convincing explanations of military intervention in 1960 is that given by G.S. Harris, 'The Causes of the 1960 Revolution in Turkey,' *Middle East Journal*, XXIV, 4 (1970), 438–54.
14. *Managers of Modernization*, Cambridge, Mass., 1971.
15. It is possible here to deal with only a few of the many and important questions raised in the work by Roos and Roos, which relates to the situation in 1960's.
16. Roos and Roos, 125.
17. *Ibid.*, 158.
18. *Ibid.*, 160.
19. *Ibid.*, 170.
20. *Ibid.*, 186.
21. F.T. Bent, 'The Turkish Bureaucracy as an Agent of Change,' *Journal of Comparative Administration*, May (1969), 53. Prof. Bent found only 16 graduates of the Political Science Faculty among 276 higher civil servants with higher education, in 1966, in seven ministries, excluding Interior and Finance. My own 1964 study found 33 out of a sample of 150, but employed chiefly in the ministies of the Interior, Finance, and Labour and Commerce. See my *Politics and Government*, 294.
22. Bent, 'Turkish Bureaucracy,' 53.
23. *Ibid.*
24. *Ibid.*, 56–57.
25. *Ibid.*, 59 and *Politics and Government*, 228–29.
26. *Politics and Government*, 237–39.
27. Bent, 62.
28. D.A. Rustow, 'Turkey; The Modernity of Tradition,' in *Political Culture and Political Development* ed. by L.W. Pye and S. Verba, Princeton, 1965, 189–90.
29. M. Heper, *Türk Kamu Bürokrasisinde Gelenekçilik ve Modernleşme* (Traditionalism and Modernization in Turkish Bureaucracy) Ist., 1977.
30. It is not possible to do anything like justice to Dr. Heper's interesting study, which has not yet, to my knowledge, appeared in English.
31. See also İ. Sunar, *State and Society in the Politics of Turkey's Development*, Ankara, 1970, 137. Dr. Sunar writes, 'Whilst the bureaucracy

tends to espouse reformist or populist measures, it is indeed a more moderate and conservative force than it seems.'
32. See M. Heper and C.L. Kim, *The Role of Bureaucracy and Regime Types: A Comparative Study of Turkish and Korean Higher Civil Servants*, University of Iowa, Comparative Legislative Research Center, Occasional Paper, No. 12, 1977, and M. Heper, "Political Modernization as Reflected in Bureaucratic Change: the Turkish Bureaucracy and a 'Historical Bureaucratic Empire' Tradition", *Int. J. Middle East Stud.*, 7, (1976), 507–21. This lattter study is concerned with the attitudes of higher civil servants of the period 1945–60. A comparison of these 36 higher civil servants with 118 present-day civil servants (both studies are restricted to four ministries—Finance, Interior, Public Works and Health and Social Assistance) is found in Dr. Heper's 'Traditional Tendencies in the Upper Reaches of the Bureaucracy in a Changing Turkey,' *Turkish Public Administration Annual*, 1975.
33. Heper, 'Traditional Tendencies,' 140.
34. *Ibid.*, 141.
35. See Heper and Kim, 'The Role of Bureaucracy and Regime Types,' 11–16.
36. Heper and Kim, 18.
37. Heper and Kim, 24. 57% generalists, 42% specialists. Over half say that expertise is the most important criterion used in promotion, a good personality being ranked next (24%) but expertise is not defined.

VIII PRESSURES ON POLITICS
WORKERS EMPLOYERS AND STUDENTS

1. See W.M. Hale, 'Labour Unions in Turkey, Progress and Problems,' in *Aspects of Modern Turkey* ed. by W.M. Hale for the best account in English of the political role of trade unions. The standard history in English is by T. Dereli, *The Development of Turkish Trade Unionism*, Ist., 1968. See also T. Ataöv, 'The Place of the Worker in Turkish Society and Politics,' in *Türk Yıllığı, The Turkish Yearbook of International Relations*, VIII, 1967, Ankara, 1970. An earlier article by O. Tuna, 'Trade Unions in Turkey,' *International Labour Review*, XC, 5, (1964) is by a well known scholar in this field. I am indebted to his work in Turkish as well as to that of T. Dereli, B. Dereli, Anil Çeçen, Alparslan İşikli and Kemal Sülker.
2. Ataöv, 'The Place of the Worker,' 87.
3. Dereli, *The Development of Turkish Trade Unionism*, 57.
4. The law is translated in Dereli, *Development*, 76.
5. Hale, 'Labour Unions in Turkey,' 65–66.
6. *Ibid.*, 67.

7. In the 1969–73 National Assembly there were four Justice Party and five People's Party members who were *Türk İş* officials. (A. İşıklı, *Sendikacılık ve Siyaset*, Ankara, 1974, 470.

8. During discussion of the 1963 legislation prohibiting support of trade unions for political parties and vice versa the government made it clear that the broad involvement of the unions in political affairs was not proscribed, but that it was the intention that the trade union movement should not be subordinated to political objectives and should not be engaged in a class struggle against the political regime. See Dereli, *Development*, 133.

9. A Ceçen, *Türkiyede Sendikacılık*, Ankara, 1973, 186. The reference is to the twenty-four principles accepted by *Türk İş* in 1968 which, it is often claimed, constitute nothing less than a blue-print for social democracy, though this is arguable.

10. *Milliyet* (Newspaper) 18.1.1971, reported in Cecen, *Turkiyede Sendikacılık*, 193.

11. The information which follows is derived from an Istanbul survey by T. Dereli, *Aydınlar Sendika Hareketi ve Endustriyel İlişkiler Sistemi*, Ist., 1975. See also N. Abadan, The Politics of Students and Young Workers in Turkey,' *Ank. Univ. Siyasal Bilgiler Fak. Dergisi*, XXVI, 1 (1971), 103–5, where there is evidence to show that young workers show some preference for parties at either end of the political spectrum.

12. According to Dr. Hale *Türk İş* was in fact demonstrating its 'above politics' policy by this move. See his 'How Significant is Tunç's support for Ecevit?' *Briefing*, 5th July, 1977, 26. I am grateful to Dr. Hale for much of this later information.

13. *Yankı*, (A Turkish Weekly) 9th April 1978, 22.

14. A discussion of these and many other matters is contained in P. Esin, *Türkiyede İşveren Sendikacılığı* (Employers' Unionism in Turkey) Ankara, 1974. I am indebted to this work and to that of K. Sayıbasılı, *Chambers of Commerce and Industry in Turkey and the United Kingdom with Special Reference to Economic Policy, 1960–70* (Unpublished Ph.D. thesis, University of Glasgow, 1975). For an abstract of some of this material see the same author's 'Chambers of Commerce and Industry, Political Parties and Governments: A Comparative Analysis of the Turkish and British Cases,' *Studies in Development*, Mid. East Tech. Univ., Ankara, 11 (1976) and his 'Türkiyede Özel Teşebbüs ve Ekonomi Politikası,' *Studies in Development*, 13, 1976.

15. Sayıbaşılı, 'Chambers of Commerce,' 130.

16. Sayıbaşılı, 'Türkiyede Özel Teşebbüs,' 94.

17. *Ibid.*, 88–90.

18. P. Esin, *Türkiyede İşveren Sendikacılığı*, 254.

19. *Ibid.*, 273.

20. There is an extensive literature on student activism. For a useful intro-

duction see S.M. Lipset (ed.), *Student Politics*, New York, 1967. This section on students and politics in Turkey owes much to the work noted in the list of books for further reading by N. Abadan-Unat, L.L. and N. Roos and G. Field, J.S. Szyliowicz (a very useful monograph) and in Turkish by M. Taylak, *Öğrenci Hareketleri*, Ankara, 1969 and A.T. Kişlalı, *Öğrenci Ayaklanmaları* Ankara, 1974.

21. The sources for this and similar information in this section are Ozankaya, *Üniversite Öğrencilerinin Siyasal Yönelimleri*, and A.T. Kışali, *Öğrenci Ayaklanmaları*. Ankara, 1974. The former work is based on questionnaires returned in 1965 by 317 students of all faculties of Ankara University, save for religious studies and medicine. In additon 109 members of student organizations received questionnaires. The second study is based on questionnaires returned by 266 students of Atatürk University, Erzurum, and Hacettepe University, Ankara, in 1969/70.

22. Conversations with teachers in the Middle East Technical University, Ankara, in 1975 and 1978 suggested the point that there is little intellectual contact between students and lecturers over political questions. One professor in the Political Science Faculty of Ankara University expressed the view in 1978 that the students had become more Marxist. There is certainly a very wide range of Marxist literature in the bookshops. Either students have changed since 1965, or the social sciences students who were the subject of these conversations are untypical, which is very likely. Further well designed studies would be of great interest.

23. Of the fathers of these respondents 58 per cent were in the officials' class.

24. Those who preferred no party or did not reply amounted to 38% (1969/70) and 32% (1965).

25. See Szyliowicz, *A Political Analysis of Student Activism: the Turkish Case*, 26–34.

26. *Ibid.*, 33.

27. Prof. Dr. Turhan Feyzioğlu, now leader of the Republican Reliance Party. For a detailed account of this incident see my 'Academic Freedom and University Autonomy in Turkey,' *Science and Freedom*, XII, 1958. See also, Weiker, *The Turkish Revolution*, 48–52.

28. D. Barchard, 'The Intellectual Background to Radical Protest in the 1960's' in *Aspects of Modern Turkey* ed. by W.M. Hale, 33.

29. The visit in July, 1968, had also occasioned severe disorders.

30. The government claimed that thanks to the autonomy granted to the universities in the 1961 Constitution, the police could not enter universities unless requested, and without a two-thirds' majority the government could not amend the Constitution. The government could, however, have declared a state of emergency, rather than watch the rightist groups attack those of the left. See G. Lewis *Modern Turkey*, 4th ed., 1974, 182.

31. See Landau, *Radical Politics*, 216—17.
32. N. Abadan, 'The Politics of Students and Young Workers,' 93.
33. Barchard, 'The Intellectual Background,' 32—33. He describes how in the 1960's students instructed themselves in Marxist doctrines through reading and through discussions in 'Ideas Clubs', but how far university students are Marxist is by no means clear, as earlier indicated. Moreover, it is easy to forget when writing about students how quickly the student universe changes.
34. Szyliowicz, *Political Analysis*, 70.
35. *Ibid.*, 71.

IX CONCLUSION:
DEMOCRACY AND DEVELOPMENT

1. A comprehensive and thorough treatment of democratic theory is by B. Holden, *The Nature of Democracy*, London, 1974, on whose approach I much rely. See also J. Plamenatz, *Democracy and Illusion*, London, 1973, R.A. Dahl, *A Preface to Democratic Theory*, Chicago, 1956, and G. Sartori, *Democratic Theory*, New York, 1962. For provocative analyses see the works of C.B. Macpherson, including his latest, *The Life and Times of Liberal Democracy*, Oxford, 1977. A succinct statement of liberal-democratic theory is given by S.E. Finer, in *Comparative Government*, London, 1970, and a highly relevant discussion of important problems is contained in B. Crick, *In Defence of Politics*, London, 1962.
2. Following the categories developed by Holden, *The Nature of Democracy*.
3. For interesting observations see Ş. Mardin, 'Opposition and Control in Turkey,' *Government and Opposition*, 1 (1966) and by the same author, 'Ideology and Religion in the Turkish Revolution,' *Int. J.M.E. Stud.*, 2, (1971). See also M. Tamkoç, 'Stable Instability of the Turkish Polity,' *Middle East Journal*, Summer (1973).
4. Mardin, 'Opposition,' 380.
5. For an instructive comparison see E. Özbudun, 'Established Revolution vs. Unfinished Revolution: Contrasting Patterns of Democratization in Mexico and Turkey,' in *Authoritarian Politics in Modern Society: The Dynamics of Established One-Party Systems*, ed. by S.P. Huntington and C.H. Moore, New York, 1970.
6. The problem was much discussed in the 1950's and after the 1960 revolution in the serious journals. (See K.H. Karpat, 'Ideology in Turkey after the Revolution of 1960' in K.H. Karpat *et al.*, *Social Change and Politics in Turkey*, 351—52). In the subsequently dominant socialist climate the focus of the argument shifted. It was claimed that the rural rich, not the populace generally, was responsible for consuming in-

vestment resources,the poorer peasant simply being exploited. For an informative and realistic study in English, however, see J.S. Szyliowicz, *Political Change in Rural Turkey, Erdemli*, especially pp. 158—60. The general problem has also been discussed in the African and Indian contexts. For the latter see B.K. Nehru, 'Western Democracy and the Third World', *Third World Quarterly* 1,2 (April 1979), 53—70, and a comment, forthcoming, in the same journal by Prof. W.H. Morris-Jones.

APPENDIX I

NATIONAL ASSEMBLY ELECTION RESULTS 1961–77

Party	1961			1965			1969			1973			1977		
	% of Votes Cast	Seats	% of Seats	% of Votes Cast	Seats	% of Seats	% of Votes Cast	Seats	% of Seats	% of Votes Cast	Seats	% of Seats	% of Votes Cast	Seats	% of Seats
New Turkey Party	13.7	65	14.4	3.7	19	4.2	2.2	6	1.3	—	—	—	—	—	—
Justice Party	34.8	158	35.1	52.9	240	53.3	46.5	256	56.9	30.6	149	33.1	36.9	189	42.0
Democratic Party	—	—	—	—	—	—	—	—	—	12.5	45	10.0	1.8	1	0.2
Nation Party	—	—	—	6.3	31	6.9	3.2	6	1.3	9.6	—	—	—	—	—
National Salvation Party (a)	—	—	—	—	—	—	—	—	—	11.9	48	10.6	8.6	24	5.3
Republican Peasant's National Party	14.0	54	12.0	2.2	11	2.4	—	—	—	—	—	—	—	—	—
National Action Party	—	—	—	—	—	—	3.0	1	0.2	3.4	3	0.6	6.4	16	3.5
Republican Peoples Party	36.7	173	38.4	28.7	134	29.8	27.4	143	31.8	33.5	185	41.1	41.6	213	47.3
Republican Reliance Party (b)	—	—	—	—	—	—	6.6	15	3.3	5.3	13	2.8	1.9	3	0.6
Turkish Worker's Party	—	—	—	3.0	15	3.3	2.7	2	0.4	—	—	—	0.1	—	—
Turkish Unity Party (c)	—	—	—	—	—	—	2.8	8	1.8	1.1	1	0.2	0.4	—	—
Independents	0.8	—	—	3.2	—	—	5.6	13	2.9	2.8	6	1.3	2.5	4	0.8

(a) Its forbear was the National Order Party, set up in 1970; (b) Reliance Party until 1973; (c) Unity Party until 1971

APPENDIX II
AGRICULTURAL REGIONS AND PROVINCES OF TURKEY

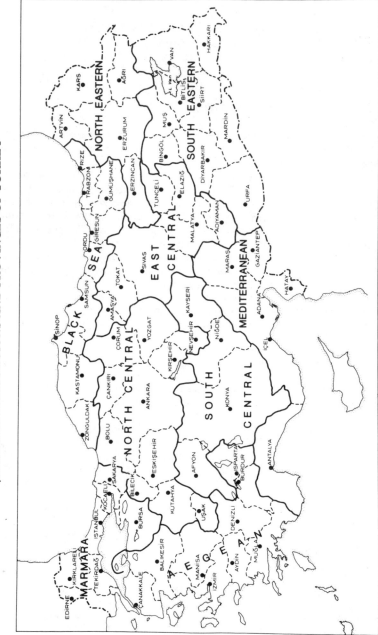

EXTRACTS FROM THE TURKISH CONSTITUTION (1961)
(including Amendments to 16.4.1974)

THE PRESS AND PUBLICATION

ARTICLE 22 — The press is free, and shall not be censored.

The State shall adopt the measures to assure the freedom of the press and gathering of information.

Freedom of the press and the gathering of information can be restricted by law solely to safeguard the integrity of the State with its territory and people, public order, national security, and the secrecy demanded by national security, or public morality; to prevent attacks on the dignity, honour and rights of individuals; to preclude instigations to commit crimes; or to assure proper implementation of judicial functions.

Barring a court order passed in cases specified by law in order that the judicial functions may be carried out properly, no ban shall be imposed on the publication of any item of information.

Newspapers and periodicals published in Turkey can be confiscated in conformity with a court judgement in the event where offences specified in the pertinent law are committed; and by decision of the competent authority clearly empowered by law in cases where delay is deemed prejudicial for the protection of the integrity of the State with its territory and people, national security, public order or public morality. The competent authority making the decision for confiscation shall inform the court of its decision within 24 hours at the latest. If such a decision is not ratified by the court within a maximum of three days, the decision for confiscation shall become null and void.

Newspapers and periodicals published in Turkey can be closed down by court judgement in the event of conviction for offences carried out against national security, public order, public morality, the national, democratic, secular and social principles of the Republic based on human rights and freedoms, or against the basic provision of indivisibility of the State with its territory and people.

The right to publish newspapers and periodicals:
ARTICLE 23 — Publication of newspapers and periodicals shall not be subject to obtaining authorization prior to publication nor to the depositing of a guarantee fund.

The publication and distribution of newspapers and periodicals, their financial resources, and the conditions pertaining to journalism shall be regulated by law. Such law shall lay down no political, economic, financial or technical restrictions liable to curb or coerce the free propagation of news, ideas and opinions.

Newspapers and periodicals shall avail themselves of the media and facilities provided by the State and other public corporate bodies or associations affiliated with them, and these facilities shall be equally available to all.

The right to publish books and pamphlets:
ARTICLE 24 — No authorization shall be necessary for the publication of books and pamphlets, nor shall they be subject to censorship.

Books and pamphlets published in Turkey shall not be confiscated except in cases provided under paragraph 5 of article 22.

The protection of printing equipment:
ARTICLE 25 — Printing houses including their presses and other equipment and fixtures shall not be seized, confiscated, or prevented from operation, even though the underlying charge may be that they are instrumental to a criminal act.

The right to make use of communications media other than the press:
ARTICLE 26 — Individuals and political parties are entitled to avail themselves of the communication and publication facilities other than the press which are owned by public corporate bodies. Conditions and procedures for such utilization shall be regulated by law in conformity with democratic principles and standards of equity. The law cannot impose restrictions impeding the public from receiving information, reaching an opinion or the free formation of public opinion through these means for reasons other than those concerned with safeguarding the integrity of the State with its territory and people, the national, democratic, secular and social Republic based on human rights, and national security and public morality.

PERSONAL SECURITY

ARTICLE 30 — Individuals against whom there exists a strong indication for indictment can be arrested by court judgement for purposes of preventing escape, destruction or alteration of evidence, or in similar cases which necessitate detention, and in other instances specified by law. The prolongation of detention is subject to the same conditions.

Arrest is resorted to only in *flagrante delicto* or in cases where delay is likely to thwart justice. The conditions for such detention shall be specified by law.

Individuals arrested or taken into custody shall be notified immediately in writing of the reasons for their detention or arrest as well as of the charges against them.

The person arrested or detained shall be arraigned within forty-eight hours, excluding the time spent to send him to the court nearest to his place of seizure, or within the time specified by law for offences falling under the jurisdiction of State Security Courts, and in cases clearly defined by law where offences are committed collectively, and, in general, during the state of war or martial law. This duration cannot exceed fifteen days. After the lapse of this period, no person can be deprived of his liberty without a court decision. When a person arrested or detained has been arraigned, his next of kin shall be immediately notified thereof. (As amended by Law No. 1699 of 15th March, 1973 and published in the *Official Gazette (Resmi Gazete)* of 20th March, 1973, No. 14482).

The person arrested or held in custody shall be arraigned within 48 hours excluding the time taken to send him to the court nearest to the place of seizure, and within seven days in cases clearly specified by law where offences are committed collectively; and after the lapse of this time, such person or persons cannot be deprived of their liberty without a court judgement. When a person detained or arrested is arraigned, his next of kin shall be immediately notified thereof.

All damage suffered by persons subjected to treatment other than that specified herein shall be indemnified by the State according to law.

LAND OWNERSHIP AND NATIONALIZATION

Land ownership:

ARTICLE 37 — The State shall adopt the measures needed to achieve the efficient utilization of land and to provide land for those farmers who either have no land, or own insufficient land. For this purpose the law may define the size of tracts of land according to different agricultural regions and types of soil. The State shall assist farmers in the acquisition of agricultural implements.

Expropriation:

ARTICLE 38 — The State and other corporate bodies, where public interest deems it necessary, are authorized, subject to the principles and procedures as set forth in the pertinent law, to expropriate the whole or part of any immovable property under private ownership, and to impose an administrative servitude thereon, provided that the equivalent value is immediately paid in cash.

The equivalent value to be paid cannot exceed the tax value stated by the owner of the property in conformity with the form and procedure prescribed by law in cases where the whole of the immovable property is expropriated, nor can it exceed the relevant amount of the tax value where part of the property is expropriated.

The owner reserves the right to protest and prosecute in cases where the equivalent value of the expropriated immovable property in appraised at less than the tax value.

The form of payment of the equivalent value of immovable property and land expropriated for the purpose of enabling farmers to own land, for the nationalization of forests, for afforestation, for accomplishing the establishment of settlement projects, for the protection of coastal areas and for touristic purposes shall be prescribed by law.

Where the law deems it necessary that payment be made by installments, the period of payment shall not exceed twenty years where expropriation is made for the purpose of enabling the farmers to own land, for the nationalization of the forests, for afforestation, and for the establishment of settlement projects. Likewise, this period shall not exceed ten years in the case of expropriations made for the protection of coastal areas and for touristic purposes. In such cases, the installments shall be paid in equal amounts and shall be subject to the interest rates prescribed by law.

The value of that part of the expropriated land which is tilled by the farmer himself, the amount of land to be indicated by law which is essential within equitable measures, to provide him with a living, and the value of the land expropriated from the small farmer shall be paid in cash under all circumstances.

Nationalization:
ARTICLE 39 — Where it is deemed necessary in the public interest, private enterprises which bear the characteristics of a public service, may be nationalized provided that the true equivalent value thereof is paid as indicated by law. Where the law deems it necessary that payment be made by installments, the period of payment shall not exceed ten years, and the installments shall be paid in equal amounts; these intallments shall be subject to interest rates prescribed by law.

TRADE UNIONS, COLLECTIVE BARGAINING AND STRIKES

The right to establish trade unions:
ARTICLE 46 — Workers and employers are entitled to establish trade unions and federations of trade unions without having to obtain prior authorization, to enroll in them as members, and to resign from such membership freely. Forms and procedures to be implemented in the exercise of these rights shall be regulated by law. The law may impose restrictions for the purpose of safeguarding the integrity of the State with its territory and its people, national security, public order, and public morality.

The regulations, the management and the operation of trade unions and federations thereof shall not conflict with democratic principles.

The right of collective bargaining and striking:
ARTICLE 47 — In their relations with their employers, workers are entitled to bargain collectively and to strike with a view to protecting or improving their economic and social status.

The exercise of the right to strike, and the exceptions thereto, and the rights of employers shall be regulated by law.

POLITICAL PARTIES

The right to found political parties and their place in political life:
ARTICLE 56 — Citizens are entitled to found political parties and to join in or withdraw from them pursuant to pertinent rules and procedures.

Political parties can be founded without prior authorization and shall operate freely.

Whether in power or in opposition political parties are indispensable entities of democratic political life.

Financial assistance to political parties which have won at least five per cent of the total valid votes in the latest general elections for the National Assembly or to those which have gained enough number of seats in the National Assembly to enable them to form a group in the said Assembly shall be regulated by law.

Principles to which political parties must conform:
ARTICLE 57 — The statutes, programs and activities of political parties shall conform to the principles of a democratic and secular republic, based on human rights and liberties, and to the fundamental principle of the State's territorial and national integrity. Parties failing to conform to these provisions shall be permanently dissolved.

The internal affairs and activities of political parties, and the circumstances and manner according to which they shall be accountable to the Constitutional Court, and the cases and manner in which this Court shall audit their finances shall be regulated by law in accordance with democratic principles. (As amended by Law No. 1699, adopted on 15th March, 1973 and published in the *Official Gazette (Resmi Gazete)* of 20th March, 1973, No. 14482).

Actions in law involving the dissolution of political parties shall be heard at the Constitutional Court, and the verdict to dissolve them shall be rendered only by the same Court.

ELECTIONS AND REPRESENTATION

ARTICLE 75 — Elections shall be conducted under the control and supervision of judicial organs.

To implement and cause to implement all procedures necessary to the fair and orderly conduct of elections from inception to completion, to review and pass final judgement on all irregularities, complaints and objections regarding election matters during and after elections, and to certify the validity of election credentials are functions devolving upon the High Election Board.

The High Election Board shall be composed of seven regular members and four alternates. Six of the members shall be elected by the general assembly of the Court of Cassation, and five by the general assembly of the Council of State from among their own members by secret ballot, and by an absolute majority of their plenary session. These members in turn shall elect from among themselves by secret ballot and by absolute majority, a chairman and a vice-chairman.

The four alternate members of the High Election Board shall be elected by lot, two from the members chosen by the Court of Cassation and two from the members chosen by the Council of State. The Chairman and Vice-Chairman of the High Election Board are exempt from the drawing of lots.

ARTICLE 76 — Members of the Grand National Assembly represent neither their constituencies nor their constituents, but the nation as a whole.

MILITARY ORGANIZATION

The office of the Commander-in-Charge and the Chief of the General Staff:
ARTICLE 110 — The office of the Commander-in-Chief is integrated in the moral existence of the Turkish Grand National Assembly and is represented by the President of the Republic.

The Council of Ministers shall be responsible to the Turkish Grand National Assembly for ensuring national security and preparing the armed forces for war.

The Chief of the General Staff is the Commander of the armed forces.

The Chief of the General Staff shall be appointed by the President of the Republic upon his nomination by the Council of Ministers, and his duties and powers shall be regulated by law. The Chief of the General Staff is responsible to the Prime Minister in the exercise of his duties and powers.

The functions and prerogatives of the Ministry of National Defence and its relations with the Chief of the General Staff and the Commanders of Forces are regulated by law.

The National Security Council:
ARTICLE 111 — The National Security Council is composed of the Prime Minister, the Chief of the General Staff, the Ministers as provided by law, and

the Commanders of Forces.

The President of the Republic shall preside over the National Security Council, and in his absence this function shall be discharged by the Prime Minister.

The National Security Council recommends to the Council of Ministers the necessary basic views for decisions to be taken in connection with national security and coordination.

Redress for Administrative Acts:
ARTICLE 114 — The way to prosecution shall be open against all acts and proceedings of the administration.

Juridical power cannot be exercised in such manner as to restrain the fulfillment of the executive function carried out in conformity with the forms and principles prescribed by law.

In court actions instituted as a result of administrative acts, prescription shall start as of the date of written notification.

The administration is liable for the damages resulting from its acts and operations.

CIVIL SERVANTS

ARTICLE 119 — Civil servants and staff members employed in an administrative or supervisory capacity in public economic enterprises, and those who are employed in the central offices of public welfare institutions, whose private facilities and sources of income are provided by law, may not join political parties or trade unions. Civil servants and those employed in public economic enterprises may, in the performance of their official duties, make no discrimination whatsoever among citizens on account of their political views.

Those whose violation of the above principles is established by court judgement shall be permanently dismissed from public service.

The provisions binding the organisations having the aim of safeguarding and promoting the professional interests of employees not qualified as workers shall be regulated by law.

UNIVERSITIES

ARTICLE 120 — Universities shall be established only by the State and in virtue of a law. The Universities are public corporate bodies enjoying autonomy. The autonomy of the universities is exercised within the provisions designated in this article, and the said autonomy shall not prevent legal proceedings against offenses and offenders within the university buildings and its annexes.

Universities shall be governed, under the supervision and control of the State, by the organs chosen by themselves. Provisions concerning the State universities founded in pursuance of a special law are reserved.

The organs, members of the teaching staff and their assistants may not, for any reason whatsoever, be removed from their office by authorities other than those of the universities. The provisions of the last paragraph are reserved.

Members of the teaching staff of the universities and their assistants may freely engage in research and publication activities.

The establishment and functioning of the universities, their organs and the election held to form such organs, the functions and powers thereof, the manner in which the State shall exercise its right of supervision and control over the universities, the responsibilities of the organs of the university, the measures to prevent all acts directed toward impeding learning and teaching, the assignment, when need be, of the members of the teaching staff and their assistants attached to one university to duties in other universities, and the rules for the execution of learning and instruction in freedom and under guarantee and in conformity with the exigencies of modern science and technology, and principles of the development plan are regulated by law.

The budgets of universities are enforced and controlled in conformity with the principles applied for general and supplementary budgets.

The Council of Ministers shall take charge of the management of the universities, or of the faculties, organisations and establishments attached to such universities, in case the freedom of learning and teaching in these universities and their faculties, organisations and establishments is endangered, and should such danger be not averted by the university organs. The Council of Ministers shall submit each decision without delay to the approval of the joint session of the Turkish Grand National Assembly. Cases necessitating such undertaking, procedures of publication and implementation regarding decisions of seizure, its duration, and the nature and extent of the powers of the Council of Ministers during its application are regulated by law.

BROADCASTING

ARTICLE 121 — The broadcasting and television stations are instituted only by the State, and their administration in the form of public corporate bodies is regulated by law. The law cannot impose any provisions violating the principle of impartiality in the administration, control and establishment of its administrative organs.

All radio and television broadcasts shall be made with due regard to the principles of impartiality.

Conformity to the requisites of the integrity of the State with its territory and people, to the national, democratic, secular and social Republic based on human rights, and to the national security and public morale in the selection of news and programs, in their elaboration and presentation, and in the performance of their functions to assist culture and education, as well as in the principles of ensuring the authenticity of news and in the selection of the organs, their powers, their duties and their responsibilities shall be regulated by law.

Impartiality is the rule for news agencies established or subsidized by State.

MARTIAL LAW

ARTICLE 124 — In the event of war, or of a situation likely to lead to war, or in case of a revolt or of a forceful and open uprising against the motherland and the Republic endangering the indivisibility of the land and the nation from within or without, or the emergence of definite indications of widespread acts of violence directed towards suppressing the free democratic order or the basic rights and freedoms recognized by the Constitution, the Council of Ministers may declare martial law in one or more regions or the whole of the country for a duration not exceeding two months, and shall submit such decision immediately to the approval of the Turkish Grand National Assembly. The Assembly, when it deems necessary, can reduce the duration of the martial law, or lift it entirely.

The extension of martial law, not exceeding two months each time, is subject to the decision of the Turkish Grand National Assembly. Such decisions shall be taken at the joint session of both legislative bodies.

In the event of martial law, or war in general, specific provisions to be enforced, the manner in which government operations shall be conducted and he manner in which freedoms shall be curtailed or suspended, or the obligations that may be imposed on citizens in the case of outbreak of war, or a situation likely to lead to war, shall be regulated by law.

THE JUDICIARY

Independence of courts:
ARTICLE 132 — Judges shall be independent in the discharge of their duties. They shall pass judgement in accordance with the Constitution, law, justice and their personal convictions.

No organ, office, agency or individual may give orders or instructions to courts or judges in connection with the discharge of their duty, send them circulars, or make recommendations or suggestions.

No questions may be raised, debates held, or statements issued in legislative bodies in connection with the discharge of judicial power concerning a case on trial. Legislative and executive organs, and the Administration are under obligation to comply with the court rulings and not delay their execution.

Guarantees for judges:

ARTICLE 133 — Judges may not be dismissed. Unless they so desire, they may not be retired before the age limit provided in the Constitution; they may not be deprived of their salaries even for reason of the abolishment of a court or of a post therein.

The exceptions prescribed by law concerning those convicted for an offence entailing dismissal from office, those whose incapacity to discharge duty for reasons of ill-health is definitely established, and those pronounced unsuitable to remain in the profession, are reserved.

Provisions concerning judges:

ARTICLE 134 — The qualifications of judges, their appointment, rights and duties, salaries and allowances, their promotion, the temporary or permanent change of their functions or places of service, the initiation of disciplinary proceedings, and the subsequent disciplinary actions taken against them, for offenses arising from the discharge of their functions; decisions to question and try them for offenses connected with the discharge of their functions, conviction, for crimes necessitating dismissal from the profession on instances of incompetence and other matters concerning their career are regulated by law in accordance with the principle of independence of the courts.

Judges shall remain in office until they complete their sixty-fifth year. The age limit, the promotion and the retirement from service of the military judges is prescribed by law.

Judges may undertake no private or public duties other than those prescribed by law.

All court verdicts shall be put down in writing and shall be accompanied by the justification of the verdict.

Organisation of courts:

ARTICLE 136 — The organisation of courts, their functions and jurisdiction, operations and trial procedures shall be regulated by law.

There shall be State Security Courts with jurisdiction to prosecute offences committed against the integrity of the State with its territory and people, free democratic order and the character of the Republic as defined in the Constitution, as well as those concerned directly with the security of the State. However, provisions concerning state of war and martial law are reserved.

The State Security Court is composed of a presiding judge, four regular and two substitute judges, a public prosecutor, and sufficient number of assistant public prosecutors. The presiding judge, two regular and one substitute judge, and the public prosecutor are chosen for appointment from among first grade judges and public prosecutors of the Republic, two regular and one substitute judges from among first grade military judges; and the assistant public prosecutors from among public prosecutors of the Republic and military judges.

For appointments to vacancies in the offices of the presiding judge, regular and substitute judges, the public prosecutor and assistant public prosecutors of the State Security Court, the Council of Ministers nominates two candidates for each vacancy. The appointment of the judges for the State Security Court from among these nominees shall be made by the High Council of Judges; that of the public prosecutor and his assistants by the High Council of Public Prosecutors.The appointment of the regular and substitute military judges and assistant military public prosecutors shall be made in conformity with procedures prescribed in the relevant special laws.

The term of office of the presiding judge, regular and substitute judges, the public prosecutor and the assistant public prosecutors of the State Security Courts shall be three years. However, they may be re-elected after the said term expires.

The competent authority to review the decisions and verdicts rendered by the State Security Courts shall be one or more special departments in the Court of Cassation to be set up to examine the decisions and verdicts of these courts alone; whereas the General Assembly shall be the one of [the] Penal Departments of the Court of Cassation.

Other provisions concerning the organization and functions of the State Security Courts, their duties and authorities, and their trial procedures shall be defined by law. (The above paragraphs of 2, 3, 4, 5, 6 and 7 were inserted into the Turkish Constitution on the basis of Law No. 1699 of 15th March, 1973, published in the *Official Gazette (Resmi Gazete)* of 20th march, 1973, No. 14482).

THE COUNCIL OF STATE

ARTICLE 140 — The Council of State is an administrative court in the first instance for matters not referred by law to other administrative courts, and an administrative court of the last instance in general.

The Council of State shall hear and settle administrative disputes and suits, shall express opinions on draft laws submitted by the Council of Ministers, shall examine draft regulations, specifications and contracts of concessions, and shall discharge such other duties as prescribed by law.

The members of the Council of State shall be elected by a two thirds majority vote of the Constitutional Court composed of its permanent and reserve members, and by secret ballot from among the two lists of nominees corresponding to the number of vacancies, submitted separately by the Council of Ministers and the General Assembly of the Council of State. If such majority is not obtained in two ballots, an absolute majority shall suffice.

The Council of State shall elect its Chairman and its Chief Attorney from among its own members by secret ballot and a two thirds majority. The term of office of the Chairman, the Chief Attorney and Heads of Departments is four years. However, they shall be eligible for re-election.

The organisation, functions, judicial procedure and methods applicable to the election of Heads of Department of the Council of State, the qualifications and appointment, rights and duties, salaries and allowances, and promotion of its members,the initiation of disciplinary measures and the execution of disciplinary penalties against such members, shall be prescribed by law in accordance with the principles of independence of the courts and tenure of judges.

Juridical control of administrative acts and deeds concerning military personnel shall be held by the Military Administrative court. The organisation, judicial procedure, the qualifications and appointment of the Chairman and members of the Military Administrative Court, and the career and disciplinary affairs of members, shall be prescribed by law in accordance with the principles of tenure of judges and the requirements of military service.

THE CONSTITUTIONAL COURT

Organisation:
ARTICLE 145 — The Constitutional Court consists of fifteen regular and five reserve members. Four regular members are elected by the General Assembly of the Court of Cassation, three by the General Assembly of the Council of State from among its Chairmen, members, the Chief Prosecutor of the Republic and the Chief Attorney by the absolute majority of their plenary session and by secret ballot; one member is elected by the Court of Accounts from among its Chairmen and members according the above procedure. Three members are elected by the National Assembly, two by the Senate of the Republic and two by the President of the Republic. One of the two members designated by the President of the Republic is selected from among three candidates nominated by the General Assembly of the Military Court of Cassation by absolute majority of its plenary session and by secret ballot. The Legislative Assemblies make these selections by absolute majority and by secret ballot, from among individuals outside the Grand National Assembly. Principles and procedures concerning application for candidacy and the elections to be made by the Legislative Assemblies shall be regulated by law.

The Constitutional Court elects a Chairman and a Vice-Chairman from among its own members by absolute majority and by secret ballot for a term of four years; re-election is permissible.

A regular or reserve member of the Constitutional Court shall have completed his fortieth year and shall have served as Chairman, member, Chief Prosecutor or Chief Attorney in the Court of Cassation or the Council of State, or the Military Court of Cassation, or the Court of Accounts; or he shall have served on the teaching staffs of the Schools of Law, Economics, or Political Sciences of the universities for at least five years; or he shall have practiced law as a barrister for fifteen years.

The Court of Cassation shall elect two, and the Council of State, and each of the legislative bodies, one reserve member, respectively, to the Constitutional Court. The procedure followed in the election of the reserve members shall be the same as in the case of the elections of regular members.

The members of the Constitutional Court shall undertake no public or private duties.

Functions and powers:
ARTICLE 147 — The Constitutional Court shall review the constitutionality of laws, the internal regulations of the Turkish Grand National Assembly, and the conformity of the Constitutional amendments within the set conditions prescribed by the Constitution.

The Constitutional Court shall bring to trial as a High Court of Justice, the President of the Republic, the members of the Council of Ministers, the Chairman and members of the Court of Cassation, the High Council of Judges and the Court of Accounts, the Chief Prosecutor of the Republic, the Chief Attorney, the Chief Prosecutor of the Military Court of Cassation, as well as its own members for offenses connected with their duties; and it discharges such other duties as prescribed by the Consitution.

In case the Constitutional Court sits as a High Court of Justice, the duty of public prosecutor shall be discharged by the Chief Prosecutor of the Republic.

Procedures governing trials and functions:
ARTICLE 148 — The organization and trial procedures of the Constitutional Court shall be determined by law; its method of operation and the division of labor among its members shall be determined by its own self-drafted by-laws.

The Constitutional Court shall perform its task on the basis of written records, except in cases in which it acts as a High Court of Justice, and in cases referring to the closing down of political parties. However, when it deems necessary, it may call the interested parties to present their oral explanations. (As amended by Law No. 1699, of 15the March, 1973 and published in the *Official Gazette (Resmi Gazete)* of 20th March, 1973, No. 14482).

Rulings of the Constitutional Court:

ARTICLE 152 — Rulings of the Constitutional Court are final. They cannot be made public before statement of reasons for the ruling is written out.

Laws and regulations or their provisions which have been invalidated by the Constitutional Court for being contrary to the Constitution shall become void as of the date of publication of the decision, together with the motivations for it, in the Official Gazette. The Constitutional Court may, in certain cases, set the date for the annulment decision to go into effect. Such dates may not exceed one year from the date of its publication in the Official Gazette.

The annulment decision cannot be retroactive.

The Constitutional Court may also rule that its decisions, based on claims of unconstitutionality by other courts, are restricted in scope with the case in question and binding only the parties involved.

Decisions of the Constitutional Court shall be published immediately in the Official Gazette, and shall be binding on the legislative, executive and judicial organs of the State, as well as on the administration and real and corporate bodies.

FURTHER READING

GENERAL

Hotham, D.	*The Turks.* London, 1972
Lewis, G.	*Modern Turkey.* 4th ed. London, 1974.
Mango, A.	*Turkey.* London, 1968.
Mango, A.	*Turkey, A Delicately Poised Ally.* Beverley Hills and London, 1975.

HISTORICAL

Ahmad, F.	*The Turkish Experiment in Democracy 1950–75.* London, 1977. (Very useful recent detailed history).
Berkes, N.	*The Development of Secularism in Turkey.* Montreal, 1964.
Davison, R.H.	*Turkey.* New Jersey, 1968. (Short historical introduction).
Karpat, K.H.	*Turkey's Politics, The Transition to a Multi-Party System.* Princeton, 1964.
Kinross, Lord	*Atatürk, The Re-birth of a Nation.* London, 1964.
Lewis, B.	*The Emergence of Modern Turkey.* 2nd ed. London, 1968.
Mardin Ş.	*The Genesis of Young Ottoman Thought: A Study in the Modernization of Turkish Political Ideas.* Princeton, 1964.
Shaw, S.J. and Shaw, E.K.	*History of the Ottoman Empire and Modern Turkey, Vol.II. Reform, Revolution and Republic: The Rise of Modern Turkey, 1808–1975.* Cambridge, 1977.
Ward, R.E. and Rustow, D.A.	*Political Modernization in Japan and Turkey.* Princeton, 1964.
Weiker, W.F.	*The Turkish Revolution, 1960–61.* Washington, D.C., 1963.

POLITICS AND SOCIETY

Akarli, E.D. with Ben-Dor, G., eds.	*Political Participation in Turkey.* Istanbul, 1975.
Frey, F.	*The Turkish Political Elite.* Cambridge, Mass., 1965.
Hale, W.M., ed.	*Aspects of Modern Turkey.* London and New York, 1976.

225

Karpat, K.H. and Contributors	*Social Change and Politics in Turkey.* Leiden, 1973.
Özbudun, E.	*Social Change and Participation in Turkey.* Princeton, 1976.
Sunay, İ.	*State and Society in the Politics of Turkey's Development.* Ankara, 1974.

POLITICAL THEORY

Berkes, N. ed.	*Turkish Nationalism and Western Civilization.* New York, 1959.
Heyd, U.	*The Foundations of Turkish Nationalism.* London, 1950.
Kili, S.	*Kemalism.* Istanbul, 1969.
Kushner, D.	*The Rise of Turkish Nationalism, 1876–1908.* London, 1977.
Landau, J.M.	*Radical Politics in Modern Turkey.* Leiden, 1974.

INSTITUTIONS IN POLITICS

Dereli, T.	*The Development of Turkish Trade Unionism.* Istanbul, 1968.
Dodd, C.H.	*Politics and Government in Turkey.* Manchester and Berkeley/Los Angeles, 1969.
Kili, S.	*Turkish Constitutional Developments and Assembly Debates on the Constitutions of 1924 and 1961.* Istanbul, 1971.
Özbudun, E.	*The Role of the Military in Recent Turkish Politics.* Harvard, 1966.
Roos, L.R. and Roos, N.P.	*Managers of Modernization, Organizations and Elites in Turkey (1950–1969).* Cambridge, Mass., 1971.

FOREIGN AFFAIRS

Harris, G.S.	*Troubled Alliance, Turkish-American Problems in Historical Perspective, 1945–1971.* Washington, 1972.
Karpat, K.H. *et al.*	*Turkey's Foreign Policy in Transition, 1950–1974.* Leiden, 1975.
Tamkoç, M.	*The Warrior Diplomats.* Salt Lake City, 1976.
Vali, F.A.	*Bridge Across the Bosphorous. The Foreign Policy of Turkey.* Baltimore and London, 1971.

For valuable periodic accounts of Turkish political developments derived from the world's press see *Keesing's Contemporary Archives*. Bristol, England, and for immediate comment, *Briefing*, a weekly magazine in English published by Ekonomik Basın Ajansı, Ankara.

INDEX

Aegean Sea, 14
Ağa's 121, 124, 140
Almond, G.A., 69
Ali Pasha, 5, 42, 56, 79
Arabic speakers, 16
Armed Forces Union, 136—37
Arms embargo, 14
Atatürkism, 84—88
Atatürkist reforms, 6
Atatürk, Mustafa Kemal, 5, 6, 8, 18, 34, 44, 48, 50, 59, 69, 60, 62, 63, 72, 82, 84, 86,97, 98, 107, 134, 135, 142, 170, 179, 185, 187
Avcioğlu, Dogan, 87, 91, 92
Aybar, Mehmet Ali, 91, 110
Aydemir, Talât, 137

Baghdad Pact, 13
Baştürk, Abdullah, 163
Batur, Muhsin, 139
Berkes, N., 87
Bilgiç, Saadettin, 122
Boran, Behice, 11
Bureaucracy, 39, 43, 49; as an elite, social origins and careers, 55—58, 143—53 (status and job satisfaction, 144, and politics, 144—145, personnel problems, 146—47, general characteristics, 148—50, and democracy, 150—52), 182
Byzantine Empire, 1—3

Cabinet, see Council of Ministers
Çakmak, Fevzi, 135, 136
Caliph and caliphate, 42, 48, 62, 79
Carlowitz, Treaty, 3
Central Treaty Organization, 13, 15
Cevdet, Abdullah, 80
Chamber of Deputies, 95—96
Chambers of Commerce Union, 163—65
Chambers of Industry Union, 164—65
Clientilism, 124—65
Commerce and Industry 163—165
Constitution, 94—105; 1876, 5, 43—44, 95; 1908—09, 44, 95—96; 1924, 27, 97—98; 1961, 10, 18, 27, 98—105, 210—23 (text with amendments); 1971 amendments, 32, 101—104
Constitutional Court, 30—31, 103—104, 140, 158
Council of Judicial Regulations, 46
Council of Ministers, 31, 46, 48, 65—66, 97
Council of State, 31, 45, 103—104
Cuba Crisis, 13—14
Cyprus, 14

Declarations of Wealth, 140
Demirel, Süleyman, 10, 12, 15, 66, 102, 122
Democracy — radical democracy, 176—78, people's democracy, 177, liberal democracy, 177—78,

Turkey is one of the crucially located states of the modern world. Situated in both Europe and Asia, bordered on the North by the Soviet Union and her allies and on the East by the Islamic world, Turkey is in some ways an outpost of the West. Yet Turkey is politically and socially subservient to no-one and has created a culture which, whilst a rich amalgam of many others, is distinctively Turkish. Over the past decades the Turks have sought to develop their historical society economically and socially. More remarkably, they have tried to do so within a framework of liberal and democratic political institutions whose importation they owe to no-one but themselves. This book is about Turkey's courageous and unusual attempt to combine economic development with democracy.

But is is also a comprehensive analysis of the modern Turkish political system. To this end the author examines the development of the political and administrative institutions of Turkish democracy, the political ideas that have been, and still are, important and the influence of significant groups in Turkish society like the military, trade unions and students. These are examined against the backcloth of a political culture which incorporates elements of an Islamic tradition, limited but still vibrant in important respects.

Professor C.H. Dodd began studying Turkish language and literature at the School of Oriental and African Studies in London during and just after the last war, completing these studies later in Edinburgh. Having also read modern history and political theory at university he has subsequently made his career in the teaching of politics and has lectured in the universities of Leeds, Durham and Manchester. From 1959 to 1962 he served as Visiting Professor of Public Administration in the Middle East Technical University, Ankara. His previous books include *Politics and Government in Turkey*, Manchester and California, 1969, *Israel and the Arab World* (with Mary Sales), Routledge, 1970 and *Political Development*, Macmillan, 1972. In 1970 he was appointed Head of Department and Professor of Politics in the University of Hull. He is currently President of the British Society for Middle Eastern Studies.

Cover designed by Gary Sargeant

The Eothen Press

Paperback U.K. £4.95 Overseas $12.00

42, Northgate, Walkington, Beverley, N.Humberside, HU17 8ST, Gt. Britain